MILTON E. POLSKY

You Can Write a Play!

MILTON E. POLSKY

You Can Write a Play!

APPLAUSE
THEATRE & CINEMA BOOKS

YOU CAN WRITE A PLAY!
BY MILTON E. POLSKY

Copyright © 2002 by Milton E. Polsky

You Can Write a Play! was previously published, as part of The Theatre Student Series, by
The Rosen Publishing Group, Inc., in 1983

LIBRARY OF CONGRESS CATALOGUING-IN-PUBLICATION DATA
   Library of Congress Card Number: 2001097610

BRITISH LIBRARY CATALOGUING-IN-PUBLICATION DATA
   A catalogue record for this book is available from the
   British Library

ISBN: 1-55783-485-7

APPLAUSE
THEATRE & CINEMA BOOKS
151 West 46th Street
New York, NY 10036
Phone: 212-575-9265
Fax: 646-562-5852
email: info@applausepub.com

SALES & DISTRIBUTION
North America:

HAL LEONARD CORP.
7777 West Bluemound Road
P. O. Box 13819
Milwaukee, WI 53213
Phone: 1-414-774-3630
Fax: 1-414-774-3259
email: halinfo@halleonard.com
internet: www.halleonard.com

UK:

COMBINED BOOK SERVICES LTD.
Units I/K, Paddock Wood Distribution Centre
Paddock Wood, Tonbridge, Kent TN12 6UU
Phone: (44) 01892 837171
Fax: (44) 01892 837272
United Kingdom

FOREWORD

Playwright, master teacher, humorist — these are just a few roles at which Dr. Milton Polsky excels. Often, I return home from a long day of teaching to find a hilarious message from Milt nesting in my answering machine. Sometimes it features a funny voice or a rhyme introducing his topic. Inevitably, I smile and usually I laugh. He always amazes and delights me with his creativity and quick wit.

On many occasions, I've been in workshops conducted by Milt. What fascinates me the most is his ability to charm both students and adults and pull them into an activity. Milt's skills at improvisation are legendary. His "twist and turn" lead-ins to improvised scenes have been adopted by legions of my colleagues. Milton is brilliant at generating ideas that lead to stories and eventually to plays.

His newly revised book, *You Can Write a Play,* is a compendium of terrific suggestions not only for germinating ideas but also for helping make these seeds grow to fruition. Milt has excellent suggestions for expanding concepts and ideas for the development of fully realized characters and plots. His book guides the beginning playwright with clear illustrations from established writers. *You Can Write a Play* has invaluable information on giving and receiving feedback. Milt clearly reminds the writer that theatre is a collaborative art.

It has been my pleasure to work with Dr. Milton Polsky over the last twenty years. I have learned much from both the man and his books. Thanks, Milton, for your invaluable contributions to American educational theatre.

John A. Shorter
President of the New York State Theatre Education Association

ABOUT THE AUTHOR

MILTON E. POLSKY has served as a drama specialist with the New York City Board of Education and the New York City Board of Higher Education. He has taught playwriting in the public school system, at the City University of New York, and at New York University, where he was a Shubert Fellow in Playwriting. His plays have been widely produced and published, and he is the author of numerous articles and books, including *Let's*

Improvise: Becoming Creative, Expressive, and Spontaneous through Drama; The Improv Workshop Handbook: The Object Is Teamwork; Celebrate Your School Namesake: Creating Across the Curriculum; and *Aquadrama: Acting in Waist-High Water.* He is currently a mentor for the New York City Board of Education and serves as an Associate Professor at Hunter College. He is also Associate Chair of the UFT Players. Dr. Polsky has received the Rod Marriott Award for Outstanding Lifetime Achievement in Theatre Education. He lives in New York City with his wife, Roberta, and two children, Jay and Madelyn.

ACKNOWLEDGMENTS

I wish to acknowledge gratitude to my playwriting instructors from whom I learned so much: Ronald Johnson, Eric Barnouw, Jerry McNeeley, Lowell Swortzell, Morton Wishengrad, and Edwin Wilson. I wish also to thank all my playwriting students from whom I also learned so much. I could not have completed this project without the help of Sharon Brunson, Gail Chin, Hazel Cones, Ana Flores, Sonia Hernandez, Marisa Jimenez, Joseph Lesser, Chandra Mack, Estee McKee, Monica Mitchell, Judith Morris, Marisol Pinero, Sylvia Torres, Linda Trotman, Amanda Udis-Kessler, and Ruthie Velez. I am also grateful to Cherie Miller for stellar typing service. Thanks to the JELL-H team that advised me so astutely on all aspects of this edition: Howard Berland, John Fredricksen, Elana Gartner, Louis Nemec, and Larry O'Connell. Thanks to Sally-Anne Milgrim, my colleague at Hunter College, for insightful suggestions regarding the text. Thanks always to my family for their encouragement: my wife, Roberta and children, Jay and Maddy. Special thanks to my agent at Writers House, Michele Rubin, and to my publisher Glenn Young, and his associate, Shannon Reed, for their confidence in the project from the beginning. I would especially like to thank my editor, Greg Collins, for his wonderful suggestions and astute attention to detail throughout the publishing process.

CONTENTS

INVITING YOUR IMAGINATION . . .

(*The time and place is here and now.*)

MEP: Hi — (*Seeing YOU holding this book.*) Have you read it yet?

YOU: No, I haven't . . . (*Looks through book.*)

MEP: You know what it's about, right?

YOU: (*Thumbing through.*) About 200 pages?

MEP: Something like that. (*Pause.*) It's also about using your imagination.

YOU: Using your imagination — that all?

MEP: Sure. Want to try something right now? (*YOU scratch your head.*) Okay, imagine the book you're holding isn't *about* playwriting, but a different kind of book —

YOU: Like what — ?

MEP: Let's say it's a book in a play . . .

YOU: I still don't get it . . .

MEP: You know . . . it could be what Hamlet is reading as he ponders the question, "To be or not to be" or —

YOU: I get it . . . a prop. Like the book Otto Frank finds, telling what happened to his daughter, Anne.

MEP: Her diary, right. I see you're getting into this now . . . want to try something?

——————— WHAT IF ———————

someone came into the room you're in and suddenly grabbed a book from you? Who is the mysterious intruder and what is so important about the book? Is it a Bible, secret plans, a fabulous diet, or what?

YOU:

HE or SHE:

YOU:

HE or SHE:

(*Keep on going . . . for at least a page.*)

YOU: A snap! (*Putting down pen or pencil.*) What do we do now?

MEP: Well, actually, this book is mostly about doing. In fact, that's what the word "drama" means — to do — and our goal here is simple — to help you write a play.

YOU: Wait! — I've never written a play before, only stories and —

MEP: Take it easy. There'll be plenty of examples, exercises and R-A-W materials for you to work with.

YOU: R-A-W materials?

MEP: Reading-Acting-Writing, with the emphasis on the latter.

YOU: I see. All that will help me write a play?

MEP: If it helps to get those creative juices flowing, why not? And if you're an aspiring actor or director you'll see from the inside — the playwright's view — how characters relate under different circumstances.

YOU: Look, I just want to write a play.

MEP: I'm with you. Let's get started!

YOU: Wait — another book in a play — just thought of it — I remember seeing a movie on TV about a young scoundrel who reads a book and becomes a very big success in business: What was the name of it? Yeah — *How to Succeed in Business* . . .

MEP: *Without Really Trying*. Right. First a stage play, you know. But listen: If you want to succeed in this business you *definitely* have to try: Write . . . Want to take another crack at it? For now, just write whatever comes to your mind. Let yourself go spontaneously, okay?

Hamlet ponders "To be or not to be . . ." in the What If exercise. What kind of book — and experience — will stimulate your imagination for this improvisation?

—————— JUST FOR YOU ——————

(*Write a dialogue between HE and SHE or YOU and ME on any subject you like.*)

HE:

SHE:

HE:

SHE:

HE:

SHE:

HE:

YOU: Hey, that wasn't so bad. Not bad, at all. Hold it, I left something out . . .

MEP: Don't worry about it, you can always rewrite.

YOU: That's all there is to it, writing and rewriting?

MEP: Not quite . . . but it's a start, no?

YOU: I don't know . . . that exercise was pretty short . . .

MEP: Short? Samuel Beckett wrote a whole play that consisted of forty lines.

YOU: Some TV commercials are even less —

MEP: Let's stick to the stage, partner.

YOU: When do we get started?

MEP: You already have! But remember, this isn't a cookbook with easy rules and set formulas. No quickie short cuts — there'll be lots of hard work. But if we can help you to find your own individual voice on the page, your imagination's own special ideas — well, then —

YOU: You can write a play ....

MEP: Hey, not a bad title for a book . . .

YOU: We'll see —

(They exit.)

MORE RAW MATERIALS

Read . . . any one-act or longer play of your choice. Whenever possible, see a play, a live stage production playing in your community or a movie adapted from a stage play.

Act out . . . a conversation with a friend or a member of your family. Now inject a conflict into the conversation. Discuss how the mood and actions changed after conflict was introduced.

Write . . . if you like, a one-act play, either based on the dialogue in this Introduction or something else on your mind. If you are wondering how you can write a play even before reading the rest of this book, the results may be surprising. The play may be raw, but remember that clay comes from mud. And from clay — who knows what fabulous creations might come forth?

Daydreaming in *How to Succeed in Business Without Really Trying* ... How to succeed in playwriting? Write!

chapter I

EXPLORING THE DRAMATIC MEDIUM

... the purpose of playing, whose end, both at the first and now, was and is, to hold, as 'twere the mirror up to nature ...
— *Hamlet*

δραμα
"Drama" — of Greek origin, meaning "to do" or "to act"

Let your eyes glance casually around the room. Now close your eyes for a moment, then open them again slowly and imagine that the surrounding walls are suddenly collapsing and the furniture is magically whisked away. You no longer find yourself in an enclosed, familiar space.

Instead, you are sitting on the ground in a circle in the company of your fellow villagers facing a smoldering fire. You are huddled together, not only because there is a chill in the air, but because you fear something. An attack. An attack by a hostile tribe or perhaps an unfriendly animal. But you also sit in awe of the wondrous things you hear and see in front of you.

Through the wisps of curling smoke, you can barely make out the shadows of two dancers quietly circling the fire, stalking each other. One of them is a hunter, erect, alert, spear in hand, approaching his quarry — a fearsome lion. You know it's not a real lion; you wouldn't be sitting still if it were. No, this lion is portrayed by one of the villagers wearing a mask and bedecked in lion skins.

Skillfully miming the lion's movements, as if the spirit from the skins were absorbed into the human body, the person playing the lion attacks. You and the rest of the villagers chant in unison — cries of disappointment, now cheers, as the hunter retreats, spins around, jumps up, avoiding the lion's sharp teeth. The hunter suddenly slips, the animal is ready to attack again — it looks as if it's all over as the lion leaps high. The chanting becomes faster and curiously softer as if careful control could turn the

tide. The hunter lunges with a spear, and the lion leaps forward —

The moment is filled with danger — tension — crisis —WHO WILL WIN?

In this chapter, we focus on exploring the dramatic medium by asking:

- What are the beginnings of drama?
- What is a dramatic experience in life?
- What is the nature of dramatic action on stage?
- What is a play?
- What are the parts of a play?
- What are the types of plays?
- What are the differences between a one-act and a longer play?

THE BEGINNINGS OF DRAMA

As stage designer Robert Edmond Jones suggests in his book *The Dramatic Imagination* , [1] the origins of drama were really magical rites, half danced and half mimed. Tribal chanting, cheers of encouragement, and groans of frustration accompanied the first musical instruments, the bodies of the actors themselves.

As seen from the example, if hunting tribes during the Stone Age lacked meat they enacted a hunting scene. To us, this is a ritual; to them it was seri-

---

[1] Robert Edmond Jones, *The Dramatic Imagination* (New York: Routledge 1987).

The primitive origins of theatre — dealing with survival — are reflected in modern ritual drama, as in this production of *Gilgamesh*.

ous business. Some of the actors became the hunting party, and others, the hunted game. These dramas developed into emotionally charged life-and-death struggles. There was fascination in the magic of hiding your own identity by impersonating someone else. And such a variety of characters: foe, demon, deity, or supporter-in-arms. The overriding issue in these dramas was the very survival of the human race.

With issues of life and death at stake, you can be assured that the primitive plays were far from aimless exercises. In fact, they were enacted with great purpose — a way of playing out in the imagination an actual or projected event difficult to manage in real life. By imitating the event, the tribespeople believed they were better able in make-believe to control their fears, wishes, and destinies than normal means would allow.

Employing the imagination to become someone or something else was a powerful discovery. As hunter progressed to farmer and town dweller, the rituals of life and death assumed new forms. For example, if the hero or god of a tribe were portrayed

as slain, it was imperative that he or she be magically resurrected as well. This enactment could be allegorically represented by the death of winter and the renewal of spring and summer. The spirit of corn and other symbols of the harvest became important concepts and characters in the fertility rites of ancient Egypt. In the earliest dramas then, long before the advent of the Greeks to the stages of Epidaurus, plays might recount a daily event of the tribe, an act of bravery or other such accomplishment. Drama, in addition to being a depicter of events, therefore could be a healer, an instructor, an entertainer. Entertainment in its most literal and universal sense means to hold or capture attention and interest.

DRAMA, THE REFLECTIVE ART

The history of playwriting is as old as the history of people. For whenever people have had problems — and when have they not? — people have had a strong need. This is to express their deepest concerns in some art form, much as a young child might act out in fantasy those things that make a strong impression in life:

All drama springs from life:
people — problems — particular time and place

As we have seen, the earliest communal dramas reflected primitive people's concern with survival. Those dramas were handed down from one generation to the next by word of mouth. As civilization progressed, dramas reflecting other kinds of problems evolved into *written* expression, usually unified by a single playwright's vision.

The Greeks with their majestic, ennobling tragedies and down-to-earth comedies, the Roman farces, spicy medieval morality plays, the towering Shakespearean repertory, the Molière satirical delights, the social concerns of Shaw and Ibsen, and today's plays of merit have in their own ways mirrored humanity at its highest and lowest points of existence.

What are our deepest concerns, our hopes, desires, fears? How do we live with others — and alone? How do we "find ourselves" and struggle for self-worth and inner dignity, happiness, and love? In what ways do we avoid pain, suffering, and death? How ought we live in the face of adversity or threat of conflict? What are the values we cherish or abuse? What are the myriad ways of expressing behavior that conforms to or resists these values? These concerns — or lack of concerns — are as diverse and complicated as there are kinds of people. A playwright, as one person, uses a special vision in which dramatic experience acts as a mirror to look more closely at life in personal and dramatic ways.

——————— WHAT IF ———————
your mind were slowly enlarged into a gigantic movie screen, flashing images of what bothers you most in life? Spontaneously write down some of those things, brainstorm with yourself, the *first* things that come to mind:

Big things   Happy things   Familiar things
Little things   Sad things   Far-off things

Pick just *one* of those things and on-the-spot enact a three-minute scene with a friend. Concentrate on *who* you are, *what* you want, and *where* you are as the scene develops.

————————————————————

THE NATURE OF DRAMATIC EXPERIENCE

The British playwright J. B. Priestly, in his book *The Art of the Dramatist*, described "dramatic" as the "rare moment in our lives — perhaps when we are physically exhausted but alert in spirit when we find ourselves in great danger — when reality itself turns into dramatic experience as if the whole world were a giant theatre and all this life a drama, so much playacting compared with some unknown deeper reality." [2]

We have all experienced problems that have their moments of heightened conflict and periods of crisis, those times when what is happening to you is most intense — an accident, a near death, a high-risk situation, an embarrassing moment. Emotions run high. Perhaps during these heightened moments you have been expecting one thing and get another that arouses a strong feeling of disappointment or triggers a call to action. It could be a quiet action like waiting for someone important in your life who doesn't appear, or perhaps shows up in a way totally unfamiliar to you. Perhaps a problem has produced a heated argument, challenge, or fight because what you want is blocked by someone else. Maybe one of your own goals is being blocked by yourself and you don't know it.

One of the main reasons we go to the theatre is to see how interesting and vital characters resolve human conflicts and crises under specific circumstances. Simply put:

Dramatic Experience in Life	Dramatic Action on Stage
People (have wants) — —	Characters (have goals)
Problems (wants — — — are denied)	Conflicts and Crises (goals are blocked)

[2] J. B. Priestly, *The Art of the Dramatist* (London: Heineman, 1973), p. 5.

Time and Place — — — Specific Circumstances
(when and where)   (when and where)

Just minutes ago your mind turned into a movie screen and you explored images. To a great extent what you decide to write about further will take the shape of what Robert Edmond Jones calls a "synthesis of dream and actuality" — magical images that *find form in dramatic action.*

Images on Stage

• On one side of the stage, a learned physician is lecturing to a group of medical students. The slides he shows are of a curious nineteenth-century phenomenon known as John Merrick. Is Merrick man or beast? We see his crippled body hideously deformed. A mammoth lopsided head rests tenuously on his frail, twisted body. As the slide demonstration continues, a handsome actor dressed only in a loin cloth on the other side of the stage slowly contorts his body and almost magically assumes the shape of what the audience sees graphically displayed on the slides. The actor lifts his shoulder slightly to the side, tilts his body forward, and begins to walk with a painful limp. The image fills the minds of the audience through the rest of the play. Although they will never see the real John Merrick of the slides (afflicted with the genetic disease neurofibromatosis), they will feel his anguish and aspirations. Such is the power and the magic of the theatre to transform experience in Bernard Pomerance's *The Elephant Man.*

• The off-Broadway theatre is dark as the audience waits for the play to start. The stage is still bare as a breezy melody is heard — a popular World War II tune called "Don't Sit Under the Apple Tree." Suddenly, a different kind of sound is heard. A gun shot. The nostalgic mood of the song is shattered. A black, middle-aged tech sergeant staggers on stage, wounded. Another shot. The man stumbles around in the shadows of the stage. In a drunken, gravelly voice he shouts, "They hate you!" and collapses on the roadway near a woods. Who killed the sergeant? The Ku Klux Klan, white officers, or his own men? The scenes leading up to the fateful shooting poignantly unfold in Charles Fuller's masterful work *A Soldier's Play.*

• The play is almost over. Three sisters are joyfully digging into an enormous cake covered with candles. They're celebrating the birthday of Lenny, the eldest sister. It's strange — and funny — and sad, but the play began with one measly candle on a little cookie. Now, as we approach the end, Lenny has grown to reveal a dormant tough side of her personality. Her sisters have also gone through some amazing comic-tragic changes in Beth Henley's Pulitzer Prize-winning play *Crimes of the Heart.*

• On another stage, a skillful actor impersonates a beaten up Russian piebald horse, which we sense carries the very yoke of humanity on its broad shoulders. The play, *Strider,* by Robert Kalfin and Steve Brown, is an all too real allegory of rejection and defiance, a bittersweet folk tale not really about horses, but hailing the spirit of humanity.

With this magical image in mind, are we really too far afield from our first example, when people portrayed lions to show the spirit of survival?

With the passage of time, a slight shift of character, and a change of lights and makeup, the fearsome lion becomes the cowardly lion in *The Wizard of Oz;* the transformed feline who cleverly reveals her charms in *My Fair Lady;* the hunted, wounded prince known as Hamlet; or two friendly foes sharing a meal that turns into a comic shambles in *The Odd Couple.*

DRAMATIC ACTION ON STAGE

Writing a play is an art as well as a craft. Playwriting is a reflective art that not only mirrors the concerns of society but reflects artistic forms as well. A play springs from life, reflects life, but strictly speaking, is not life. The materials of a play, much like a potter's clay, must be selected and shaped into an artistic form that has some kind of beginning, middle, and end.

Dramatic action comes out of an image or an image emerges from an action. Each reinforces the

The universal drama of hunter and prey finds continuing creative expression in *The Wiz*.

other. Dramatic action is developmental. A central character has a goal — it is blocked — new problems are created out of old strategies and game plans. Life on stage is as complex as the intersecting lives of its characters require it to be.

It is important to distinguish between action in a play and dramatic action. Dramatic action is not mere physical movement; it is movement in which characters develop, grow, and change or intensify patterns of development and relationships.

Consider the famous "battle" scene (Act II, Scene 3) in William Gibson's *The Miracle Worker*, in which Annie Sullivan, Helen Keller's teacher, makes a last-ditch effort to get the six-year-old to sit down at the table, fold her napkin, and eat with a fork. Helen resists. Annie chases Helen around the table,

pushes her into a chair; Helen breaks away, crawls under the table, is picked up and subdued for a bit, then breaks away again, licks her plate like a voracious animal, pounds on the table, tries to throw the fork away. There is more grappling, tussling, and she is finally held to the chair.

It is a stirring turning point in the play because, as beaming Annie Sullivan explains, the "room is a wreck, but she folded her napkin."

The emotional ups and downs of the play shape the dramatic action. It is Helen's struggle to learn to use language to (in her mother's words) "be like you and me." Remember, Helen's father had wanted to put the girl in an asylum for mental defectives before Annie arrived. So really the dramatic action includes the ultimate acceptance of Helen's condition and the challenges of the girl to assert herself, as well as Annie's heroic efforts to help Helen discover the miracle. The rest of the family, too, must undergo change, especially Helen's elder brother, who finally comes to understand his sister and challenges his father to understand her better too, so that the "seeing blind" can surrender their prejudices. A line like Annie's "it's less trouble to feel sorry for her than to teach her anything" reverberates with meaning and feeling when we consider how the Keller family was treating Helen before the advent of Annie. The play is a stirring story of faith and courage, the testing of the human will to survive and soar.

——————— JUST FOR YOU ———————

Based on your experience of going to the theatre or seeing movies and television plays, what do you think a play is or *seems* to be? Discuss this with friends or make an artistic or photographic collage of what you love about the theatre ... pour your soul into it. (See page 28.)

We know, for example, that a play is a kind of story that is enacted on the stage before an audience. We know it deals with a problem or a question that has to be solved by a central character who is opposed by at least one other character in a struggle (or conflict) that reaches an emotional crisis of some sort.

Here are two definitions you may find helpful:

The drama presents a sequence of situations in which characters express themselves through what happens to them, what they do or (even) fail to do. [3]

A play is an image of human life created in the minds of an audience by the enactment of a pattern of life. [4]

PARTS OF A PLAY

The Greek scholar and theoretician Aristotle

[3] John Gassner, *Producing the Play* (New York: Dryden Press, 1953), p. 11.
[4] James H. Clay and Daniel Krempel, *The Theatrical Image* (Baltimore: Rowman and Littlefield, 1985), p. 26.

(384-322 B.C.) divided the play (based on tragedies he had seen) into six main parts. This categorization still serves as a useful guide for the would-be playwright to sort things out and get the wheels of the imagination moving:

A. THEME: According to Aristotle, theme is the ability to say what the circumstances allow and what is appropriate to them. You could say theme is the central idea that *emerges from the dramatic action of the play*, never a message or a statement imposed upon the action by the playwright. In the drama of the hunter and the lion, the theme might be (1) the universal struggle of humankind with the forces of nature, or perhaps (2) an early account of the survival of the fittest.

B. PLOT: According to Aristotle, the "fable" (as he termed plot) is "... the arrangement (structure) of the incidents." A practical way of looking at plot is to ask:

Who is doing what to whom
where, when, and why?

Helen Keller and her teacher, Annie Sullivan, struggle in the famous "battle" scene of *The Miracle Worker*. Physical action is not the same as dramatic action.

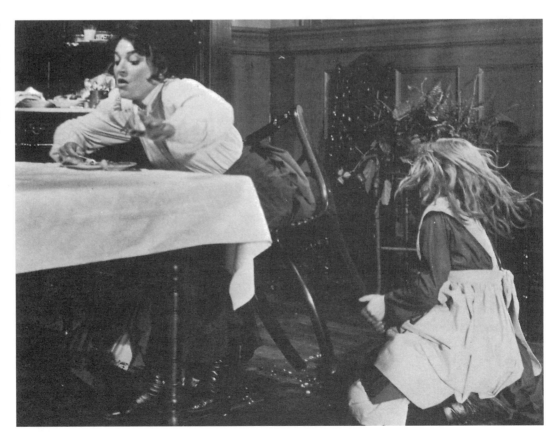

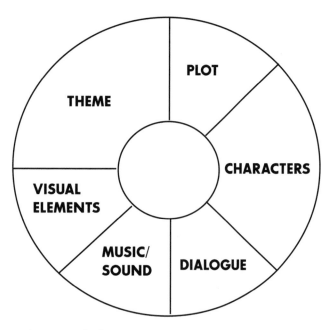

Elements of Plot

1) *Point of attack:* The point or time in the play when the dramatic action begins. (In the drama of the hunter and lion, food runs out in the village; hunter must go out to search for food.)

2) *Exposition:* Incidents or events from the past or happenings outside of the play of which the audience must be aware in order to comprehend characters and plot (i.e., village has been without food, hunter chosen to search for food is brave, lion is feared).

3) *Preparation:* The earlier "planting" of certain information, so that a particular character or scene will be believable (i.e., last chance to find the food, hunter blessed with good spirits for a successful hunt, stake great).

4) *Conflict:* An internal struggle within one person or between two or more characters; the heart of plot (i.e., hunter vs. lion).

5) *Complications:* The introduction of a fact or character already in the play that grows out of the conflict and delays the climax. (Hunter at several points loses spear: lion gains advantage.)

6) *Crisis:* The protagonist has to make a major decision that is also a key turning point in the dramatic action. (How will the hunter evade the lion's claws?)

7) *Dramatic question or problem:* The suspense question related to the fate of the central character's major goal. (Will hunter defeat lion?)

8) *Climax:* The highest emotional peak in a play. (Hunter triumphs over lion.)

9) *Resolution:* The point after the climax, during which any remaining questions are answered. (Lion brought back to village for tribespeople to see, lion becomes food, hunter rewarded for brave achievement.)

C. CHARACTERS: According to Aristotle, "the agents of the incidents." In practical terms, there are three general kinds of characters in a play:

1) *Central characters:* These are characters around whom the dramatic action revolves or who have the dominant objective in the play (hunter, to defeat the lion and bring back food).

2) *Opposing characters:* These are characters who provide the basic obstacles by blocking the central character's objective (lion, to defeat hunter).

3) *Contributing characters:* These are characters who line up with the central character (hunter's helpers) or with the opposing character; sometimes both, at different times.

D. MUSIC: Termed "melody" by Aristotle, this part refers to any music that may appear in a play. Not all plays today include the element of music (chants supplied by tribe sitting in circle, songs of hunter and lion).

E. DIALOGUE: According to Aristotle, "diction" in the play. Quite simply, what a character says and how he or she says it, be it street language, poetry, or slang (sounds of hunter and lion).

F. SPECTACLE: According to Aristotle, the "embellishments" in a play. Today, referred to as all the visual elements: scenery, costumes, lighting, movement, gestures, and other nonverbal elements (masks, spears, lion skins, and so forth).

There are at least two major kinds of production styles:

1) *Stage as "picture":* These are attempts to create a "realistic" picture or illusion of life as though you

were peeking through a fourth wall. Realistic scenery is portrayed in varying degrees.

Examples: Realistic plays such as Lorraine Hansberry's *A Raisin in the Sun* or Goodrich and Hackett's *The Diary of Anne Frank.*

2) *Stage as "platform":* Presents life on stage rather than represents it as a picture. Stage is a stage, with no pretense of "realism."

Examples: Lerner and Loewe's *My Fair Lady* and Samuel Beckett's *Waiting for Godot.*

TYPES OF PLAYS

A. *Tragedy:* Themes are serious in depth and worthiness; the central character (hero) struggles to overcome overpowering obstacles but instead is overcome by them, resulting in death.
Examples: Shakespeare's *Hamlet;* Arthur Miller's *Death of a Salesman; West Side Story* by Leonard Bernstein, Arthur Laurents, Jerome Robbins, and Stephen Sondheim; Euripides' *Oedipus Rex;* John M. Synge's one-act play *Riders to the Sea.*

B. *Drama:* Themes are serious in nature; but unlike tragedy, the central character in overcoming obstacles does not die at the end of the play.
Examples: A Raisin in the Sun; Harold Pinter's *The Homecoming;* Terence Rattigan's *The Browning Version; The Miracle Worker.*

C. *Melodrama:* Themes are exaggerated in their seriousness; the central characters (heroes/heroines) overcome villains in sensational plots usually crowded with action and conflict.
Examples: Eugene O'Neill's *The Personal Equation,* Mrs. Henry Wood's *East Lynne.*

D. *Comedy:* A humorous play with light or serious themes whose central characters succeed in overcoming all obstacles.
Examples: Neil Simon's *The Odd Couple;* Anton Chekhov's *The Boor;* Shakespeare's *As You Like It;* musical comedies such as *My Fair Lady.*

In turn, comedy can be subdivided as follows:

1) *High Comedy:* A humorous play whose central characters reside in the upper stratum of society and whose verbal wit pokes fun at societal conventions and manners.
Examples: Oscar Wilde's *The Importance of Being Ernest;* plays by Noël Coward.

2) *Serious Comedy:* A humorous play whose central characters are to be found in all strata of society and who overcome obstacles in dealing with serious themes.
Examples: Beth Henley's *Crimes of the Heart* and Neil Simon's *The Odd Couple.*

3) *Satire:* A humorous play whose themes criticize or ridicule human foibles, showing the absurdity of characters who take themselves too seriously.
Examples: Burrows' and Loesser's *How to Succeed in Business Without Really Trying;* Brecht's and Weill's *The Three Penny Opera.*

4) *Farce:* A humorous play whose improbable characters find themselves in unlikely and ridiculous situations featuring zany and unexpected kinds of actions.
Example:s Michael Frayn's *Noises Off,* Nikolai Gogol's *The Inspector General.*

5) *Situation Comedy:* A humorous play in which strongly contrasting characters find themselves in unexpected "fluff" situations, which are generally happily resolved.
Examples: TV situation comedies such as "*Friends*" and "*Seinfeld.*"

6) *Low Comedy:* A humorous play whose improbable characters overcome obstacles and whose behavior depends more on physical action and slapstick than on verbal wit.
Examples: Sugar Babies; vaudeville skits such as "Dr. Kronkite"; baggy-pants burlesque revues.

E. *Fantasy:* A serious or humorous play (often a combination of both) in which "unreal" characters with human traits overcome obstacles in a

land of make-believe.
Examples: *The Wizard of Oz*; Jean Giraudoux's *The Apollo of Bellac*.

F. *Allegory*: A play serious or humorous (or a combination of both), often written in a poetic or fairy-tale style featuring abstract characters.
Examples: Maurice Maeterlinck's *The Blue Bird*; the medieval morality play *Everyman*.

Such play forms as monodramas, docudramas, revues, and story theatre are discussed in Chapter X.

A Word About Terms

Playwrights are often intentionally unaware of the kind of play they are writing until they are well into it or have completed it. When Anton Chekhov, for example, thought he was writing a comedy, it turned out to be poignantly mellow or in the vein of tragicomedy. One scene in Neil Simon's *The Odd Couple* had the cast in tears during rehearsal but turned out uproariously funny when played before an audience. Some college students asked satirist Abe Burrows, coauthor of *How to Succeed in Business Without Really Trying*, if he ever aspired to write something serious. Burrows laughed and responded

that all comedy is based on serious concerns.

Relying only on terms to describe something can be misleading. *The Wizard of Oz*, one of the plays referred to in this text as an example of fine plotting, is both a musical fantasy and a serious comedy with elements of finely tuned satire. Whereas Hamlet is universally acknowledged as a tragedy, *Death of a Salesman* is considered a tragedy or a serious drama. Its author, Arthur Miller, calls it a "play in two acts with a requiem." *The Odd Couple* is a serious comedy with elements of farce. Pinter's *The Homecoming* is a serious drama with aspects of allegory. Ansky's *The Dybukk* is a towering tragedy, a folk drama, and a musical fantasy.

Content often colors the form, which in turn leaves wide open the question of the kind of play the work is. The great *Sweeney Todd* by Hugh Wheeler, Stephen Sondheim, and Harold Prince has been called a musical comedy, a "grim" comedy, and a "musical thriller." Joseph Stein's *Fiddler on the Roof* is a folk drama, a musical comedy, an allegory. *Blithe Spirit* is a pungent satire on mediums and the medical profession but also (with its array of ghosts) a delightful fantasy. Noël Coward, its author, subtitled the play "An improbable farce in three acts."

An excellent example of "stage as platform," which is a presentation of life rather than a representation of life. The final scene of *West Side Story* as staged in a constructivistic setting. (See page 125.) The production style also has elements of ritual.

Though it is important to be intellectually aware of the various kinds of drama and comedy, don't get trapped in terms when you write your own play. Instead, be concerned about characters and the situations they find themselves in that make for vital drama presented in a form that best expresses what the characters have to say and do under specific circumstances.

DIFFERENCES BETWEEN A ONE-ACT AND LONGER PLAY

The motto for writing a one-act play could be:

One Sitting — One Setting — One Sighting

That is, generally there is no need for an intermission or many changes (if any) of scenery; and what one sees on stage is unified in theme, characters, and plot. Here are some other key differences:

Theme

A theme can be effectively conveyed in any of the theater forms discussed. Shortness is by no means a measure of quality of work. Neither is there a limitation on content. Sophocles' *Oedipus Rex*, a long one-act play, is one of the finest dramas ever written.

The short play is more likely to be successful when it impresses upon its audience one basic idea or theme explored as fully as possible within a time span of fifteen to thirty minutes.

Plot

A one-act play usually explores a single dramatic action. There are usually no subplots. Characters and conflicts are sharply drawn, and exposition must be brief with no wasted dramatic action.

Characters

Because of the relatively short time span of a one-act play (ten minutes to an hour), there is less opportunity to fully explore too many characters.

Dialogue

Be especially wary of long "talky" speeches except when benefiting character (such as Ivan Vassiliyitch Lomov's defensive speech in Chekhov's one-acter *A Marriage Proposal*). Songs or music may be included if they belong organically to the play as a whole.

Setting

Usually one set is sufficient, as there is no time to change scenery, unless changes are effected through use of levels, light projections, reversible scenery, mime, narration, story theatre (Chapter X), or other imaginative techniques that blend into and are an integral part of the play.

THE PLAYWRIGHT'S TASK

In writing a play, your job will be to transform real-life or imagined experience based on life into a theatre experience. The experience, dramatic in nature, may not have happened to you directly. You may have heard, or read about, or altogether made up the experience. But in any case, you will most likely feel strongly enough to want to discover more about the experience (or gaps in the experience) to invest the time, energy, and love to write a play about it.

——————— JUST FOR YOU ———————

In your notebook list some of the things in life that concern you the most.

• Problems in the world
• Personal problems (yours or someone else's — who?)
• Could any of these concerns form the basis of a play?

Write down which problem interests you the most. Now start acting it out in your mind. Write some dialogue. It does not have to add up; the important thing is to get it down.

IN SUM: DRAMA, THE REFLECTIVE ART

Concepts explored in this chapter will become

more meaningful as you reread or think about them, especially when you are in the process of writing and rewriting your play. Writing will help you reflect on and discover what your play is attempting to communicate.

From its very beginnings, drama has sprung from life, reflecting the problems and pleasures of people at a particular time and place.

A play is a patterned sequence of situations or images in which characters reveal who they are and how they feel through what they *do*. Drama means "to do" or "to act." Dramatic action on stage takes the form of characters in conflict with each other. This conflict builds through details of characterization and plotting to a crisis and resolution of the problem.

The six parts of a play include theme, plot, character, dialogue, music, and spectacle (visual elements).

As we shall see, any or all of these parts can spark ideas for your own play, whether it is a one-act or longer, tragedy, drama, melodrama, high comedy, satire, low comedy, farce, fantasy, or allegory. Any of these kinds of plays can be mixed. For example, *Oedipus Rex* is a poetic tragedy in one act, a suspenseful mystery, a detective story, and a play of character and ideas. A play, however, should have a unity of form and/or purpose.

Drama not only reflects the concerns of society and the vision of the artist, but through rewriting gives the playwright a chance to rethink or further reflect on the substance and style of the play and particular aspects of life.

PLAYWRIGHT'S PAGE

1) Do you have any ideas on what your play will be about? (When asked this question, some writers quip, "About an hour too long. ")

2) Which part of your play do you think will come easiest — dialogue, character, plotting, or what? Try some dialogue right now (write now), and see how it turns out.

3) Drama has been referred to as "the reflective art." Reflect about this for a moment. What does the word "drama" mean to you?

4) How would you describe the difference between *action* and *dramatic action*? Give an example or two from life. Try an example from a play.

5) What is your favorite play — read or seen? What do you especially like about it?

MORE **RAW** MATERIALS

Read . . .*Oedipus Rex*, by Sophocles, the majestic tragedy of suffering and redemption. Also read the story and one-act play version of *The Devil and Daniel Webster* by Stephen Vincent Benét.

Act ... out some scenes with conflict. With a partner play "Twist 'n' Turn," an effectively easy way to experience drama first-hand. Here's how:

Both you and your partner Twist 'n' Turn in space for a few seconds. One of you quickly yells out "Freeze!"

One maintains the frozen position (say your hand is out, palm up) while the other unfreezes. The one who unfreezes starts the dialogue using the position of the other to spur the imagination. For example, say B is the one who is frozen with the palm up:

A: I don't give to beggars.
B: I just need a little —
A: Forget it.
B: Aw, please — etc., etc.,   (see photo, p. 26)

Remember to introduce conflict into the scene; carry through a confrontation rather than just hold a conversation. Each of you pursue your goal strongly. Play the scene for a few minutes, then switch. Twist 'n' Turn again. Enact not only familiar situations, but go back into history or project into the future. Reach for interesting, vital characters who have strong goals. Don't use your own names; make up names. This acting exercise is valuable because it spontaneously explores a fundamental unit of drama—two people who either want to do something *for* each other or *to* each other; or who want something *from* each other.

Here's another easy, yet challenging exercise: "Bag-o-Drama." With some people (from three to six) place in an ordinary shopping bag some unrelated objects, such as a comb, a book, a tie, beads. Take ten to fifteen minutes to make up a short play with a beginning-middle-end and strong conflict. (The props can also symbolize other things; e.g., the tie can be a tourniquet or a snake.) Don't plan the dialogue. It's more fun when "it just happens." Do, however, plan an ending, and discuss main physical and vocal traits for each character:

- WHO he or she is
- WHAT he or she wants
- WHERE the scene takes place

After the skit, talk about what worked out best and why.

Write . . .

1) Your own version (update it, if you like) of the dialogue between the hunter and the lion.

2) Some of the scenes that developed during the Twist 'n' Turn exercises.

3) The sketch you made up for "Bag-o-Drama."

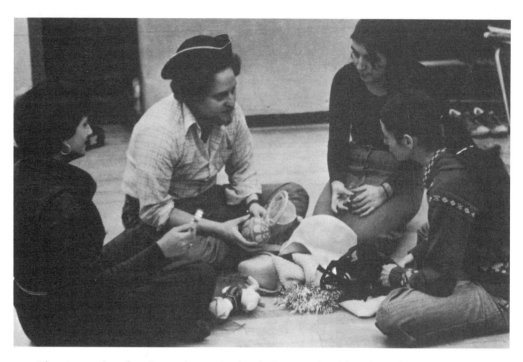

Planning and performing an improvisational play stimulated by a bag of unrelated props.

—— SUGGESTIONS FOR CLASSROOM ACTIVITIES ——

You may be reading this at school, in a summer theatre barn, or in a community center classroom. Along with developing as a playwright, would you want to become an actor, director or simply expand your knowledge of theatre? Perhaps you wish to explore and express yourself through another form of writing. No matter where or why you are using this text, these solo and group activities will help you draw — from yourself — ideas that you can develop in playwriting. Everybody has different creative instincts, impulses and learning styles. Browse through these exercises and choose the ones of interest to you and your group.

Discuss these questions in your group:
• Has seeing, reading or writing a play ever changed or affected how you think or feel about some aspect of life? Share some examples.
• Look at the photos in the book. Share some examples of dramatic feelings, situations and images (such as mentioned in the chapter) that are meaningful in your life. How so?

ONGOING CLASS OR GROUP PROJECT
This activity can be extended over a period of time to fit the needs of the class/group. Create a dramatic collage of what drama/theatre means to you. Your collage can include drawings of your impressions of plays, props, people, playbills, bits of dialogue from plays you have read or seen — or from plays you are writing. (See examples on page 28.)

Read
You may wish to share, in your group, some of your "What If?" (page 16) responses and "Playwrights Page" (page 24) responses. Any surprises? Why?

Act
• Try some more "Twist 'n' Turn" and "Bag-o-Drama" exercises explained on page 24 — with different combinations of people. Doing improvisations like these can help free the imagination and impart a sense of what is dramatic.

    • Improvise a real-life situation. For example, someone is coming home very late at night during mid-week. Assign CHARACTERS and CIRCUMSTANCES: Who is it? (A student coming home from a date? Grandparent coming home from a binge? A homeless person coming home to a home that is not a home?) Why is he or she coming home so late now? Determine the ACTION. Who is waiting? (A strict parent, nosy neighbors, the cops?) What happens when the latecomer arrives? Play out the CONSEQUENCES. (What is the outcome?)

Write . . .
    • a one- to three-minute scene on ANY topic of your choice. Then identify the central and opposing characters, what each wants in the scene, and the basic

Twist 'n' Turn: Be careful with that basin of water, Mom!

In this depiction of a Navajo medicinal drama, the goddess at the right performs initiation rites on a youth. At the left, the masked man who portrays a god of healing is driving evil spirits from a patient. In what ways do you think drama reflects the concerns of modern-day society?

conflict between them. How does action differ from *dramatic* action?

If you've ever tried to write a story, you're aware that dramatic action can play an important part in a narrative's development. But a story need not have a strong dramatic line to work as a story, especially if it focuses on only one character or is a mood piece.

• a letter to yourself about a moment when you felt a strong emotion. Could this be the beginning of

a play? Does it come from the heart? Is the subject matter important to you? How so?

NOTEBOOK (JOURNAL) FEATURE

Your journal provides a wonderful opportunity for you to collect, explore, and express personal observations and reflections about so many varied subjects. It can become so personal that you may even decide to give your journal a name. That's what Gemma Cooper-Novack, a winner of a Young Playwrights Conference national playwriting contest (see "Contests" in Chapter X), did when she named her notebook "RMPN" (Random Multi-Purpose Notebook). She especially enjoys writing down ideas, quotes, lists, dreams, and bits of overheard dialogue.

Keep a running record of the play you are writing — notes, images, questions, bits of dialogue, sketches, doodles, whatever fancies the imagination. Remember that inspiration can come from anywhere: advertisements, interactions between people, artwork, music, photographs or the newspaper. You can include, alter, update your ideas and feelings in the "Just for You" and "What If" and "Playwright's Page" sections. Or you may decide to start from scratch. In any case, for now

come up with at least *one* idea for a play you would like to write. Here are some examples of journal suggestions to get you started:

• Once I was in real trouble when . . .
• My friend (or family member) was really angry when . . .
• I felt sorry for _____ who I heard did _____ because . . .
• I read in the paper that _____ wishes he or she could . . .
• If I could take a time machine back in time or into the future, I would . . .
• If I could change one thing about school it would be . . .
• My (parents) (boss) (neighbor) . . .

Your memories and flashes of insight about any of the above may provide a starter for your current play or become part of other plays you write in the future. That is why a notebook is so valuable — to capture the flashes and keep them together.

Ntozake Shange's *for colored girls who have considered/ suicide when the rainbow is not enuf* is grounded in specific stories of women abused by men. This poetic play is a cry for survival and an anthem of strength of "everywoman" in society. In what ways do you think plays, serious or light, reflect or reveal some aspect of the human condition?

DRAMATIC EXPERIENCE — SOME FEELINGS AND REFLECTIONS

Creative Ongoing Collage: A company of young people participating in the "Looking for Shakespeare" summer workshop (sponsored by the New York University Program in Educational Theatre under the direction of Alistair Martin-Smith) integrated scenes from Shakespeare with parallel contemporary scenes and monologues they wrote. In the "Room of Possibilities" at the theatre, walls were papered with a collage of cut-out images. Surrounded by this visual environment, the students created their silhouettes of characters, drawings, and designs.

In Jonathan Larson's Pulitzer Prize-winning musical, *Rent*, Mimi and Roger have AIDS, but never completely abandon hope.

MIMI: I should tell you. I blew the candle out/Just to get back in.
ROGER: I'd forgotten how to smile/until your candle burned my skin …

Why is the expression of feelings so important in plays?

chapter II

NARRATIVE VS. DRAMATIC

> Play out the play . . .
> And thereby hangs a tale
>
> —Shakespeare

By contrasting essential differences between the story and play forms, the nature of the dramatic medium can be further clarified. In this chapter we ask:

- What are the essential differences between the narrative and dramatic forms?
- What are the unities of action, time, and place?
- Why is form especially important in writing a play?

To help answer these questions, let's compare the original story and the one-act play version of *The Devil and Daniel Webster*, both written by Stephen Vincent Benét. It is suggested that both works be read for a fuller comprehension of this chapter.

SYNOPSIS OF STORY [1]

The story concerns Daniel Webster, "the biggest man" in the U.S., and how he saved the Union from the devil himself. Webster was so eloquent that when he spoke, stars and stripes seemed to pop right out of the sky. Trout jumped out of the streams into his pocket when he went fishing. And there simply was no use trying to challenge him in a legal fight. But, somehow, Webster's biggest case never made the history books. Here's what happened:

Jabez Stone, a hard-working farmer, lived in Cross Corners, New Hampshire. His luck at farm-

[1] *The Devil and Daniel Webster and Other Writings of Stephen Vincent Benét* (New York: Viking Penguin, Inc., 1999).

ing was so miserable that instead of potatoes he got blight, and the rest of the crops were just as poor. Jabez was blessed with a wonderful wife and children. But the more young ones the family had, the less Jabez was able to feed them because of his hard times. Things got so bad that Jabez vowed it was enough "to make a man want to sell his soul to the devil! And would, too, for two cents!"

Almost as soon as he made the rash vow, strange things began to happen. The very next day there appeared a soft-spoken, well-dressed stranger, whose flashing white teeth were filed to razor-sharp points. The stranger presently proposed a deal that would make Jabez wealthy. Jabez agreed. The stranger mysteriously pricked Jabez's finger, leaving a little white scar. And so the bargain was sealed.

Jabez's fortunes immediately changed for the better, and he began to prosper mightily. His crops were the envy of the neighborhood. Nothing or nobody could harm him. If, for example, lightning struck the valley, it curiously passed right by the Stone farm. Jabez Stone became so popular that he was overwhelmingly elected a state senator.

Then, just as mysteriously as he first appeared, the stranger with the sharp teeth called again. He was ready to claim Jabez as a "closed account" and stuff him into his little black box. Jabez pleaded with him and managed to get a three-year extension. Two years passed. Jabez continued to prosper; there were those who wanted him to run for governor.

Jabez was deeply worried, for he knew the stranger would soon be returning to collect on his "mortgage." So he hitched up his wagon and drove off to see Daniel Webster. The great man was so touched by Jabez's plight that he immediately dropped his Missouri Compromise antislavery case, journeyed to New Hampshire and, drawing up a jug of brew, prepared for a long siege. As the two men sat in Stone's kitchen, Jabez begged Daniel to leave. After all, he couldn't let the devil take the Union's pride and joy. Daniel Webster responded that he never left a jug or a case half-finished.

As soon as the devil appeared, Daniel faced off with him. The argument began in earnest. First, Daniel tried to compromise with the devil. Now that Senator Stone was so well known, his life ought to be worth more than that of a farmer. So the mortgage should be defaulted! The devil didn't buy that argument, so Webster had to switch tactics. Wasn't it true, he asked, that no American could be forced into the service of a foreign prince?

Scratch — as the devil called himself — laughingly countered that as a "foreign prince" he fit very nicely into the American scheme of things: "When the first wrong was done to the first Indian, I was there. When the first slaver put out for the Congo, I stood on her deck . . ."

Seeing what he was up against, Daniel demanded an immediate trial for his client. Jabez was sick with terror. What would Scratch do now? There suddenly materialized a jury of twelve of the most terrible renegades, traitors, and thieves ever assembled in one room. The deadly roster included the despicable Walter Butler, a loyalist traitor who spread fire and horror through the Mohawk Valley during the Revolutionary War; Governor Dale, a despot who broke men on the torturer's wheel; and Teach, a bloodthirsty pirate. All twelve had played the cruelest roles in America's most nefarious deeds. Justice Hathorne, who presided at the witch trials in Salem, was summoned by Scratch to be judge.

Daniel Webster knew that this was going to be the hardest case of his life. For the first time, he could see clearly that Scratch was not only after Jabez's soul, but his own too.

Daniel spoke first. He began by talking about the beautiful and simple things that make a country and a man a man — like the freshness of a fine morning. Webster waxed eloquent. He made the point that when young any person can make a mistake. Hadn't Jabez admitted that he had been wrong? Still, out of all the suffering and deprivation something good could yet come.

Daniel's summation was, in fact, so powerful

Scratch, the Devil, taunts Jabez and Mary in the dramatization of "The Devil and Daniel Webster."

The central and opposing characters in *The Devil and Daniel Webster* confront each other over the future of Jabez Stone.

that the jury found Jabez innocent. The jury was deeply touched. Webster's speech had evoked for them memories of the freedom they all once had felt and loved. The familiar crow of a rooster split the gray morning. Judge and jury were instantly gone, and Jabez was declared a free man.

Daniel still had one piece of unfinished business. He was determined to wrestle with Scratch because he knew that once the devil was beaten in a fair case, his powers were virtually gone. After winning the wrestling match hands down, Daniel made the devil sign a document promising never to bother Jabez Stone and his heirs again. And to make sure the devil kept his promise, Daniel allowed as how his rambunctious ram in the fields back home could be instantly turned loose if the devil ever came to meddle again.

Now there was a sad turn of events. As if to get back at Daniel, the devil made a number of predictions concerning Webster's future. First, the devil predicted ominously that Daniel's two beloved sons would die in the war. Webster took this news with a sad but stoic heart. The devil further said that Daniel's most famous speech would be turned against him. " . . . Will I see that fight [the Civil War] won against those who would tear [the Union] down?" Webster asked. "Not while you live," said the stranger grimly, "but it will be won." Daniel was so pleased by this news that he kicked the devil right out of the house.

SYNOPSIS OF THE PLAY [2]

The play opens in the main room of a new Hampshire farm house. The year is 1841. A country wedding is coming to an end. Jabez Stone, a husky farmer around thirty, and his bride, Mary, are square-dancing with their neighbors, who include New England doctors, lawyers, storekeepers, and schoolteachers. The newlyweds congratulate the guests, then dance a happy duet. Off to the side, the guests gossip about how Jabez has come into so much money, wondering how he got to be a prosperous state senator. The wedding guests excitedly anticipate the arrival of U.S. Senator Daniel Webster

[2] New York: Dramatists Play Service, 1966.

("the greatest man in the U.S.").

We learn that Jabez and Mary have known each other since they were youngsters and that Mary is deeply proud of him. Jabez turns to Mary, and whispers, "Mary, whatever happens, it was all for you, and nothing's going to happen. Because he hasn't come yet — and he would have come if it was wrong." Mary, of course, thinks Jabez is talking about Mr. Webster. Jabez is about to tell Mary his secret when Webster arrives amid cheers from the guests.

Webster pays tribute to Jabez, telling the guests that Jabez Stone wears no man's collar (on this speech there is a discordant note from the fiddler's bow) and that ten years ago he started out with a patch of land that was mostly rocks and mortgage, and now he is a popular state senator. The frustrated fiddler remarks that the devil himself must have gotten into the violin because he just can't seem to play a right note.

The devil suddenly appears dressed like a rather conservative attorney, wearing long black leather gloves and holding a large, thin black box. Scratch takes the fiddle, draws his bow across in discord, and plays a moody song that frightens Mrs. Stone. Webster demands that Scratch leave immediately. The fiddler tampers with Scratch's box, throwing open the lid. Lightning flashes amid an ominous clap of thunder.

A white moth flies out of Scratch's black box. It's the voice of a lost soul, Miser Stevens. As the guests question if it really is Miser Stevens, the church funeral bell is heard. The crowd begins to taunt Jabez on how he really got all his money as it occurs to everyone that Jabez has sold his soul to the devil.

The guests scoop up their presents just as Scratch drives them out into the night. At last, Jabez confides to Mary that he sold his soul to the devil because he couldn't stand being poor anymore. Mary wants to run away with Jabez and hide.

Webster decides to defend Jabez, taking on the job as a mortgage case. He would "fight ten thousand devils to save a New Hampshire man!" Webster requests that Mary leave to pray for them, and she obligingly exits.

The trial starts. When Scratch demands possession of Jabez Stone, his property, Webster counters that the document is not worth the paper it's written on — the law permits no traffic in human flesh. Scratch contests Webster's assertion. Webster thunders that Mr. Stone is an American citizen, and no American citizen may be forced into service of a foreigner.

SCRATCH
And who with better right? When the first wrong was done to the first Indian, I was there. When the first slaver put out for the Congo, I stood on her deck. Am I not in your books and stories and beliefs, from the first settlements on? Am I not spoken of, still, in every church in New England? 'Tis true, the North claims me for a Southerner and the South for a Northerner, but I am neither. I am merely an honest American like yourself — and of the best descent — for, to tell the truth, Mr. Webster, though I don't like to boast of it, my name is older in the country than yours.

WEBSTER
Aha! Then I stand on the Constitution! I demand a trial for my client!

SCRATCH
The case is hardly one for an ordinary jury — and, indeed, the lateness of the hour —

WEBSTER
Let it be any court you choose, so it is an American judge and an American jury . . .

The devil summons Judge Hathorne of Salem witch trial infamy to preside. Webster moves to dismiss the case on the grounds of improper jurisdiction, then flagrant bias — all to no avail. The jury and the impartial judge offer Webster no chance for cross-examination. At long last, Daniel is given his chance to respond:

WEBSTER
Be still!
I was going to thunder and roar. I shall not do that.
I was going to denounce and defy. I shall not do that.

You have judged this man already with your abominable justice. See that you defend it. For I shall not speak of this man.

You are demons now, but once you were men. I shall speak to every one of you.

Of common things I speak, of small things and common.

The freshness of morning to the young, the taste of food to the hungry, the day's toil, the rest by the fire, the quiet sleep.

These are good things.

But without freedom they sicken, without freedom they are nothing.

Freedom is the bread and the morning and the risen sun.

Slowly, each juror wakes up as if from a dream as Webster continues his speech " . . . now here is this man with good and evil in his heart. Do you know him? He is your brother . . . "

The jury unanimously finds for Jabez, setting him free. The devil tries to escape with the document, but Webster captures him and destroys the paper. The wedding guests return singing:

We'll drive him out of New Hampshire!
We'll drive old Scratch away!
Forever and a day, boys,
Forever and a day!

They fling Scratch out of Stone's house. Jabez and Mary are reunited, and Webster happily joins hands with them.

MAJOR DIFFERENCES BETWEEN THE NARRATIVE AND DRAMATIC FORMS

1) *Page/Stage*

There is an enormous difference, of course, between *reading* what is on a page and seeing what takes place on the stage. The essential difference is that a story tells what took place, while a play shows what is actually taking place. As Arthur Miller has pointed out, the novelist or storyteller sees events through the medium of another person's mind. The dramatist, on the other hand, permits an audience to see another person's mind through the medium of events.

It is true that a skillful author of stories and novels may appeal to the entire sensory makeup of readers, engaging them to see, hear, taste, feel the emotional life of the characters portrayed.

On the stage it is imperative that the sensory and emotional makeup of the characters portrayed be fully communicated to the audience; and, in drama, this is possible through the performability of live actors. In a story, the writer-to-one-reader relationship appeals to the mind, whereas the actor-audience relationship is a whole body-to-body phenomenon.

A reader can rest his or her mind, put a story down, or reread certain passages. As Peter Shaffer, author of *Equus* and *Amadeus*, has observed, a live play is not a book; an audience can't turn the pages back. In the theatre the emotional intensity is direct and immediate, a flowing, uninterrupted, concentrated experience. A story or novel can take its time to build up to an emotional peak. On stage, there is a built-in urgency, a "dramatic clock" of sorts, which helps to coalesce elements of conflict, crisis, and suspense to heighten the emotional response of the audience.

For example, early in the story version of *The Devil and Daniel Webster* we read: " . . . all of a sudden, things began to pick up and prosper for Jabez Stone. His cows got fat and his horses sleek, his crops were the envy of the neighborhood, and lightning might strike all over the valley, but it wouldn't strike his barn. Pretty soon, he was one of the prosperous . . . "

In the beginning of the play version, we discover that Jabez has just been married. Expository information evolves naturally as the guests celebrating the wedding gossip about his former circumstances, revealing that Jabez was once poor and got rich overnight. The stage *shows* what we see in our minds on a page.

2) *Subjective/Objective*

A narrator often tells us what a character in a story is thinking and feeling. Characters on stage reveal themselves through objective behavior, that is, through vital dialogue and meaningful dramatic actions. For example, in the story, Jabez is having incredibly bad luck — a sick wife, ailing children, and broken plowshares. Everything is going wrong. The story continues: "I vow," he said, and he looked around him kind of desperate, "I vow it's enough to make a man want to sell his soul to the devil! And I would, too, for two cents!"

The story continues:

Then he [Jabez] felt a kind of queerness come over him at having said what he'd said; though, naturally, being a New Hampshireman, he wouldn't take it back. But, all the same, when it got to be evening and, as far as he could see, no notice had been taken, he felt relieved in his mind, for he was a religious man. But notice is always taken, sooner or later, just like the Good Book says. And sure enough, next day, about suppertime, a soft-spoken, dark-dressed stranger drove up in a handsome buggy and asked for Jabez Stone.

Compare the above passage with how the play treats this action. The subjective feelings of Jabez's uneasiness that the narrator relates in the story are *shown* in the play when Jabez confides to Mary that he has an uneasy feeling because "he [the devil] hasn't arrived yet." Jabez thinks nothing will happen, but Mary feels his uneasiness and asks if anything is wrong. Thus, through an objective two-character interaction, the subjective feeling of the character's uneasiness on the page is conveyed visually to the audience.

——————— JUST FOR YOU ———————

In your own mind see if the idea for your play can be dramatized *objectively*. That is, are there opportunities for *interaction between characters?* Is there possibility for dramatic development?

3) *Past Vs. Present Tense*

Another fundamental difference between narrative and dramatic writing is the matter of tense. Thornton Wilder, author of *Our Town*, refers to the action of a play taking place in a "perpetual present time." He explains that

Thornton Wilder's stage manager/narrator in *Our Town* is also a vivid character, as seen here in the "soda fountain scene."

Novels are written in the past tense. The characters in them, it is true, are represented as living moments in their present time. But the constant running commentary of the novelist . . . inevitably conveys to the reader the fact that these events are long past and over with. The novel is the past record in the *present. On the stage it is always now.* This confers upon the action an increased vitality which the novelist longs in vain to incorporate into his work. [3]

A common mistake for a beginning playwright is to overload the incidents in a plot. This happens because it is often difficult to select those dramatic incidents that can be unfolded in the present tense. When structuring your play, it is helpful to outline a dramatic development (that is, a central character working to and away from a crisis under specific circumstances) that can unfold in the *here* and *now.*

For example, in the story of "The Devil and Daniel Webster," seven years have passed by the narrator's account from Stone's adversity to prosperity. In the play version, Benét has selected one specific time to spin out the action — shortly after Jabez and Mary are married. The wedding celebration is a perfect metaphor, a way of making the story coherent in stage terms, and yet preserving the theme. One way of describing it concerns the consequences of selling one's soul for the promise of success. The couple are happy and have something good to look forward to together. We are concerned for their happiness and *want* them to succeed. At the same time, we *worry* about Jabez as the events of his past gradually funnel into the present. We both understand and *feel* his problem of having sold his soul to the devil and how this fact, alone, could ruin his future.

Even though the part of Daniel Webster becomes crucially important during the crisis of the trial, Jabez, in fact, is the central character of the play:

[3] Thornton Wilder, "Some Thoughts on Playwriting," in *Playwrights on Playwriting*, ed., Toby Cole (New York: Hill and Wang. 1966), p. 114. Emphasis added — MP.

Central Conflict

Central Character ——> *Goal*
(Jabez)   (wants to stay alive and
                           have a happy marriage)

Goal <—————— *Opposing Character*
(to claim Jabez)   (Scratch–Devil)

Crisis

Will Webster be able to save Jabez even as the devil loads the jury with his own kind?

Special Circumstance — The year is 1841. Slavery exists in the U.S.; this is a fact that the devil uses to disarm Daniel during the trial.

By making Jabez — and not Daniel — the central character in the play version, the author ensures that the drama will have the emotional *immediacy* of the present tense because Jabez's recent marriage is threatened by the arrival of Scratch, the grim living reminder of Jabez's past.

A common mistake for beginning playwrights is to use a narrator to *tell* events rather than to select the characters and incidents that can be most effectively dramatized. It is true that Shakespeare, Bertolt Brecht, Thornton Wilder, and others have used narrators in inventive ways. Too often, though, a neophyte playwright uses a narrator as a crutch merely to get across information.

When a lazy playwright does not take the time to dramatize the action, boredom — the cardinal sin of the theatre — sets in.

————— JUST FOR YOU —————

Will you be able to write your play without the use of a narrator, unless one is *absolutely* indispensable?
_____

4) *Unities of Action, Time, and Place: The Beginning of Form*

When asked if he believed a movie should have a beginning, a middle, and an end, one of the great French movie directors responded, "Oui, but not necessarily in that order."

Au contraire, good advice to the beginning playwright is not only to have a beginning, a middle, and an end for your play (and in that order) but to have a *clear focus* as well. This focus could be a central character, a significant dramatic incident, or a major thematic thrust. In the case of *The Devil and Daniel Webster*, the wedding celebration of Jabez and Mary provides the focus. (The *stake* of their happiness is one the audience can worry about.) Your *focus* should include a plot or structural framework that holds the characters together dramatically. Themes will emerge from the dramatic interaction of characters.

Now, as we know, those very elements that may make a story or novel exciting — atmosphere or mood, rambling philosophical discourse, and inner conflict — may not help a play.

Instead, we expect a compact arrangement of action, clarity of circumstances, and immediacy of the present. Action, time, and place are structural units that help give a play its cohesive form.

This is why, as poignant as the ending of the story version is (Webster learns that his sons will die during the war), Benét has chosen as the climax of the play the banishment of the devil and the play ends then; therefore, the unity of theme is also preserved.

A. *Unity of Action*

Observe how the structural elements in *The Devil and Daniel Webster* play version come together in a unified way:

a) *Exposition:* Things from the past that help the audience to understand ongoing plot and character interaction. (Webster needs to know that Jabez is prosperous in order to prepare for the reversal of his fortune when Scratch arrives.)

b) *Preparation:* Things planted or foreshadowed well ahead of the point at which they make a scene or characters more believable. (Jabez mentions to his wife that "he's coming" and Mary thinks Jabez is referring to Webster.)

c) *Complication:* A fact or character already planted in a play brought forward to spur the plot into mounting suspense. (Scratch, the devil himself, endangers the happiness of Jabez and Mary.)

d) *Suspense:* Dramatic problem or question — worry over the possibility of a conflict and its outcome. (Who will claim Jabez — Webster or Scratch?) A dramatic time clock often enhances suspense. (Scratch has come to claim Jabez *today*.)

e) *Conflict:* A tension between two or more characters (Webster vs. Scratch).

f) *Crisis:* A major development or outgrowth of conflict; the turning point. (Webster must persuade the jury to free Jabez.)

g) *Climax:* Emotional high point of crisis. (Jury is convinced by Webster's eloquence that Jabez should be freed.)

h) *Resolution:* Dramatic question is resolved (Will Jabez and Mary continue their happy state?), and all previous questions are cleared up. (Scratch is banished — the couple is reunited.)

B. *Unity of Place*

In the story version, over a dozen locales are referred to where some kind of action takes place. Benét — as playwright — has chosen one set to coalesce and unify all the action. Places mentioned in the story that are essential for understanding are woven into the play through skillful exposition; all other references to place are dropped.

You probably can think of a number of plays that have multiscenic settings. (*The Miracle Worker* is an excellent example.) The forms of these plays are unified through the playwright's vision and the staging.

For example, Arthur Miller, in writing *Death of a Salesman*, felt that if Willy Loman remembered enough of his past he would eventually destroy himself. Willy recalls his tortured past not really as flashbacks; rather, the scenes appear as subjective remembrances as the past rushes into the present. Thus, Willy steps out of the imaginary walls of his Brooklyn house or restaurant in New York, and we are back in his world as a younger man with his teenage sons or with a woman buyer in Boston. We see the optimistic as well as tormented images of his life played out in several scenes, all unified by Willy's subjective perceptions of what has happened. Visually, there is no need to construct separate sets for these locales, as they really all fall on the tortured landscape of Willy's mind.

A short story or novel can wander, but a play must have a riveted center of action; must be designed so that a sense of place is used in an economical manner with coherence and clarity. Whatever is *essential* on stage should be included. For example, in *The Miracle Worker* the set must include the Keller homestead, the gardenhouse, and the pump downstage. These three elements are all unified on stage through movement and lighting. You may decide to concentrate all the locales in your play artistically into one place.

C. *Unity of Time*

In *The Devil and Daniel Webster* real time equals stage time. The actions unfold in straightforward time in the present tense. Other plays feature other kinds of time unities. For example, in Bernard Slade's *Same Time Next Year*, each new scene takes place a set number of years apart for the illicit reunion of the two central characters. The unity of time in *The Wizard of Oz* is a series of episodic scenes in Dorothy's odyssey to reach the wizard and get back to Kansas, which first must be shown so that we have a mental idea of her goal. *Hamlet* is a counterpointal succession of the prince's struggles with Claudius and himself.

As Benét has demonstrated, you do not need a narrator to bridge time, place, and action. Charles Fuller, who patterned his powerful *A Soldier's Play* after the structure of Melville's novel *Billy Budd*, decided to forgo the use of a narrator so common in novels because a narrator is unseen in a play. Instead, Captain Davenport fulfills the role of narrator in the sense that while conducting his investigation of the tech sergeant's murder, he binds all the elements of the play together. Davenport's investigation calls for flashbacks in which all the soldier-suspects reappear to enact various scenes leading to the fatal gunshot. These scenes are able to leap boldly through time and space because of Davenport's dramatic role as a kind of narrator, though he is a fully fleshed character.

A common temptation is for beginning playwrights to have a narrator say what should really be stage or speech directions. For example:

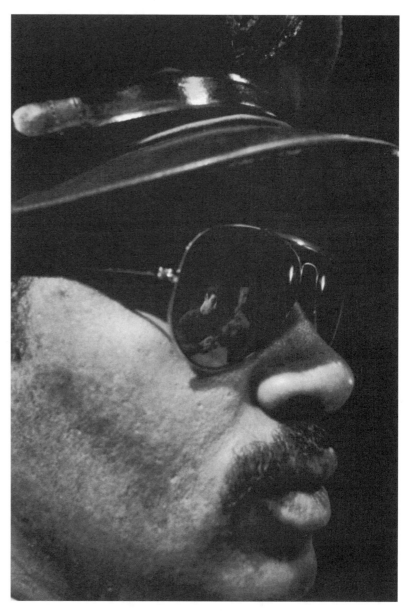

Instead of using a narrator, dramatize your action. Captain Davenport in Charles Fuller's *A Soldier's Play* was originally conceived as a narrator but later became a fully fleshed character.

NARRATOR: The scene takes place at Melissa's house on a bright, Sunday afternoon.
MELISSA: Where did Nancy go?
NARRATOR: After looking around, Melissa went to the door.
NANCY: (*Coming into Melissa's house.*) Hi, Melissa!
MELISSA: Hi, Nancy!
NARRATOR: Melissa was happy that Nancy had returned to help her.

Two tramps, Vladimir and Estragon, wait by a barren tree for Godot in Samuel Beckett's *Waiting For Godot.* They quarrel, make up, sleep, wonder and worry, eat a carrot. By the end of the play, the tree has sprouted some leaves, and the tramps are still waiting. Is the waiting a dramatic action? Why or why not?

Music plays an important role in creating moods, as in "the shower scene," above, in the serious comedy *The Heidi Chronicles* by Wendy Wasserstein. In what other ways can mood, so important in a play's texture, be evoked?

The text, of course, should read, *without* the narrator, something like this:

Place: Melissa's house in Akron, a tidy, neat living room. One door, stage left.

Time: A bright, sunny Sunday afternoon in July, the present year.

MELISSA: (*Looking around.*) Where did Nancy go?
[*Melissa goes to the door.*]

NANCY: (*Opening the door.*) Hi, Mom!

MELISSA: Nancy, I really am glad you came back to help. You know, for dinner.

In other words, your play should *show* the action as it *unfolds* in the *"here and now."* The characters' dialogue interwoven into a character's speech can easily take care of place and time. Stage and speech directions will give the actor, director — and audience — a good idea of what the characters should look and sound like. But some modern plays include a narrator who is also a character (for example, Tom in *The Glass Menagerie*). In such cases, the purpose is not to provide stage or speech directions, but to reinforce or contrast a character's spoken thoughts with what is happening in his or her life on stage.

IN SUM

As you begin to search for your play idea, keep in mind that form is vital. The dramatic action, as we have shown, should be compact with a definite unity of time and place.

Also keep in mind the words of playwright Rolf Hochhuth: "I believe the opposite of art is not nature but arbitrariness." [4] Do not get lost in labels. *The Devil and Daniel Webster* deals with a serious theme in a fantasy form, has lots of comedy, and beautiful poetry. It is a historical drama, a melodrama, and a drama of character. The important thing is that it works beautifully.

Do get involved in content. But remember, you are writing a play and a play is dramatic structure, a focus of a central character who has a problem (conflict with someone else), which is somehow resolved within the framework of the play. As you conceive the idea for your play —which is what the next chapter is about — remember that a play:

- takes place in the present tense
- deals with objective, performable behavior
- shows, not tells

---

[4] Martin Esslin, "A Playwright Who Drops Political Blockbusters." *New York Times Magazine.* November 19, 1967, pp. 158-60.

- has a unity of action, time, and place
- has a definite form

PLAYWRIGHT'S PAGE

1) Of all the *major* differences between the story and play forms, which do you feel are the *most* important?
2) What if a play had *no* form at all — what would it be?
3) Write a dialogue between A and B on the merits of writing a formless play. If A and B argue (which they should), introduce C, with still another point of view.
4) In a few words, tell why your idea would make a better play or story.
5) Whether you are writing a play or a story, you will need a central character. Who is yours and what does she or he want? Who gets in the way? Why? State the central conflict of your play.

MORE **RAW** MATERIALS

Read . . . both the story and play versions of *The Devil and Daniel Webster.* Discuss what you like about both versions.

Act . . . Dramatize a selected short story you like with a group of friends or aspiring playwrights. Break the story down into scenes. Then assign characters. When you enact a story be mindful of:
- Who you are (physical/vocal)
- What you want (goal in scene)
- Where you are (specific environment)
Make sure that the sketch has a beginning (conflict); a middle (crisis); and an ending (climax). Do not use a narrator. Let it happen in the present tense, *here and now.*

Write . . . Individually or together, jot down the scenes that emerge from the story. Another way is to audiotape the scene and transcribe the dialogue. Listen to the tape and discuss what you've learned from it.

—— SUGGESTIONS FOR CLASSROOM ACTIVITIES ——

Browse through these exercises about the nature of drama, and select one or two that work well for you.

A Venn diagram is a useful graphic aid to compare similarities between things as well as differences between things. Here's an example:

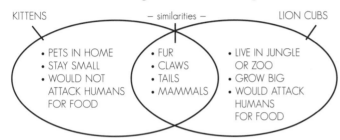

Draw a large Venn diagram with a partner. Then compare and contrast narrative and dramatic writing. Do not write full sentences — just notes, words, or phrases.

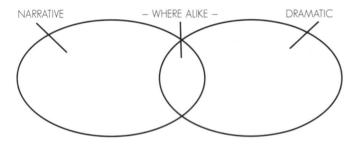

"Step into the Venn" and have the circles talk to each other. You may wish to enlarge your Venn diagram and add it to the class dramatic collage. (See page 28.)

Read . . . a published play or scene aloud that the group likes and then discuss these points briefly. Add some questions of your own about the characters.

- What's going on in the play — or scene? What is its major conflict?
- Does the central character change in some way? If so, how?
- In the play as a whole, is the past action reflected in the present? How so? What can you envision for the future of the characters?

NOTEBOOK (JOURNAL) FEATURE

Jot down some thoughts on how you can make the play that you are writing more dramatic. For example, what's really driving your central character? Who or what is getting in his or her way? Why? Why do you think we should care about the characters in your play?

Act out informally

- A scene from a published play. Discuss *why the play starts when it does for the central character.* Why is this day different from all other days for the central character?
- Get in a group and tell an anecdote, a *brief* story of an interesting or amusing incident that happened to you (e.g. the misguided trip, that ill-fated date, your lucky day, meeting an unusual person). Have the group reenact it. Does the enactment capture the essence of your experience? What did you learn from telling your anecdote and/or seeing and hearing it being acted out? This technique is known as Playback Theatre. [5]

Write . . .

- a brief *personal experience* in a paragraph or two. Then rewrite it in dialogue form. Read the versions aloud with a partner.
- a *group poem.* On a sheet of paper write some words and phrases that express what "dramatic" means to you. Exchange sheets with a partner and circle three of the words on the sheet you have received. Form a circle. Choose someone to start off and someone to end. Spontaneously, in a steady flow, take turns reading the circled words and phrases. You have created, together, a beautiful group poem. Save it!

[5] For more information on Playback Theatre, read *Gathering Voices: Essays on Playback Theatre* by Jonathan Fox and Heinrich Dauber, 1999; and *Improvising Real Life: Personal Story in Playback Theatre* by Jo Salas, 1993; both published by Tustiala Publishing Company, New Paltz, New York.

chapter III

DISCOVERING YOUR IDEA

> The beginnings of all things are small. — Cicero

> The poet seeks what is nowhere in all the world and yet somewhere finds it. — Terence

The previous chapters were designed to help you prepare the soil for working creatively in drama. Now let's discuss some of the ways you can discover the seeds of an idea that can grow into a play. We ask:

- How can a feeling or an image get you going?
- What are some general and specific sources of ideas?
- How can ideas too close to experience be distanced?
- How can you begin to think about form?
- How can you get feedback on your idea?

START WITH A FEELING OR AN IMAGE

When Paddy Chayefsky was asked how he began a play, he responded " . . . with a feeling . . . something inside." Most likely this is some kind of a problem that you feel needs to be solved. Maybe it's something that is troubling you personally. Perhaps it's an unusual problem of others that arouses your curiosity. In any case, there's a gap inside that has to be filled — by your urge to create. The feeling may be as simple (and profound) as, "Hey, this is the play I want to write, about a . . ."

Your mind begins to go to work, becoming a sort of "image blender" preparing you for the creative process, shifting, sorting, eliminating, synthesizing, so that now you are *actively* thinking. But even when you have your idea (or it has you), you discover that there still are gaps. The solving of one problem seems devilishly to create new ones. It's a little bit like the working of a corset — a bulge here, some tightening there, another bulge gone here, a new one there. In the early stages of writing, considerable time will be spent working out those "bulges" while groping in the dark. How can you see everything from the beginning? When you work in the dark, certain of your senses are naturally more closed off than others. So, you're forced to work from *within*, to rely on your *inner* vision. This inner vision, the wonderful human radar flowing from your subconscious, is known as intuition.

Because most ideas are so vague in the beginning, intuition may be your best friend. Learn to listen to it and trust it. For example, Tennessee Williams stated that it was almost impossible for him to pinpoint the start of a play. For him, as well as for most writers, plays grow out of an inner tension of longing to say something that can only be discovered during the *actual process of writing*. There's a good reason Harold Pinter has been equally vague about the genesis of some of his ideas: the ideas themselves are only dimly conceived. He recalls, for example, that the origins of one play came about while he was sitting on the sofa reading the newspaper. Something flashed into his mind, nothing really to do with the paper —maybe the first couple of lines of the play. He recalls that " . . . two people were, talking about something else." That image propelled him forward to write *Old Times*.

Most play ideas evolve from personal experience. The idea for David Mamet's *American Buffalo* grew out of his experiences in frequenting junk shops when he was growing up in Chicago.

Another example of starting with an image is the first one Arthur Miller had while creating *Death of a Salesman*. The image was a large head of Willy Loman covering the entire proscenium of the stage. (In fact, one of the play's first titles was "The Inside of His Head. ") Miller felt if his central character remembered enough of the painful contradictions in his life, he would be compelled to destroy himself. Therefore, the structure and texture of the play eventually combined the key events of Willy's past with work and family problems in the present.

The process of playwriting involves the creative combination of the *subconscious* intuitive process — often difficult to explain — and a keen *conscious* awareness of dramatic form. Both processes are interdependent and equally important for molding a dramatic shape from the materials you work with. Using the analogy of a car, an idea can be considered the spontaneous spark plug of the creative process while the fuel line is the actual synthesis of writing and rewriting, playfulness, and hard work. You — as always — are the pump. Now let's get that pump activated!

WHAT ARE SOME GENERAL SOURCES OF IDEAS?

The greatest source of ideas is, of course, right inside you — your own reservoir of thoughts, feelings, and experiences. What's deep inside may be a sense of restlessness, uneasiness, a puzzlement of some sort. Perhaps it's a feeling of depression, elation, or some other strong emotion that might be difficult to define or articulate for the moment — or ever. You may have feelings for several plays. Gradually, you will filter those feelings through a priority system that finally flashes "This is it — I'll go with this — for now!" Paddy Chayefsky urged beginning writers to draw from their own experiences, and when these were "drained," to draw on the experiences of others through research and observation.

Mark Medoff, prize-winning author of *Children of a Lesser God* and a fine playwriting teacher, also advises his students to draw on experience —though not exclusively about themselves. (In fact, he cautions, the only excuse many playwrights have for writing at all is to justify their lives and

Like personal experience, imagined experience must find an appropriate form. Patterning the structure of *A Soldier's Play* on Melville's novel *Billy Budd*, the playwright transformed the ship into a World War II army barracks.

make themselves look good.) When you write, be objective about yourself.

There are two general kinds of writing experiences — personal and imagined.

Personal Experience

Say you do decide to write about what you know firsthand. Fine. Most impulses start with firsthand, "felt" knowledge. The question arises, though: Does this mean that you, *directly*, have to be the central character?

Arthur Miller worked in an automotive parts plant in Brooklyn when he was a young man. Years later he wrote *A Memory of Two Mondays*, which concerns a cross section of women and men who work in an auto-parts warehouse. One of the characters, who is dying, has one last pathetic fling with life. The play is a poignant and poetic slice of life with well observed characters and is told with tender feeling. With the passage of time (contrasting the seasons of winter and spring as an emotional metaphor), Miller looks back lovingly at the characters he once worked with. There probably is a little bit of him in all the characters, although he most resembles the young man, Burt. Burt is one of the peripheral characters in the play, the one who is able to escape the humdrum existence of the warehouse.

Likewise, David Mamet writes about what he

knows, though not necessarily about himself. Mamet used to play poker in the back of a junk shop in his hometown of Chicago. He vividly recalls the junk shop being frequented by an assortment of odd-ball people. Years later Mamet's interest in his youthful haunt was rekindled in his imagination. His idea for *American Buffalo* was to dramatize what happens when a couple of people meet in a junk shop and devise an elaborate plan to steal a rare American Buffalo nickel. The men are so incompetent, and there is so much bickering among them, that the plan backfires and ends in violence.

Eduardo Machado's semi-autobiographical *Havana Is Waiting* is a moving drama about a man who visits his birthplace, Cuba, in 1999 for the first time in 38 years. He remembers when he was 8 years old being airlifted with thousands of other unaccompanied Cuban children to America because their parents feared Castro's new revolutionary regime. During his return visit to Cuba, the man faces conflicting and ambivalent perceptions of the land and himself. Machado, like Mamet and Miller, was able to filter his personal experience into an imaginative play with a definite shape and form.

Imagined Experience

Charles Fuller's impulse to write *A Soldier's Play* was to honor the memory of a close friend who had recently died. The idea came to him to pattern the play after Herman Melville's novel *Billy Budd*. But instead of a ship, it would be an army barracks — where men were confined to one place. In the play there would be talk of a mutiny in a World War II setting. Fuller then proceeded to read everything he could about World War II. Feelings and facts and form combined to make an exciting idea.

The first full-length play I wrote was called *The Four Winds of Heaven*, an adventure story set during the period of Emperor Charlemagne. I wanted to write about the fate of the Jewish people during their dispersion throughout Europe during the Middle Ages. While I was doing research for the play, I learned that in honor of Charlemagne's coronation, the Eastern caliph Harun al-Rashid had dispatched three items — a tent, a water clock, and something until then unseen by Western eyes — an elephant.

While I was working as a lifeguard at the University of Wisconsin, the conundrum that has to be solved by the central character came to me in a flash. (I was so happy I dove right into the lake.):

Six foot thick
Twelve feet high
Its greatest offender's
A common fly
Tho an arrow's sting
Won't make it die.

Of two things more
You should beware
Its nose is a hose where
The water goes
And two of its feet
Are lacking toes!

The idea of the elephant slowly evolved into a puzzle that became the central focus of the play. My research, to a great extent, was based on the customs of medieval times, but the *feeling* that propelled me to write the play was my emotional connection with the historic struggle of my ancestors, an attempt to find roots in the past. Those feelings then had to find a form.

You may wish to take your imagination back into history or project an idea into the future. And if you feel you don't have the necessary on-the-spot observation to make the play work, remember that Stephen Crane wrote the stirring novel *The Red Badge of Courage* without having personally witnessed any part of the Civil War. Martin Cruz-Smith, who wrote *Gorky Park*, the masterful novel about espionage in Russia, spent only a couple of weeks in that country. Tony Kushner, author of *Angels in America*, had never been to Afghanistan before writing *Homebody/Kabul*, but he immersed himself in research, including reading an historical guidebook about Kabul. You may wish to delve into the rich imaginative depths of your mind to come up with a mythical place to explore. Sam Shepard did with Nogoland (strangely resembling some of the bleaker aspects of our society) in *The Unseen Hand*. So did Amlin Gray with Amboland (paralleling Vietnam) in *How I Got That Story*.

Stimuli from books, magazines, and newspapers can trigger all kinds of ideas. For example, the French playwright Jean Anouilh got the idea for *Becket* when he least expected it. He was rummaging through a used-book store and ran across *The Conquest of England by the Normans* by Augustin Thierry, a somewhat forgotten historian. While reading the thirty-page story, Anouilh was surprised to learn that the famous historical figure was not just another unapproachable saint, but a man of flesh-and-blood dimensions — a discovery that prompted him to write *Becket*.

The summer I was working on this book, I read an interesting newspaper story about a daring fireman whose company answered a fire-alarm call. When the fireman reached his destination, he discovered, to his horror, that it was his own house on fire, and he made a hair-raising rescue of his wife and children. I had to smile thinking about all the TV and movie treatments this newspaper story would generate. My smile broadened when I remembered one of my favorite one-act plays, *The Still Alarm*, by Kaufman and Hart. The play concerns two friends in a hotel room who nonchalantly carry on their business in the most polite terms, oblivious to the fact that their room is on fire. The example shows that the most serious of themes can be treated in a variety of styles and forms.

Paul Zindel's inspiration for *The Effect of Gamma Rays on Man-in-the-Moon Marigolds* grew out of his high school teaching experiences.

—————— JUST FOR YOU ——————

Writing is talking made permanent.

Start an "Image File" in your notebook. Jot down any and all images you have for a play (I can show you napkins I have scribbled ideas on when my notebook wasn't handy). Write it down, no matter how fuzzy or clear the idea seems to you now. [1] Hoard your ideas, work with them, play with them. When your mind begins to wander, follow its bends and curves and surprises. It's great when work can be playful too. When you *work* on a *play*, that happens. Trust yourself to let go.

Brainstorm with Yourself — Write down what is important to you, from personal values to topical issues. Jot down characters you like and don't like and why. What's so special about them? A look? A casual remark? A particular deed? Could any of these characters belong in a play? What kind of a play — suspense story, mystery? Historical or biographical? Farce? What? Think about your own family and friends for ideas. Write the images or draw them.

Be as Specific as Possible — What has *specifically* touched off these images? Stress, pressure from school — teachers, grades, other kids? Pressures from the inside to prove to somebody (who?) your self-worth? Do you know of friends or acquaintances who are under pressure to cut classes, to try drugs, to go to a special place? Can you think of specific instances of these people being in trouble? Does a specific line touch off sparks? A funny remark? Something sad? For now, get the ideas down.

Don't worry if they're good, bad, or indifferent. You'll probably see relationships and connections later. Value judgments don't help at this point. At this point also refrain from being critical about your writing.

—————————————————————

After brainstorming with yourself, put your ideas away and also look more closely at them. If this sounds contradictory, so what? Life is full of contradictions, and plays, thank God, can't exist without them. Listen to your own voice — which is the idea you really want to do and feel you might have *a chance at finishing*? *Try a scene or character sketch* based on the idea.

—————— ASK YOURSELF——————

Does your idea have an inherent dramatic action, an

[1] As the Romans used to say, "What is spoken flies away, what is written endures." Writing is like exercise — it keeps you in shape if you do it every day.

interesting character who wants something, goes after it, and comes into conflict with at least one other character?

IDEAS CAN COME FROM THE CRAZIEST PLACES

You may brainstorm until you become blue in the face and then all of a sudden (out of the blue?) your idea will pop into your mind, or your mind will pop into your idea.

The idea for Eugene Ionesco's first play, *The Bald Soprano*, came about in a strange fashion. The playwright was trying to learn English from a phrase book for tourists. The absurd repetition of words and phrases in the book triggered the idea that thought residing below the surface of language is often incomprehensible. Ionesco took it one step further that human behavior itself is absurdly lacking in comprehension.

A chance glance at his filing cabinet's section O-Z provided Frank Baum with both the name of the magical land and the title for *The Wizard of Oz*.

When Alan Jay Lerner was writing the script of *My Fair Lady*, he was cautioned by Rex Harrison (who was to star as Henry Higgins) to stick as closely as possible to George Bernard Shaw's *Pygmalion*, the stage play upon which the musical was based. One day Harrison and Lerner were having a heated conversation. Mrs. Lerner had some thoughts on the matter. Lerner suggested that she not get involved in the debate. Mrs. Lerner then remarked that what her husband really meant was "Why can't a woman be more like a man?" And so was born the idea for one of the most delightful songs in the great musical. Yes, ideas come the craziest ways . . .

IDEAS FROM SPECIFIC PARTS OF THE PLAY

Looking at the specific parts of a play may help you find a *focus* for your idea based on personal or imagined experience, or both.

Characterization

Always a good starting point is to fix your idea on an unusually interesting character. Paul Zindel, author of the novel *My Darling, My Hamburger*, based the idea for one of his plays on his high school teaching experience. A girl in his chemistry class took a first prize for her science exhibit entry. The girl, according to Zindel, was charmingly advanced, but her mother thought she was crazy. Why? Her dreamy daughter spent all her time at night looking through a telescope. Zindel puzzled and dreamt about both characters. Both mother and daughter became the basis of the idea that was to evolve into the beautifully tender *The Effect of Gamma Rays on Man-in-the-Moon Marigolds*.

My colleague Jerome Coopersmith likes to focus the central character's problem in the form of a succinct story statement. For example: (1) This is the story of Willy Loman, whose delusion that he can be successful clashes with his son's newly discovered sense of reality. (2) This story starts out as a bet and turns into a romantic clash between a professor and a flower girl. Such statements have also been referred to as premises, notions, or hooks. "What if" is another way of starting a premise: "What if this college kid discovers that his uncle has murdered his father and . . . " (See page 55.)

─────────── JUST FOR YOU ───────────

Ask yourself: Does the central character in your play have a goal, what he or she wants in life? Is the problem that there is a gap between the aspiration and attainment of the goal?

Who or what *specifically gets in the way* of attaining this goal? What are the special circumstances that color the central character's struggle or plan? What is your central character like — what special features or traits will contrast him or her markedly with other characters in your play?

Plot

The incidents of a story may be so unusual in themselves, the events so dramatic, that you will either see the possibilities for a whole play in a flash, or parts of the plot will come into slow focus, hinged on maybe a common thread or image that begins to connect with other images.

A second approach is to hinge the idea of your play on a myth, fairy tale, or legend and rework it into a contemporary framework. Such plays include Giraudoux's *Amphitryon 38*, George Bernard Shaw's *Pygmalion*, or *Joseph and the Amazing Technicolor Dreamcoat* by Webber and Rice.

You may decide to rework a story you have already started into a play. For example, Tennessee Williams patterned his poignantly haunting masterpiece *The Glass Menagerie* after an earlier short story he had written about his delicate, handicapped sister, Rose. In the drama, Laura and her dominating mother, Amanda Wingate, become the focus. In the form of a memory play, Tom recalls the stormy time when his stern mother invited an outgoing Gentleman Caller to visit his sister.

Character and plot offer the greatest sources for play ideas, but as you know, ideas can and do come from anywhere.

——————— JUST FOR YOU ———————

Write what you feel is the central image of your play in this manner: This is a play about a (woman, man, teenager, worker, etc.) who (goal) BUT (*conflict or obstacle*). As an alternative, make a collage of colors or fabrics that convey the essence of your play's central idea.

Dialogue

We have already related how Harold Pinter got the idea for his *Old Times* (two people talking about somebody else). Tennessee Williams recalled that some of his ideas evolved by just writing dialogue — something in a page of dialogue will spark something in the way of character and situation.

——————— JUST FOR YOU ———————

Right now try writing a page of dialogue in your notebook; hold onto it. It may spark an idea most anytime for a play, scene, or situation.

Visual Elements

When playwright Howard Sackler first saw a photograph of fighter Jack Johnson, he wondered who the person was behind the photo. Sackler was especially struck by the accusation that Johnson had thrown the championship fight. Was this, indeed, so? Inspired by the photo, Sackler proceeded to find an almost cinematic form for *The Great White Hope*, a sweeping multiscenic drama culminating in the climax of the fight.

Tom Stoppard saw in his mind the images of acrobats first forming, then tumbling off an inverted pyramid. A dead body was another image he envisoned. These images became the basis for his play *Jumpers*. Stoppard knew that if he could eventually solve the mystery of who the dead body was, he was on his way to a very theatrical play. This is a classic example of a play's visual cues paving the way for verbalization.

——————— WHAT IF ———————

your play contained no dialogue at all? What is the most striking visual image in your play? Describe where the action of your play will take place.

Music

Any part of a play can trigger the evolution of its eventual theme. One day playwright Arthur Kopit was reading a newspaper account of how General Westmoreland had expressed regret for the accidental killing and wounding of innocent people in Vietnam. While Kopit was reading he was also listening to music — two orchestras playing against each other (one chamber music, the other marching music). It was just then that the potential theme popped into his mind for his new play that would be entitled *Indians*: the mythology created when a social and political power imposes itself on a lesser power. Thus, both the idea and the form seemed to come in a flash. In the play, Wild Bill Cody (Buffalo Bill) creates a Wild West Show to assuage his guilt for helping to wipe out the Indians.

——————— JUST FOR YOU ———————

Mull over the cast of characters you have chosen so far for your play and think about some of the action in musical images. Is there a special kind of sound that occurs anywhere in the play? What is it? Make

The conflict between a father and son over opposing values triggered the idea for the author's first one-act play, *A Night of Mourning*.

the sound for yourself or share it with somebody.

IDEAS CHANGE AND GROW

Because an idea sets off all kinds of creative sparks, it is usually visualized in cartoons as a light bulb. Now the light bulb is a radiating but somewhat static image, I believe. I prefer to think of an idea — at least one for a play — as a harmonious, colorful balloon, which not only expands to its fullest natural shape but can be twisted into interesting new shapes when it is already blown up.

Do ideas change? All the time!

West Side Story, for example, was originally conceived in the late 1940's by Jerome Robbins as taking place around Easter and Passover time, with the central conflict between a Catholic boy and a Jewish girl. Ten years later he shifted the idea — still based on the passion he felt in the original model, *Romeo and Juliet* — to reflect the social conflicts between Puerto Ricans and so-called "native" Americans fighting each other on the upper West Side of New York during the early 1950's. Because the play is so universal, the specific dates no longer matter.

Even when a play has already been written and produced, the original idea or concept can be subject to all kinds of changes.

For example, after *Equus* was in production, playwright Peter Shaffer revised the concept of the parents from "crazy" and "puritanical" to more "normal" so that the idea of the attack on environmental

psychology could be preserved. The second act of Shaffer's *Amadeus* was rewritten after the British production.

Neil Simon feels that his Broadway musical *Little Me* did not really work when it was first produced in 1962. One of the main things wrong with the show, he thinks now, was the characterization of the central character. In the first produced version, the leading lady was a wealthy Southampton woman writing her memoirs. In the latest version she is a washed-up nightclub singer working in a run-down club in Hackensack, New Jersey. The reason for the change? The lady's wealth lost her a lot of sympathy from the audience.

Creative changes can be made at any stage of the game if they maintain the integrity of the play and serve the playwright's expanding vision of the idea.

There does come a time, however, when you have to tie down an idea, just as you would a balloon before it blows away. When do you know? You will "know." Your body will let you know that things have "jelled" to the point where you want them — at least, for now.

FOR IDEAS TO WORK, YOU MUST WORK ON THEM

You've probably heard the expression "great idea, too bad it doesn't work." To make an idea work *you* have to make it work, and this takes rewriting (plays are structured — wrought — as well as written).

Creativity has often been referred to as elaborated insight. *Periods of Illumination* (flashes where ends and means come magically together) and *Incubation* (dreamlike periods in which problems and solutions to problems are lying fallow to be rediscovered in different forms) can happen at any stage of the process. So do doubts, nagging feelings that things just aren't working out or going right, and this is where you might want to put the work away or work on some other part of the play. Robert Edmond Jones has observed that the artist works for a synthesis of dreams and actuality. How true! There will be more brainstorms and trial and error, false starts and new beginnings growing out of periods when you think you are stuck. By steadily working and reflecting on and occasionally stepping back from your idea, it will gradually become clearer.

To make what you want really clear to yourself and to others will take a number of drafts. Unless you are a super-genius, this is guaranteed. Every writer, from Sophocles to Stephen Sondheim, has experienced the pains and pleasures of discovering new insights through writing waves of successive drafts.

True, playwriting is rewriting, but it's fun when you are personally involved in every stage of the process, especially the times when you sit down to write. When the great Russian composer Igor Stravinsky was asked where he got his ideas, he replied: " . . . at the piano." (But, of course!) New problems and insights, more revisions, and who can say how much energy expended to make what's in your head come out to what you want on paper. And when it does come out, it is one of the most joyful feelings in the world. And this is why process is just as important as the final product. What you ultimately see on stage is not only problems of people, but the successful resolution of how you solved the problems of writing about the problems of those people.

HOW TO DISTANCE

You may decide to write about a subject that is too painful to you at this time. You simply may need more time to be away. You may not be ready to do the story of your life. Store it away (in a file or in your subconscious world) for a later pick-up.

On the other hand, a real-life situation that you have not actually participated in may fill your emotional need to write about a parallel situation. For example, the characters in Neil Simon's *The Odd Couple* were, in essence, based on the playwright's brother when he had a roommate and they were living in California. Simon does not deny that he has a little of both the compulsive "neatnik" and the sloppy sportswriter in himself, but he first glimpsed those parts of himself in his brother and the roommate.

The first play I ever wrote, a one-acter called *A Night of Mourning*, concerned a problem between a son and father over conflicting generational values. Specifically, the boy wanted to marry a young woman of a different religion. The father objected to the point of disowning his son. Like other young adults growing up, I had many conflicts with my father, although not about the specific one I later wrote about in *A Night of Mourning*. Although I did not know it at the time, I was inwardly interested in discovering more about the relationship I had with my father, and I distanced the feeling by making the young man a soldier who is called home on leave when his mother dies. It is then that the orthodox father discovers that his son is in love with the girl. A deeply emotional and stormy struggle then ensues between father and son.

"Did that happen to *you?*" friends asked me after the show. Not exactly, I thought. Not the girl, not the army, but the underlying strife between father and son? Yes, that feeling was true, very true.

FIND A FORM

Form is a major concern in creativity. Every worthwhile work of art has form. Some of those forms may strike you as unusual, yet "just right for the content." For example, John and Lorraine take turns writing alternate chapters in Paul Zindel's novel *The Pigman*. When the colors and shapes shift with the relationships in Picasso's painting "The Three Musicians," form matches content perfectly.

Form takes its lead and inspiration from the inevitability of nature, the way moss finds itself on the right side of a tree; the sureness of night following day; the way we walk one step at a time; or how

Structural Ways to Think About Play Ideas

LIFE	PLAY	FORM
People	Characters	Who
Plot	Conflict and	What They Want
	Crises	
Time and Place	Specific Circumstances	Where and When
Natural	Selective	*"Picture"* illusion or *"Platform"* reality nonillusionistic* Why — Theme (will be discovered when writing, through interaction of characters)

(Fill in the space with structural ideas.)

an eagle circles the sky... the wholeness of life and its asymmetries.

It is exciting when idea and form merge into a thematic whole. Not only does content influence form; form also helps to solve problems dealing with content.

If the form is realistic, the playwright selects those unities that will give the play an artistic wholeness. In *The Odd Couple*, for example, each act starts with a poker game, a sort of visual barometer of the emotional changes between Oscar and Felix that develop over a linear progression of time.

You recall Arthur Miller's image for *Death of a Salesman* of a large head filling up the proscenium of the stage. The form of the play is the fluid interchange of past and present internal conflicts in Willy Loman's life. Willy's anguished thoughts are externalized in a dreamlike expressionistic form. Thus, the play is not realistic at all, although the language is.

Another supposedly realistic play is *Waiting for Lefty*, dealing with a group of workers planning to go on strike. According to the author, Clifford Odets, the play was written in the form of a minstrel

show, to give it coherence. Even the most straightforward play imaginable will have a form based on artistic selectivity and wholeness. *Waiting for Godot*, though poetically sparse, is pervaded by theatrical song-and-dance elements as well. Form and content often intermesh in a flash of insight, when you can see ideas perceived in *theatrical* terms.

——————— JUST FOR YOU ———————

For the play you have in mind, is there a possibility of conflict? In most general terms, does your idea have an inherent dramatic problem? Does your play have a potential for beginning-middle-end? Are there possibilities for interesting dialogue, vital characters, and a worthwhile theme? Will it be a serious play, comedy, fantasy, or have elements of all? Will the set create the illusion of life (picture) or be a presentational (platform), that is, nonillusionistic style? Theme — worthwhile? Challenging? Form interesting?

Use this space for more brainstorming
Focus on *one* idea:

* In the *presentational style*, actors may speak directly to an audience. In the *representational style* the actors do not recognize the presence of an audience, which is supposedly watching real life unfold on stage. Some playwrights and directors use the term *ritualistic staging* — which may include, for example, a musical's overture or stylistic elements such as make-up, pantomime and symbolic elements.

GET SOME FEEDBACK

While searching for your idea you may find yourself totally inarticulate about what you are doing. Yet the important thing is that you *will* find yourself *doing* — that is, *writing*. In many instances, you may not be able to verbalize the idea of your play until at least a draft of it has been written. If this happens, don't worry; at least you have the draft. Now build on it.

Talking to a lot of people about an idea too early in the game may spill the creative tension needed to flesh out the idea. This is especially true when you come up with what you consider a terrific idea and someone listening to it responds, "Boring." Your description of the idea may, indeed, be dull. But the dialogue and characterization of the actual play may be truly exciting.

Consider this hardly dull but perhaps "unbelievable" idea: a college student who is called back from the university to attend his father's funeral and the second marriage of his mother discovers that his uncle (who is marrying the young man's mother) is the murderer of his father. The young man becomes a detective of sorts, dons a disguise of madness, and eventually proves — with the aid of a traveling troupe of actors — that his uncle is guilty. The uncle tries to kill the young man first and . . . This melodramatic description of the plot of *Hamlet* never can do justice to the tragedy as it is actually written. So instead of babbling all over the place, get the idea out of your system and onto the page — for your eyes only at the beginning.

Another danger of talking about your idea before it really has jelled is that an incomplete description could prompt someone to say, on one hand, that it's "too far out," or conversely, not original enough. Such thoughts could tend to dampen your enthusiasm for the project. Perhaps what will make it original is still in your head even though it sounds like an idea already done. For example, Harold Pinter's play *Betrayal* is one continuous flashback starting with the end of an extramarital love affair; the play's last scene is the beginning of the affair. The story of Kaufman and Hart's *Merrily We Roll Along* — written long before Pinter's play — is also told backwards, but this fact did not prevent Pinter from completing his own work, a play that deals with a very different theme, set of characters, and story. Many a sensitive beginning writer has been intimidated by self-styled critics who bark, "Forget it! That's been done already."

On the other hand, a certain amount of feedback may be welcome from people whose opinions you genuinely trust and who can offer constructive help, not just put you down. At the same time, those people should be able to help you discover when your energy is flowing into a potentially dead end (one that has absolutely no possibility for dramatic development). (See Appendix D, page 174.)

——— SELF-CHECK FEEDBACK ———

Amplify — How can I get all the ideas out regardless if they make sense or not?

Clarify — How can I make clear to myself what I'm really trying to say and do?

Edify — How can I make clear to others what I'm really trying to say and do?

Simplify — How can I keep the whole thing manageable and true?

I have found the ACES BASIS to be helpful and hope you do too.

IN SUM

Ideas for plays, which can come from almost anywhere, usually start with an image or a feeling. Paul Zindel has described the intuitive side of writing as dreamlike: Writing is like a dream — exactly and precisely like a dream. The job of the playwright is to interpret the dream instinctively. The dream is the writer. The playwright edits what is dramatically feasible from the dream. [2]

The other side of writing is hard work, to fashion the dream into reality. In order to do so, be prepared to go through a number of drafts. But take heart! The process of discovery and revision is a joyful one too.

[2] John S. Wilson, "The Effect of the Pulitzer Prize on Man-in-the-Moon Paul Zindel," *After Dark*, pp. 7-8.

Ideas may be triggered by a character image, a part of a plot, a song or a sound; a vision of the set; or some dialogue. Ideas also come from the craziest places and when you least expect them. Finding a form for your idea and getting feedback on it are also important aspects of the process.

Above all, go with your feelings. Don't worry if your idea is different or offbeat. The German philosopher Arthur Schopenhauer observed that every original idea is first ridiculed, then vigorously attacked, and finally taken for granted.

And don't worry how great your play is going to be. For now, concentrate on a character in crisis and his or her changing circumstances as a dramatic climax is reached.

As Gordon Rogoff has noted: "Playwrights are not required to be philosophers, psychiatrists, or saints. The only requirement is art. They may do their thinking in the shower, their analyzing in bed, if their experience is transformed by an act of will and personal magic into a play with a life of its own." [3]

[3] Gordon Rogoff, "Theatre," *The Nation*, February 10, 1964, p. 153.

PLAYWRIGHT'S PAGE

1) How do you feel about your idea for a play? Will it make the basis for a good play?

2) Do you have a central character? List some of the character's traits. What does he or she want?

3) Who is the opposing character? What does he or she want? What is the situation or problem? How is it resolved?

4) Is your play a serious drama, a comedy, or does it have elements of both or neither? If neither, what is it?

5) Can you describe your play's form or convey it visually? Will the form have a linear progression of dramatic action? Will it be a mosaic of images? Do you have in mind a literal representational setting or more of a presentational style? Could you draw — no matter how roughly — the set for your play?

A source of inspiration for the play *The Spirit of Bleecker Street* (which I wrote with Howard Berland) was Thomas Paine, who lived in my Greenwich Village neighborhood in 1806. This radical, who had spurred on the American Revolution in 1776, was later shunned for his free-thinking beliefs. Your neighborhood might be hiding some colorful happenings in its past, just waiting to be shaped into a play. Did someone live there or something happen that might be worth exploring?

The idea for my satire "Bite the Bagel" was inspired by a seventeen-year-old student who fights for her dream to be somebody. A corrupt Board of Directors tries to stop her, for their own selfish reasons. I patterned the Board after the crooked town officials in Nikolai Gogol's *The Inspector General*. Not only personal experiences and observations but also creative adaptations of classics can become springboards for plays.

MORE **RAW** MATERIALS

Read . . . Imagine you are a "drama detective" and track down the original idea for a play. You may enjoy reading about how plays have evolved and the creative process of playwrights. Some of the books I have found fascinating include: Abe Burrows, *Honest, Abe* (New York: Atlantic; Little, Brown, 1980); Toby Cole, ed. *Playwrights on Playwriting* (New York: Hill and Wang, 1960, 1995), 26th printing, includes theatre practitioners from Archer to Zola; very valuable; Arthur and Barbara Gelb, *O'Neill: Life With Monte Cristo* (New York: Applause Theatre and Cinema Books, 2000); William Gibson, *The Seesaw Log* (New York: Alfred A. Knopf, Inc., 1959); Mel Gussow, *Conversations With Pinter* (London: Nick Hern Books, 1994); Mel Gussow, *Edward Albee: A Singular Journey* (New York: Applause Theatre and Cinema Books, 2000); Moss Hart, *Act One* (New York: Random House, 1959); Arthur Laurents, *Original Story By: A*

Yip Harburg's original idea for *Finian's Rainbow* was to satirize a Mississippi senator well known for his racism in the 1940's. But Harburg didn't want to write only about real people. Extending his imagination, he wove folklore, featuring a leprechaun, a magic pot of gold, along with a mythical rainbow, into a rich tapestry of fable and fantasy.

Memoir of Broadway and Hollywood (New York: Applause Theatre and Cinema Books, 2001); Alan Jay Lerner, *The Street Where I Live* (New York: DaCapo Press, 1994); Arthur Miller, *Timebends: A Life* (New York: Grove Press, 1987); Julie Taymor, Introduction to *The Lion King, Pride Rock on Broadway* (New York: Hyperion, 1997); Walter Wager, *The Playwrights Speak* (New York: Delta, 1967); Tennessee Williams, *Memoirs* (New York: Doubleday, 1975); August Wilson, *Three Plays by August Wilson* (Pittsburgh: University of Pittsburgh Press, 1991).

Act . . . out a dialogue between two of the favorite ideas you have for your play: Idea No. 1 vs. Idea No 2.

Write . . . out some of the dialogue that develops between the two ideas in the above enactment. Do you have an idea for a play right now? Then fill in the space: This is a play about a (man) (woman) _____ who _____. (Come back to this idea later and see if and how it grows. See page 55 for variations of this graphic organizer.)

Often helping to clarify a playwright's vision are improvisations designed to explore character and to make dialogue more real. Make sure your improvised dialogue really fits your characterization. If it doesn't, you might still jot it down for use in a future play. (But in either case, improvised dialogue can be fleeting, so don't delay in getting it down on paper.)

—— SUGGESTIONS FOR CLASSROOM ACTIVITIES ——

Choose two of these plotting and characterization exercises to do now, or make a note to try them soon, before you go on to Chapter Four.

Draw one of these graphic organizers on a notebook-size sheet, and fill in with notes for your play's idea:

BIG W

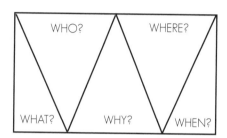

MAGIC SQUARES

WHAT IS HAPPENING	WHO IS INVOLVED
WHERE AND WHEN	WHY?

In your journal or notebook fill in the following plot prompters for your play:

This is a story about (central character)_____
who wants to (goal)_____
but (conflict)_____ *

When (central character)_____
_____ (main action) _____
then _____
until _____ **

Examples:

* (*The Miracle Worker*) This is a story about a young woman who wants to teach a blind-deaf girl language, but both the girl and her father resist change.

** (*The Miracle Worker*) When a strong-willed young woman is hired by a rich family to be the teacher of their blind-deaf daughter, she then discovers that the child is wild and battles for control until the father intervenes.

NOTEBOOK (JOURNAL) FEATURE

Continue making notes about the characters in your play (including writing bits of their dialogue). Make some of your entries as one of the characters (and later entries as other characaters):

- What are their dreams, hopes and desires? (Describe a dream they might have. Do they remember it when they wake up? Why or why not? When, where, and how do they awaken from the dream?)
- What might they want in each scene — that makes them behave like they do? Do any of them have unique, annoying, unusual behavior or habits? When and how so? Consider all kinds of qualities in a character as you write. Remember, not everyone is all "good" or all "bad." Again, ask yourself the question: "Why should an audience care about the characters?"

Read over some of your ideas for a play with your partner, if you wish. For now, don't critique the ideas. Just focus on *one* thought: Is the idea potentially dramatic?

Act out (or improvise)
- the beginning of your play. Ask yourself again. "Why does the play start *now?*" Is someone coming or leaving? Reappearing? Changing? What's happening? Act out the inciting incident of the play. Ask yourself: "Can I change the setting or time to intensify the conflict?" At this point, you may already be asking: "Is there anything I can do to intensify what I think will be the climax or emotional high point of my play?"

Write about or sketch freely your idea for your play, your story structure, or any of the characters.

Thanks to Larry O'Connell for the plot prompters idea.

chapter IV

PLOT: GETTING STARTED

If you have built castles in the air... that is where
they should be. Now put foundations under them.
— Emerson

When we mean to build, we first survey the plot.
— Shakespeare

So far in the playwriting process you have been a dreamer, searching for an idea. Now you will become a builder, turning your idea into dramatic form. Your building tools will be the elements of plot.

Not all plays, as we have shown in the first several chapters, stress plot. Intriguing character relationships, haunting elements of mood, and engaging themes may, in fact, be effectively conveyed structurally without resorting to tight or even episodic plots. Finding a form for such elements is covered in Chapter VI.

But for now, if you are planning to write a play that tells a dramatic story, a basic knowledge of plotting is essential.

Plot is the way you tell your story, not only in words, but in dramatic actions. It is the progressive unfolding of incidents, interweaving of character and situation that builds to a dramatic outcome.

FINDING YOUR OWN WAY

How Much Preplotting?

It is up to you, as the playwright, to decide how much plotting you want to do before you start to write dialogue. Instead of outlining, you may wish to start writing once you get an idea. Harold Pinter is one playwright who prefers not to plan too much in advance. He gets a flash for an idea and then, as

he says, once he gets the clues, he follows them as a detective would.

On the other hand, you may wish to plot the whole play before you start to write it. Or you can plot as far as you can go at a particular point. Regarding this, Arthur Miller remarks that he plans as far as it is possible to plan — that is, to the point where the plan is there in order to open up the way to the passion. Edward Albee relates his playwriting process: rather than getting an idea, he discovers that he has an idea. Then over the next six months or a year or two, the idea slowly develops. He thinks about it occasionally. The characters are forming at that time. Eventually, when the idea seems clear enough to start working on, and the characters seem three-dimensional enough to carry the play forward by themselves, Albee starts typing.

Balance Is Important

William Inge compared writing a play to taking a ride on a bus. One knows the general destination but is never quite sure of all the twists and turns the bus route will take. Every playwright, from Pulitzer Prize-winner Inge to a skilled television or screenwriter, experiences the excitement of false starts, periods of trial and error, and new bursts of energy. Often you will find that in the actual writing, new characters materialize who were never on your conceptual drawing board. You may find yourself writing the third scene, rethinking the first scene, and perhaps rewriting the second scene for the seventh time. The process of hard work, discovery, and new insight is always exhilarating and sometimes discouraging. Take heart. Writing is rewriting and often requires restructuring until things get to where you want them.

The question now is how to begin thinking about your plot. One working method is to start with a central character who has a strong goal, focus the central conflict, and then resolve the conflict.

This chapter focuses on how to begin working on your structure by asking the following questions:

- *Whose play* is it?
- What is the *central conflict*?
- What is *at stake*?
- Why does the play start *now*?

WHOSE PLAY IS IT?

In life we are often caught up in our own dramas — at home, at work, even during moments of recreation — with a cast of fullblooded characters. Because we are so close to the drama swirling around us, it is sometimes difficult to identify the leading characters. As a playwright you must be able to discern clearly who the central characters are in your dramatic writing.

The central character either sustains the action of the play or is the person around whom the action revolves. In classic Greek theatre, such a character was called a *protagonist*. Today we ask, "Whose play is it? Who has the dominant problem that has to be worked out, or who drives the action forward during the course of the play to achieve a goal?"

Sometimes the central character may be two people, such as the delightful sisters who poison lonely men in *Arsenic and Old Lace*, or even a group of people such as the inhabitants of a doomed city in Euripides' *The Trojan Women*, or the dancers who are auditioning in the musical *A Chorus Line*. In *Crimes of the Heart*, Lenny is probably a little more central than the other two sisters. She grows steadily throughout the play, becoming so assertive, in fact, that at the end she chases her snoopy cousin, Chick, out of the house with a broom.

A key way for you to determine your central character is to examine closely your central character's dramatic goal(s).

Major Goals

The central character usually has an urgent goal — most likely, a problem — that is not resolved until the end of the play. On stage or screen, a central character's major goal is shown primarily in action, to want or need someone or something, the more specific, the better. These dramatic goals must be made clear and believable during the unfolding of a play's action within a definite period of time so that the action takes place "here and now." For example:

- In *Hamlet*, Hamlet wants to avenge the death of his father while sparing his mother.
- In *The Wizard of Oz*, Dorothy Gale wants to get back to Kansas.
- In *The Homecoming*, the family of men wants to persuade Ruth to stay in the house and service them to their satisfaction.
- *In Death of a Salesman*, Willy Loman wants to achieve success either by himself or through his son, Biff.
- In *The Browning Version*, Andrew Crocker-Harris wants to retire from teaching with quiet dignity.

—————— WHAT IF ——————

a character in one of your favorite paintings or photos suddenly came alive? Write a short monologue in which the character expresses his or her goals, either directly or indirectly.

The goals of a central character may start strongly and clearly like Hamlet's resolve (". . . with wings as swift as meditation or the thoughts of love, may sweep to my revenge") and then because of internal and external tension falter during the play, only to regain strength later. Another possibility is for the major goal to come slowly into focus for an audience as the play progresses, such as Felix Unger's desire to be independent of Oscar Madison in *The Odd Couple*.

It may be that a stated goal (for example, Henry Higgins' desire to pass off Eliza Doolittle as a lady)

In *Death of a Salesman*, does Willy fear he may lose his son's love? Why do we care about these characters?

is surpassed by a stronger or more real goal underlying the verbal intent (Higgins' desire to control Eliza is his subtextual or unstated goal).

Sometimes a central character's goal is taken over by another character. In *The Browning Version*, for example, Andrew's desire to free himself of his wife, Millie, is overtaken by Frank Hunter. Frank must break off with Millie, his mistress, after seeing how cruelly she treats Andrew. This breaking-off action, in turn, restores Andrew's respect for Frank. Andrew is now prepared to retire in dignity, his major overall goal in the play. In *The Homecoming*, the men's goal of controlling Ruth is overtaken by her demands to dominate them.

What your central character wants in the play and the various things he or she must do to achieve the major goal depend largely on your play's central conflict.

WHAT IS THE CENTRAL CONFLICT?

As a structural foundation you now have:

Central character————> goal

If the central character reaches his or her goal too quickly, your play obviously comes to an end. Therefore, obstacles must be created that will block the attainment of the central character's major goal, create an interesting problem, and keep the play alive.

Opposing Character

Because of the dynamic nature of drama, it is often difficult to conceive of a central character without a strong counterpart. Called an *antagonist* in classic theatre, such a character is known today as an opposing character. Think of Dorothy, and the Wicked Witch of the West automatically flies to mind. Think of Willy Loman and the flesh-and-blood character of his son, Biff, appears to challenge his father's false dreams of success. In *My Fair Lady*,

Eliza Doolittle and Henry Higgins match wits verbally as well as musically. Ruth, the lone female, is pitted against a father and his three sons in *The Homecoming*. In contrast to *Hamlet*, this Pinter play does not follow a hero-villain pattern. The opposing forces are subtly understated, all to various degrees in conflict with each other and themselves.

Indeed, a play without opposing characters is the exception, for the essence of the dramatic experience is the fascination with the progression of clashing forces toward resolution; for that is essentially what conflict is — clashing forces.

Central character————> Goal
Goal <———————— Opposing character

A conflict between. your central character(s) and opposing character(s) or forces may arise from strong differences in personality or motivation, or perhaps from contrasting purposes and life-styles (e.g., superneat Felix and superslob Oscar in *The Odd Couple*).

——————— WHAT IF ———————
you could become any character you wished? As this character, tell what you want most out of life. Hit the highlights. Now invite someone to challenge you on attaining *one* of those goals. Let your conversation gradually turn into a confrontation. If necessary, improvise additional opposing characters.

On stage, as in real life, the ways of dealing with conflict are as varied as are the diverse kinds of conflict. The conflict may be between social forces as represented by class differences seen in *My Fair Lady* or *The Homecoming*. Conflicts of the personal kind are perhaps the most prevalent on stage.

An opposing character may enter headlong into conflict, as in the case of Claudius' deadly cat-and-mouse game to stop Hamlet from discovering his father's murderer. Some conflicts, like Biff's struggle with Willy in *Death of a Salesman*, are delayed up to a point and then must be faced directly. In life, we either avoid conflict altogether or settle for some sort of accommodation or compromise. In the theatre, the audience expects to see the playing out of a fight and its resolution. This fight can be tragic, comic, farcical, or melodramatic, but it must exist in some recognizable and believable form.

In structuring the basic conflict of your play, you may wish to give thought to the *thematic* implications of the plot. However, it is important to remember never to impose a theme onto your structure. Instead, the theme should naturally *grow out* of the play's interaction of character and incident. For example in Eugene O'Neill's *The Emperor Jones*, the external conflict is between Jones and the natives, but Jones' inner conflict with his past is effectively dramatized; apparitions from the past continually confound him and retard his efforts to escape from the natives.

Inner Conflict

During the course of a play the central character may be in conflict with the inner self, or with the forces of nature, such as a flood or a fire. But underlying these adverse natural or supernatural forces is a visible conflict between people. For example, in the horror film *Alien*, though the sinister, monstrous force provides the frightening chills in general, the specific struggle between the woman scientist and the robot commander on what to do about the alien provides the real tension.

Inner conflict, too, must eventually be seen in the context of *behavior between people*. Hamlet's soliloquies regarding guilt and responsibility, which beautifully show his stormy inner conflicts, are quite theatrical, but it is his outward visible conflicts with Claudius, Gertrude, Ophelia, Rosencrantz and Guildenstern, and Laertes that advance the story most noticeably.

There is nothing wrong with showing inner conflict if such conflict delineates character and is not in danger of becoming dramatic deadwood. For example, Willy Loman's tortured guilt about his affair with a buyer in Boston is all the more poignant because we see the circumstances of Biff's discovery actually portrayed on stage.

Conflict or Dramatic Tension Is Essential

As with other aspects of dramatic writing, there are no hard and fast rules or magic formulas regarding how much or what kinds of conflict or dramat-

The visible stake is a specific physical object, prop, or place—a reminder of the chamcter's fate. Here Laura contemplates her animal collection in Tennessee Williams' *The Glass Menagerie.*

—— JUST FOR YOU ——

Review and jot down your play's central conflict. Who are the central and opposing characters, what do they want, and where are the possibilities for dramatic action? What other characters will you need for your play?

WHAT IS AT STAKE?

Emotional Stake

If something intensely meaningful is involved in the life of the central character and is important enough for the opposing and/or contributing characters to challenge or defend the attainment of that goal, chances are that the audience will care more about what happens to the central character, as well as to the other characters. This emotional stake is the reason why the audience roots for the central character to succeed.

The most interesting characters on stage evoke strong emotions. We may laugh heartily at the foibles and follies of Oscar Madison and Felix Unger in *The Odd Couple.* We may shudder at the power and sexual games Max and his sons play with Ruth, and vice versa, in *The Homecoming.* We may hate and revile Regina in Lillian Hellman's *The Little Foxes* or the cunning Richard III. We may admire and revere Annie Sullivan in William Gibson's *The Miracle Worker*, or pity Blanche DuBois of Tennessee Williams' *A Streetcar Named Desire.* We can share their dreams, their high and low points, their feelings of doubt. But whatever basic emotion is sparked by our characters, we should always be

ic tension you should have in your play. As you begin to write your play, what you are trying to say (and in what form) will determine how strong or extensive your conflict should be. Be true to your characters, what they want, and their motivations. But remember you are writing a play, and the heart of a play is a believable, motivated problem. Many beginning playwrights fail in the elementary task of providing a central core of conflict or dramatic tension. It is not surprising that the primary reason for a play's rejection by agents or directors and producers — apart from the choice of subject or uninteresting characters — is lack of motivated human conflict.

Real characters, who have a real point of view. These are the starting blocks when playwright Steven Tesich, who also wrote the film *Breaking Away*, constructs a play. He used to begin with a conflict. But still, once Tesich has his real characters he sets them against each other (another way of talking about conflict).

Why does your play start now? In Terence Rattigan's *The Browning Version*, John Taplow comes to the study of Andrew Crocker-Harris to take a test.

fascinated by them and never (unless intentionally) bored. It is the responsibility of the playwright to make us *care* what happens to all the characters through what they say, what they do, or even what they fail to do.

Often, but not necessarily, a stake involves the well-being of other characters who are associated with or interact with the central character. We root for Dorothy in *The Wizard of Oz* because she wants to help not only herself but her three friends as well. Each is a character with detailed emotions, motivations, and actions. We want Hamlet to succeed, not only so that he can right a personal wrong, but because the pride and political health of country and court are also at stake. We want Higgins and Eliza to get together, especially after her transformation into a lady. And we care about the character of Ruth in *The Homecoming* even if the world she inhabits is somewhat alien to our own morality.

Visible Stake

This is a prop or place that shows the stake in action. Classic examples include the broom and ruby slippers in *The Wizard of Oz*, the copy of the Browning version of *Agamemnon*, and Laura's animal collection in *The Glass Menagerie*. Other examples of objects and places include: the rubber hose in *Death of a Salesman* that Willy is using to inhale gas and that Biff discovers and confronts Willy with during a major turning point; the appearance and upkeep of the apartment in *The Odd Couple*; in *The Homecoming*, the large, womblike room of an old house in North London, a space pervaded by mystery and menace; the fence in August Wilson's *Fences*.

Sometimes the stake may be aural; for example, the song that always reminds Charles of his deceased wife, Elvira, in *Blithe Spirit* (the visible stake is her arm in a sling).

―――――――――― JUST FOR YOU ――――――――――

Once the action of your play starts, what is at stake emotionally for your central character and the other characters? Does your play have a visible stake? (If not, don't worry; not every play does).

―――――――――――――――――――――――――――――――――

WHY DOES YOUR PLAY START NOW?

Ask yourself why your play starts when it does. What is so special about this particular day or time in the emotional or physical life of the central character? What is happening this time that is different from yesterday or tomorrow? Be careful to distinguish between your play's opening and the beginning of its dramatic action.

For example, John Guare's *The House of Blue Leaves* begins when Artie plays his songs for the audience. The audience is not impressed. Thus, the play's frame reveals that Artie has enthusiasm but no talent for songwriting. The dramatic action begins when Artie calls Billy Einhorn, a famous producer and Artie's childhood chum who could make him a star. This action shows Artie's commitment to a new life — Hollywood and stardom. Such a dramatic action is called a point of attack.

Point of Attack

This is when the dramatic action of the play starts, a *specific* point in time. You've observed from seeing and reading plays that their action often begins with the coming or going of a character. For example, Hamlet returns from the University of Wittenburg to Elsinor Castle to attend both his father's funeral and his mother's wedding. In *The Wizard of Oz*, Miss Gulch bikes to the Gale farm to take Dorothy's dog away, in turn causing Dorothy to run away. Colonel Pickering's arrival in London to meet Henry Higgins touches off the wager over Eliza Doolittle. In *The Browning Version*, student John Taplow comes to the home of his teacher, Andrew Crocker-Harris, to find out if he has passed the school term. In *The Homecoming*, Lenny asks his newly arrived sister-in-law, Ruth, to dance and then kisses her as her husband looks on.

The starting action of your play, its *point of attack,* can be likened to a small but potent pellet that serves as a catalyst when dropped into a test tube, releasing energy so that underlying forces can begin to interact.

All starting actions, and indeed all actions in your play, must be believable and well motivated. Actions should spring from what a character would really do under the *specific* circumstances *of the moment,* yet naturally fit into the entire design of your play.

——————— JUST FOR YOU ———————

Why does your play start when it does—not yesterday, or tomorrow, but today? *Now.* Jot down three possible starting actions for your play.

Exposition

There are things from the past that the audience needs to know in order to understand the characters and the plot. For example, in *Hamlet*, the audience needs to know that Hamlet's father has recently died and that his uncle plans to marry the prince's mother. Through the device of the ghost and information supplied by his friends, the audience learns pertinent dramatic information about Hamlet. The opening scene of *The Homecoming* between Max and his son, Lenny, ominously establishes the tone of power relationships within the family. Lenny and Max insult, bully, and manipulate each other to gain dominance.

In any case, keep your exposition brief and natural. For example, in *The Odd Couple*, the men are playing poker in Oscar Madison's sloppy apartment:

ROY: Hey, Oscar; let's make a rule. Every six months, you have to buy fresh potato chips. How can you live like this? Don't you have a maid?

OSCAR: (*Shakes head.*) She quit after my wife and kids left. The work got to be too much for her . . . (*Looks on table.*) The pot's shy. Who didn't put in a quarter?

Thus, in this natural banter, we learn or sense that Oscar is divorced, information that is essential to the plot because Felix Unger, recently separated, will be moving in. We also learn valuable character exposition—that Oscar is a slob — equally important to the plot, as it sets up the extreme contrasting lifestyle to Felix's supermeticulous habits. Other expositional devices include direct address to the audience: the stage manager in Thornton Wilder's *Our Town*; or a narrator in some of the "presentational style" plays of Bertolt Brecht and Shakespeare, and in Oriental drama.

Exposition Should Be Natural

You will discover that most exposition that you think so necessary in the beginning of the play can be brought out more naturally at later points and can best be revealed through dramatic action rather than by talk.

For example, say you were writing a play about a shy playwriting teacher who falls in love with a student's wife and must eventually confront his student over this sticky fact.

Say it is also very important to establish that this is the first time something like this has ever happened to the teacher. In an opening scene such exposition could come out in conversation (about other things as well) between the playwright and his close friend, a producer.

On the other hand, it would probably be more effective for the fact to be revealed naturally when the teacher confronts the student (or vice versa) in a later scene. Or even more effectively, the fact could come out when the teacher is awkwardly alone with the student's wife.

The first way is talky, the second is still talky but somewhat more dramatic, the third way substitutes an action for talk.

Preparation

Also known as foreshadowing, there are things that should be "planted" (made known well ahead of a scene so that ensuing scenes are believable). "Tolstoy's Law" of fiction can be applied to the stage: Let the viewer come to know and become emotionally involved with your characters before they enter their period of crisis. For example, in *Death of a Salesman*, we get to know and feel for Willy Loman in the first scene of the play through a dramatic conversation he has with his wife, Linda; this prepares the audience for his eventual confrontation with his son, Biff. Shortly afterward, we get a feeling for Biff through dialogue he has with his brother, Happy.

Hamlet's ambivalent feelings are expressed through several soliloquies and through dialogues he has with his mother, Gertrude, and with Ophelia.

In *The Wizard of Oz*, we get an incisive look at the major characters in Dorothy's fantasy dream through a brief but touching glimpse of them in real life on their Kansas farm.

In *The Browning Version*, there is the marvelous use of *Agamemnon*, which not only hints at one of the play's themes ("God from afar looks graciously upon a gentle master"), but also foreshadows the personal relationship of Andrew and Millie when Taplow remarks that *Agamemnon*'s plot is about "a wife murdering her husband and having a lover and all that."

In the opening scene of *My Fair Lady*, the viewer is prepared to enjoy the contrasting characters of Higgins and Doolittle through lively, witty exposition and two songs, "Why Can't the English?" and "Wouldn't It Be Lovely?"

In *The Homecoming*, Pinter subtly prepares the viewer for the brother's later disclosure that Max's wife was having an affair. This preparation comes about when Max recalls the man he used "to knock about with," MacGregor. This emotional "coloring" of Max's deceased wife prefigures the later concubine role Ruth will play out in the family.

Another good example of foreshadowing is the "battle" scene, Act II, Scene 3 of *The Miracle Worker*, in which Helen's folding her napkin prefigures the concluding scene when Annie and members of the Keller family gather at the dinner table and Helen's behavior renews the major conflict of the play. Of course, Act I, Scene 3, Act I, curtain, and Act III, Scene 1 all prefigure the famous concluding "pump scene."

"Dramatic Clock"

In the final scenes of *The Wizard of Oz* we are constantly made aware of a sand hourglass, which dramatically reminds the audience that Dorothy must get the broom to prevent the witch from ending her life. In many plays a different kind of clock is built into the structure, almost from the beginning. This "dramatic clock" serves as a framework for the action and also colors the emotional stake with urgency and concern for the central character to reach his or her goal.

In *Death of a Salesman* Willy Loman's struggle to keep his job and Biff Loman's futile efforts to find a job — both on the same day — contrast chillingly with Linda Loman's revelation at the end of the play that she has made "the last payment on the house today ... And there'll be nobody home . . . "

Higgins needs six months to pass off Eliza "as a duchess at an Embassy ball."

Teddy and Ruth, in *The Homecoming*, remark several times that they are just passing through London for a few days. We know — and fear — that her visit will be much longer, perhaps indefinite.

——————— JUST FOR YOU ———————
Does your play have a "dramatic clock"? Why does the dramatic action start *now*? Why do we care about what happens?

The inciting incident — when Stan was almost fired from his job — takes place *before* the play begins in Neil Simon's *Brighton Beach Memoirs*. The play is set into motion (point of attack) when Stan explains to his younger brother Eugene why he was almost fired — for sticking up for his principles — and that he has to apologize to his boss to get his job back.

PLAYWRIGHT'S PAGE

1) Which elements of plot did you have the easiest time with so far? Which elements were hardest to deal with?
2) Has the conception of your central character's goals changed during the *actual* process of writing?
3) Could you show your plot's basic conflict through pantomime?
4) Do you have a *visible stake* in your play? If so, what is it?
5) Do you feel more comfortable during the plotting, writing, or rewriting stages? Why?
6) Are you now more aware of structural elements of starting a play when you see a movie or play? Give an example.

IN SUM

Playwright John Galsworthy once remarked that a human being is the best plot. People — characters you know from real life, fiction, history, or from the richness of your imagination — truly make the best material for a play.

Once you have determined the major goals of the characters and the scope of the action (the incidents leading to a dramatic outcome), you can get deeper into the actual writing of the script. In the next chapter we show you how the "bare bones" of your structural beginnings will gradually become flesh and blood, vibrating with the pulse beat of a living organism.

MORE **RAW** MATERIALS

Read . . . and see plays with an eye to how the basic conflict is established. What does the conflict have to do with why the plays *start* when they do? What do the conflicts have to do with the plays' *point of attack* and *"dramatic clock"*?

Act ... out the scenes in your play in which your basic conflicts are introduced.

Write . . . an alternative opening for your play and contrast its differences with the one you have now.

—— SUGGESTIONS FOR CLASSROOM ACTIVITIES ——

The ongoing project — writing a group play — on the next page is not to be missed. Working on a group play, getting varied views on the plot, characters, and dialogue will be very valuable for your own individual work.

Draw or sketch an object or character in your play. Then make a cartoon bubble coming from either with self-descriptive words in it. Continue having the object or character talking. This can develop into a monologue, which you might later use in your play.

Read biographies or autobiographies of playwrights (such as *Playwrights on Playwrights*; see page 53). Try to get a sense of how different playwrights work when they plot or shape their plays. For example, as pointed out earlier, Edward Albee thinks about his plays sometimes for a year before committing them to paper, whereas Arthur Laurents (*West Side Story*) outlines his plays from the start. Other playwrights begin by writing dialogue freely, letting the subconscious lead the way. Still others, sure of their direction and climax, start at the end and work backwards. If possible, interview some professional/working playwrights in your community.

Act with a partner and build a scene, no more than five minutes long, with a beginning, middle, and end, using the following story starters:

> **NOTEBOOK (JOURNAL) FEATURE**
> Jot down some thoughts about the differences between writing a group play and your own play. How does writing a group play help you with your own play? In what ways does working on your own play help you to contribute to the group play? How does having your own personal vision for the play you are writing differ from the group work? Give some examples.

In Joseph Kesselring's comedy *Arsenic and Old Lace*, Mortimer announces to his sweet Aunt Abby and Aunt Martha his engagement to Elaine. Shortly after, Mortimer discovers — to his horror — that his sweet old aunts have been killing lonely old men visiting the house. From then on, the side-splitting action rolls on nonstop. Why does your play start when it does?

Conflicting Roles	Situational Starters	Conflicting Roles	Situational Starters
referee – ball player	"You're out!"/ "I'm not!"	girlfriend – boyfriend	"You can pay the check?"/ "Me?"\
rider – cabdriver	"Pull over!"/ "Wait!"		
boss – worker	"Late again?"/ "On this salary?"	tenant – landlord	"We're freezing!"/ "Pay the rent!"

ONGOING GROUP PROJECT

Writing a Group Play — In your groups:

1. Decide on your idea (or interesting conflict) for a play that your group will write together. The play can be about anything you wish. (If another group has a similar topic in mind, do not let this be a concern as its vision most likely will be different). Make sure your central character has a conflict with at least one other character in the play. Remember, conflict arises when characters having their own goals cannot agree or find a compromise. It is important to remember that opposing characters also have their own strong goals or objectives. Characters agreeing on things in life is great, but not good for drama on stage. After your group decides where your point of attack begins, make a list of MUST HAVE scenes.

Do not use names of the people in your group for character names.

2. Write the title of the play.
3. Write the specific TIME or TIMES your play takes place.

   Write the specific PLACE or PLACES of your play.

   Write down the CHARACTERS including their ages.
4. Start writing the dialogue. Plunge right in. Work together as a team. SHARE ideas. Begin anywhere. If you get stuck, improvise some scenes or move on to another part of the play. When you work on the parts, you are really working on the whole.
5. Listen to each other and be respectful of each other's ideas. Choose those that work best for the play.

chapter V

SHAPING YOUR PLOT

Content presents the task; form, the solution.
— Friedrich Hebbel

Clarify … clarify … clarify.   — Lanford Wilson

Ask yourself why you read a newspaper, story, or novel. Why do you go to see a play or movie? Why are you so often glued to your television set at home? One likely reason is that you are fascinated to read about or see how a human conflict will be resolved from start to finish.

A theatre, movie, or television audience feels cheated if the conflict or dramatic problem that has been set up is not fully resolved in some way.

This chapter focuses on helping you to shape your structure by asking:

- How is the central conflict sustained? (complications and dramatic question)
- How is the central conflict resolved? (major crisis and climax)

HOW IS THE CENTRAL CONFLICT SUSTAINED?

Complications
Complications serve to keep your play building in a steady line of development and suspense. They are, in effect, the twists and turns, the emotional ups and downs of your plot.

Structurally, each complication should be an integral part of your play's whole, just as the whole is made up of all the dramatic parts.

You can structurally think about the world of your play as follows:

Characters and incidents providing complications must be so selected as to somehow intersect with the lives of the central and opposing characters

A WAY OF LOOKING STRUCTURALLY

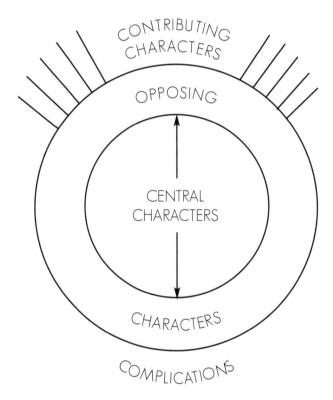

AT THE WORLD OF YOUR PLAY

and lead to a better understanding and feeling of the conflict between them.

These characters may become so real in the writing that you shouldn't be surprised if your plot must foremost accommodate to the development of the characters rather than the characters to the plot. It is quite common for a writer, referring to the characters, to say "I have to let them go their way."

A complication often is a character who has

already appeared in the play and is reintroduced to generate a new or changing balance of power in the play as a whole. For example, Hamlet mistakenly kills Polonius and must flee Denmark. The former pursuer of Claudius thus becomes the pursued. Then, through his wit and cunning, Hamlet turns this complication into a plus when he tricks his pursuers, Rosencrantz and Guildenstern, and is able to return safely to Denmark. There, new complications await him —the death of Ophelia and the burning rage of Laertes' revenge, engineered by Claudius.

By way of contrast, in the relatively plotless *The Homecoming*, Sam lets his brother, Max, know that he had witnessed the adulterous relationship of Jennie (Max's deceased wife) and MacGregor (Max's friend). The revelation of this fact, just before Sam dies, further complicates the dominant-submissive relationship of Ruth (Jennie's replacement) to Max and his sons.

——————— WHAT IF ———————

your life were free of complications? Write a *brief* dramatic sketch focusing on this theme. Then do another draft, making sure you have a central conflict and at least one complication.

———————————————————

Depending on the style of play and the world created within it, complications may range from sparse to dense. For example, in the medieval morality play *Everyman*, the title figure must find some virtue to accompany him to the grave. One by one, Fellowship, Strength, Beauty, and other virtues abandon Everyman. Only Good Deeds remains. The beauty of this play lies in the very simplicity of its "uncomplicated" complications.

On the other hand, *Hamlet*, an attempt at once to create the anguish and grief of the prince and the public world of the court he lives in, has thirty or so characters who interact dynamically. In certain melodramas and farces, plots are so often intentionally crowded with new complications that the expression "the plot thickens" becomes quite apt. A "spare and lean" plot, on the other hand, in *Waiting for Godot*, well serves the play's intentional mood of barrenness.

It is vital that complications never appear con-

trived (unless, of course, intentionally as in Shakespeare's *Comedy of Errors* or in Pirandello's *Six Characters in Search of an Author*). Complications should spring from the action, characterization and changing circumstances of the previous scenes and contribute naturally to the eventual dramatic outcome of your play.

Dramatic Question

A play lives by suspense — from action to action, moment to moment, scene to scene. [1] The audience wants to know — and *feel* — what will happen next. The *dramatic question* is the suspense question running through the course of the play that is directly related to the goal or fate of the central character. Here are some examples:

Hamlet: Will Hamlet be able to avenge his father's death while sparing his mother?

My Fair Lady: Will Henry Higgins let "a woman in his life"?

Death of a Salesman: Will Willy Loman find success either by himself or through his son, Biff?

The Odd Couple: Will Oscar and Felix remain roommates — and friends?

The Wizard of Oz: Will Dorothy Gale get back to Kansas even as she helps her friends achieve their goals?

The Browning Version: Will Andrew Crocker-Harris resolve the problems with his wife and retire in dignity?

After you have been working on your play for a while, you may feel the need to revise your central conflict and complications. Examining your play's dramatic question helps to focus the line of your dramatic action. You may discover, amazingly, that the one you thought was your central character is not really that person at all.

For example, in *The Devil and Daniel Webster* Jabez is the central character, not Webster or the devil as one could easily assume. The dramatic question is: will Jabez find happiness with his new wife, Mary? The first scene sets up the problem and shows

[1] There are always exceptions. Playwrights such as Bertolt Brecht in many of their plays have a narrator inform the audience what will happen during the next scene. This convention is built in as an integral part of the form and of the playwright's style.

The turning point in Act I of *My Fair Lady* leading to Eliza's successful masquerade as a lady: "By George, she's got it!" Higgins exclaims triumphantly.

the economic pressures on the impoverished Jabez, who is forced to sell his soul for money to Scratch, the devil. Daniel Webster must then defeat the devil before Jabez's life is snatched away. Although Jabez does not dominate the stage action in the last half of the play, he still remains the central character around whom the dramatic question revolves.

Without a strong and believable dramatic question, a play would simply lack the necessary tension and suspense to hold an audience's interest.

Drama Is Dynamic

Every scene of your play should carry within it the flow of the dramatic question. In this sense, the ultimate in your total design is in the immediate; the distant vision is in the instant moment. Choose characters who are bound to interact with each other to keep the dramatic question alive. Often the beginning scene or an early scene will contain the seeds of the dramatic outcome. Like an old record album in which Side Four is often found on the back of Side One, the opening scene of a play will contain elements of the ending.

In *The Homecoming*, Max's neurotic ambivalence about his departed wife, Jennie, is a distorted mirror of Jennie's replacement, Ruth. In *The Odd Couple*, the play begins and ends with the weekly card game in Oscar Madison's apartment. In *My Fair Lady*, Eliza's voice in the final scene echoes her situation in the first scene: "I want to be a lady in a flower shop instead of selling flowers at the corner of Tottenham Court Road. But they won't take me unless I talk more genteel. He said he could teach me ..." In *The Wizard of Oz*, the same kind of concern Dorothy's farmhand friends express for her at the beginning of the film is shown again when they peek through the farmhouse window at the end. In *Death of a Salesman* the premature return home of Willy from the road in the first scene is a harbinger of his offstage suicide in his car during the final moments of the play.

——————— JUST FOR YOU ———————

Think about your favorite stage, movie, or TV show. Can you verbalize its dramatic question? What is *your* play's dramatic question? What does it have to do with the central character of your play? What does the dramatic question have to do with your play's emotional stake?

HOW IS THE CENTRAL CONFLICT RESOLVED?

Crisis

In Chapter II, we learned that a novel can take its time, can afford to go slower in pacing while it explores the subjective thoughts and feelings of its characters. The play, on the other hand, because of time limitations and the objective world of the stage, must be more compact, immediate, and intense. That is why fiction is considered the art of *gradual* development, whereas drama may be looked upon as the art of *crisis*. In fact, a major crisis, or turning point, is indispensable to your plot because it provides the greatest amount of suspense regarding the play's outcome.

When you identify with the characters in a book or on stage or screen, you have a vicarious chance to take sides and get caught up in the drama. You have an opportunity to identify with someone having problems similar to yours. Or the problems may be so different from yours that they hold you in steady fascination.

An audience likes to see how a character will wiggle in and out of crisis. It likes to use its imagination on how the characters will use their guile, fortitude, perseverance, cunning, or whatever to overcome obstacles and strive toward their goal. "I knew it!" is a familiar cry of some theatregoers; they knew just how things would turn out. Another response of course is, "I never would have guessed it." Sometimes a major action is repeated in such a way as to set up an expectation that it will be either different or the same as the first time. Then the expectation is turned upside down. For example: Felix's return to Oscar's apartment and quick move out again; Eliza Doolittle's successful masquerade as a duchess at the Ball. Whatever reversal you use, make sure it is believable and springs naturally from both circumstance and character.

--- JUST FOR YOU ---

Theatre audiences feel cheated if the conflict that has been set up is not fully resolved. They want to see the dramatic question that pervades the play satisfactorily answered. Whether the central character gets what he or she wants. What are some things to consider in resolving your play's central conflict?

In the development of plot there are several lines of action that lead to the outcome of a play. When the goals of the central and opposing characters become incompatible with each other, a major crisis is produced. The fortunes of the central character take a crucial turn for better or worse. In this crucible of action and reaction, the central character must make a major decision that will affect his or her life and the life of the rest of the play. A major crisis is the most intense action that affects the life of the central character. It is his or her major turning point in the life of the play.

For example, during the first scene of *The Browning Version*, student John Taplow makes a mocking imitation of his teacher, Andrew Crocker-Harris, which is overheard by Andrew's wife, Millie. Later, toward the end of the play, Taplow, with all sincerity, gives Andrew an inscribed copy of Browning's version of *Agamemnon*, a gesture that moves Andrew to tears. But Millie, to get back at Andrew for his supposed inadequacy, informs him about Taplow's earlier mocking. This action produces an irretrievable crisis in their husband-wife relationship. Andrew decides to tell Frank Hunter that he knows about Frank and Millie's clandestine affair and to reveal her other affairs as well.

Because a set of relationships is maintained during the development of *The Browning Version*, Millie (the opposing character) also has a major turning point. Millie wants Andrew's retirement pension more than she wants Andrew himself. When Andrew — and consequently she — is denied the pension and she is also denied Frank (through Andrew's earlier action described above), she finds herself in a crisis that she cannot weather. She cannot have Frank and therefore must accept the "new" Andrew, who has grown considerably during the experience of his crisis.

Think about and express the major crisis of your play. What are some of the minor crises or complications leading to the turning point?

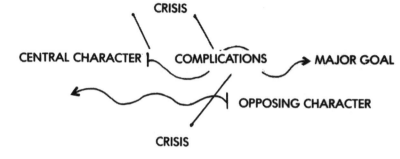

YOUR STRUCTURAL GUIDE SO FAR:

CRISIS

CENTRAL CHARACTER · COMPLICATIONS → MAJOR GOAL

OPPOSING CHARACTER

CRISIS

(TURNING POINT)

(There may be a number of minor crises leading to a major crisis or turning point in which the central character makes a major decision.)

Another Way of Looking at Crisis

We have already discussed the question of where to begin the action of your play. A good idea is to ask anew why the play starts now and not yesterday or tomorrow. What is it *specifically* in the life of the central character that is different today?

As the play reaches its end, one might ask the same question of the central character. After all the obstacles and complications have run their course, what still remains of the fate of the central character that can be revealed only through the additional element of crisis?

Michael Crichton has observed that every crisis has its beginning long before the actual onset. A crisis is a situation in which a previously tolerable set of circumstances is suddenly, by the addition of another factor, rendered intolerable.

From the examples cited so far, we can see how an additional critical element can tip the balance of conflicting forces and throw the outcome between them in doubt. In *My Fair Lady* it is the character of Freddie Hill, introduced at the very beginning of the play, who toward the end plays a more prominent role in influencing Henry Higgins to change his mind about Eliza. In *The Browning Version* the additional element, as we have seen, is Frank, who rejects Millie. In *Hamlet* it is the suicide of Ophelia, which so angers Laertes that he must seek revenge just as Hamlet up to now has been seeking revenge for the death of his father. The additional elements or turning points in *Death of a Salesman* include Willy's being fired and Biff's being turned down for a job. In *The Odd Couple* the added elements are the Pigeon sisters, who invite Felix and Oscar to their apartment after Felix's London broil is burned: but Felix, in character, turns down the invitation. This,

in turn, infuriates Oscar, whose intense anger is directed toward Felix. In *The Homecoming*, Max and his son, Lenny, propose their terms for Ruth's staying in the London household.

A crisis may be tightly constructed, or the images comprising the crisis may be more subtly drawn. For example, in *Annie* the crisis is suddenly crystallized when just as Warbucks wants to adopt Annie, she most intensely wants her parents. So instead of asking to be her father, he calls the F.B.I. The irony is that if they find Annie's parents, Warbucks loses her. The subtle crisis in *The Elephant Man* comes about when John Merrick starts as an object of pity and curiosity in a lowly freak show and winds up an object of admiration in a "freak show" attended by royalty. Throughout this transformation, John struggles to hold onto his inner beauty and sense of dignity.

What is your play's major crisis or turning point? Perhaps this was one of the first things you envisioned when you started writing your play. If so, has the vision of your play's crisis changed? How?

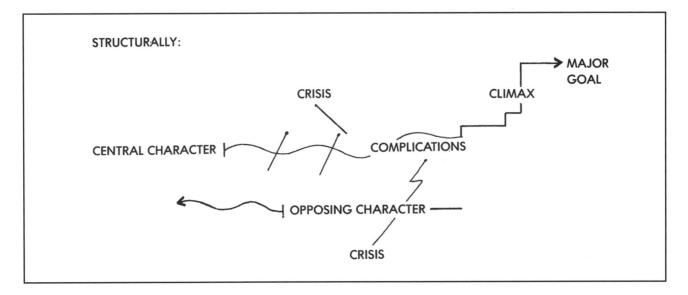

STRUCTURALLY:

Climax

A crisis may be looked upon as an onrushing river, carrying with it increasingly intense dramatic or comic situations throughout the play. The dramatic question, or the fate of the central character, eventually reaches a point where the outcome of the play is in greatest doubt.

The climax of a play is the *high point* of the flowing river, *where emotion is most intense.* All doubt produced by a major crisis is at last removed. As such, a play's climax may be considered the emotional peak of its structure. Usually there is a definite outcome regarding the central character's major goal — win, lose or draw, but never a dead halt.

In *Death of a Salesman,* Biff openly declares his love for his father and asks Willie to give up his false dreams.

In *My Fair Lady,* Henry Higgins, in a fit of passion, admits he's "grown accustomed to her face."

In *The Odd Couple,* Oscar throws Felix out of the apartment.

In *Hamlet,* Hamlet kills Claudius and loses his own life.

In *The Browning Version,* Andrew Crocker-Harris quietly informs headmaster Probisher of his rightful speaking place at school commencement.

In *The Homecoming,* Ruth agrees to remain in the family but on terms that will be in her favor so she can take control. Teddy leaves.

─────── JUST FOR YOU ───────

What is your play's climax? What if your play did not have a climax? (What does it have to do with the central character's major goal and the dramatic question?)

────────────────────────────

Resolution

Resolution of the plot is the tying together of the final strands of the play's action after the climax has been reached. The dramatic question is answered, and all previous questions in the plot are cleared up. In *Death of a Salesman,* the resolution comes in a Requiem when Biff, Happy, and Linda pay their respects to Willy at the grave site; in *My Fair Lady,* Eliza returns to Henry Higgins — on her terms. In *Hamlet,* Horatio promises that he will relate to Fortinbras the tragic events of the day. In *The Odd Couple,* the action ends with the weekly poker game, just as it had begun ("Marriages may come and go," Felix says, "but the game must go on . . ."). This time, however, things have changed with Oscar's awareness of "the two greatest things" he has done for Felix, "Taking you in and throwing you out." In *The Homecoming,* Max's power has been usurped. He pleads for attention from Ruth.

In a number of classic Greek plays, the conflict was resolved by an outside force such as a god flown on stage on a crane or a messenger carrying a change of fortune for the protagonist. This type of resolution was known as a *deus ex machina* (literally, "god from the machine"). Such endings, of course, are to be avoided unless stylistically intended for comic or ironic effect (i.e., Brecht & Weill's *The Threepenny*

A climax is a play's emotional high point. In Harold Pinter's *The Homecoming*, Ruth agrees to remain in the family, but on her terms.

Opera) or for a definite production value (*A Funny Thing Happened on the Way to the Forum*). You can think of some plays in which an outside force wins the day. The climax of Moliere's *Tartuffe* comes to mind; the dramatic problem is solved when Tartuffe is arrested by the king's officer, an outside character.

In the main, the resolution should spring from and be a natural consequence of your play's progression of dramatic interaction. For example, the renewed conflict at the dinner table in the concluding scene of *The Miracle Worker* affects not only the relationship between Annie and Helen but also that between Captain Keller and his son, James.

——————— JUST FOR YOU ———————

Create a central character and another character,

(continues on page 75)

A play's resolution ties up any remaining dramatic questions. Here Fortinbras promises to learn the tragic events of the day as the slain Hamlet is attended by Horatio.

SUMMARY OF THE PLOT OF *THE BROWNING VERSION*

POINT OF ATTACK —— On the last day of his school term, 16-year-old John Taplow goes to the apartment of his teacher, Andrew Crocker-Harris, —— CENTRAL CHARACTER

to find out how he did on his exams. Instead of finding Andrew, Taplow discovers Frank Hunter, a science teacher. They share a laugh as Taplow imitates Andrew's ("The Crock") stern and stuffy manner. Taplow thinks the play *Agamemnon* is "muck." Andrew's wife, Millie, enters, and —— OPPOSING CHARACTER

after Taplow is sent for medicine, we learn that Frank and Millie are having an affair. She wants Frank to come to her summer place. Frank is concerned that Andrew will find out about their relationship. Frank feels sorry for Andrew, and Millie is jealous of Frank's female acquaintances. Andrew enters. Frank relates warmly to him and then inquires about Andrew's new job for the next year in a school for backward —— EXPOSITION

boys. Andrew tests Taplow on the *Agamemnon*, and we find out that Andew is a scholar who loves *Agamemnon* so much

COMPLICATION —— that he did a translation of it when he was Taplow's age.

Millie returns and Frobisher, the headmaster, comes in. He —— CONFLICT

brings two pieces of news that make Andrew's world cave in: first, that Andrew has been relegated to a lower position during the speechmaking at the end-of-the-year Prize-Giving Ceremonies the next day; and more important, that the

DRAMATIC QUESTION —— Board has denied Andrew his pension despite the fact that he has been at the school for eighteen years.

CONFLICT COMPLICATIONS —— Andrew is upset. When Millie hears the news, she is very angry. Andrew's world goes further spinning when he, through a visit by his successor, learns that he is known as "The Himmler of the Lower Fifth." During this visit, Andrew says that a single success can atone for all the failure in the world. Taplow gives Andrew a copy of the Browning version of *Agamemnon* as a going-away present. Andrew is extremely touched and breaks down, sobbing.

CRISIS —— After Taplow leaves, Millie mocks Andrew, telling him how she caught Taplow making fun of him before. Frank, deeply disturbed by Millie's actions, breaks off his relationship with her. Andrew has known about Frank's affair and isn't angry at him. Frank informs Andrew that Taplow does indeed like Andrew. Frank advises Andrew to leave Millie.

In a series of revelations, we learn that Frank isn't Millie's only lover and that she had led Andrew to believe she was going to marry Frank. Frank offers his friendship to Andrew. Andrew puts Millie in her place and passes Taplow. In a last assertive —— CLIMAX AND RESOLUTION

move, he tells Headmaster Frobisher over the phone that he will not be relegated to the lower speech-giving position during the Award Ceremonies the next day.

give your central character a goal, and decide what the basic conflict will be. Introduce another character as a complicating factor in the central character's realization of the major goal. Incorporate as many plot elements as needed in your instant drama.

___

Can You Know All?

As you may be sensing or experiencing, writing a play is really a dynamic combination of dramatic instinct and thoughtful awareness of how to mold a dramatic shape or meaning from the material you work with. What makes this process invigorating is the alternating bursts of spontaneous creativity and conscious deliberation over what has been and is about to be written.

Even when thinking about your structure, you cannot be expected from the beginning to know how all the dramatic elements will coalesce in your play. Alan Jay Lerner, who wrote the book for *My Fair Lady*, for example, had to discover through much rewriting that it was Higgins' passionate love for the English language that was to be the "principal barrier separating class from class." This and Higgins' misogyny were the outstanding aspects of his character that had to be dramatized. Although Lerner had a complete play, *Pygmalion*, to work from, he still had to find the musical's dramatic structure by "trial and error." [2]

Any aspect of character or the dramatic elements discussed in this and the previous chapter may trigger ideas about your play's structure. For example, if you happen to start with the crisis in the life of your central character, you may have to work backward to discover why the play starts now and what is at stake. You may not know your point of attack until you can see the climax.

REVIEW OF BASIC STRUCTURAL ELEMENTS

Point of attack — the point in the play where the dramatic action begins

Exposition — events from the past or happenings outside of the play of which the audience must be aware in order to comprehend characters and plot

Preparation — the earlier planting of certain information so that a particular character or scene will be believable

Conflict — an internal struggle within one person or between two or more characters

Complications — the introduction of a fact or character already in the play that delays the climax and propels the play into growing suspense

Dramatic question — the suspense question related to the fate of the central character's major goal

Crises — turning points of a play in which a central character makes major decisions concerning a course of action

Climax — the highest emotional peak in the play

Resolution — the point after the climax at which all remaining questions are answered and the action is tied up thematically.

Whether a play is tightly constructed or episodic and sprawling, characters and incidents should be chosen in ways that give the greatest dramatic impact in the most imaginatively "economical" way. It is interesting, for example, how playwright Terence Rattigan has selected his characters, situations, and place so that the action of his one-acter *The Browning Version* unfolds naturally in one set in a continuous flow of time. There are no "wasted characters." Keep in mind the general dramatic elements as you review this play and your play's *specific* structure.

Although the plot of the Rattigan one-acter appears as though it just "happens," in truth the writing of this play, like most others, required a great deal of rearrangement of incidents and character interaction until a clear focus was finally found.

Plunge Right In

The best way to write is to write. Plunge in anywhere. It may be an opening scene, character capsules, a description of the setting, or stage directions. The important thing, as short story writer Guy de Maupassant said, is to capture your ideas with the black of the pen on the white of the paper. How does one start? With a feeling or specific image, almost anything might start you off.

[2] Alan Jay Lerner, *The Street Where I Live* (New York: W. W. Norton & Cb. 1978). p. 44.

These feelings can flow from any number of ideas and images you have already considered for your play. In this chapter our purpose has been to help you capture the flow of your ideas within a manageable flamework. Remember, the actual writing of dialogue will touch off more ideas for your plot as well as for characterization.

We hope the techniques found in this chapter help you make the people of your play come alive through the telling of a dramatic story whose shape and outcome is worthy of the characters, conflicts, and themes you choose to present.

IN SUM

This structural short checklist will prove helpful:

1) *Whose play* is it and *what does he or she want?*
2) What is the *central conflict?*
3) Why does the play *start now?*
4) What is *at stake?*
5) What is the major *crisis* or turning point'?
6) What is the *climax* or emotional high point?

Receiving and playing your "Mission Possible" (see page 79).

I've got five minutes to finish the last page of my novel — get out of here!

In the next chapter we will look at some writing aids that you will find useful during the process of plotting. And if you'd rather not do a lot of plotting, we'll take a look at some alternative forms that are relatively plotless.

PLAYWRIGHT'S PAGE

1) In your play do the various plot elements flow smoothly and naturally from one scene to another?

2) Can you clearly identify the major crisis and the climax of your play?

3) What is your dramatic question?

4) Do you see your idea differently now that you have had a chance to structure it? If so, how has it changed?

5) Do you find yourself rewriting your play more and more, focusing it more specifically and clearly each time?

6) In your mind review your own life or the life of a close friend or family member. Have you experienced a crisis? Would this make a basis for a play? Is it too close to you? What if you distanced it by setting it back in time or into the future, or by disguising your character as someone else?

7) React to the following statement: Writing is rewriting! (Write a short scene about it, if you like.)

MORE **RAW** MATERIALS

Read . . . or reread some of your favorite plays. Can you sense how the playwright has related the crisis and climax of the play?

Act . . . out the scenes that encompass the crisis and climax of your play. How do they "feel" to you?

Write . . . any revisions you think are necessary after hearing the above scenes read and enacted.

In *You're a Good Man, Charlie Brown* (book by John Gordon; lyrics and music, Clark Gessner) Lucy Van Pelt's overall goal is to make fun of Charlie, but learns that he is not so bad after all. In the scene at the right she reminds Charlie of his faults, but then she makes him feel better (her scene goal) by letting him know that he is the one and only, the unique, original Charlie Brown.

——— SUGGESTIONS FOR CLASSROOM ACTIVITIES ———

You may not want to miss playing the "Missions Possible," next page. It will help you feel how one character's circumstances influence and interact with another character's circumstances.

Discuss the following questions with a partner:
• Does each character in your play have an overall objective as well as a specific objective for each scene they are in? How so?
• Do the circumstances for your central and opposing characters change in any way during the course of the play, complicating the action? In which ways? What leads to your central character's crisis? For example, is it: Ambition for something? Intense desire for someone or something? Fear of losing or getting something or someone? Running away or avoiding something unpleasant? Anger, depression, or elation, by something big — or small?
• What's at stake for your central and opposing characters? Why do we *care* about what they do and what happens to them?

Read *The Browning Version* by Terence Rattigan. (New York: Samuel French, 1975.)

In the powerful, emotional climax of William Gibson's *The Miracle Worker*, Helen Keller — having made the connection between her memories of water and Annie Sullivan's signing of the word — is now able to communicate fully her love for her teacher. The water pump is a visible stake for Helen and Annie's mutual victory. They are both dynamic characters who change during the course of the play. In what way does your play, whether it is a drama or comedy, have a satisfying, emotional and truthful payoff? How does the climax achieve the classic goal of feeling *inevitable* (not artificially contrived), and yet offer a jolt of *surprise* (not boringly predictable)?

"MISSIONS POSSIBLE" GAME

Act out the "Missions Possible" game. Prepare in advance, the following tape-recorded message — spoken seriously and slowly — and played in the dark (while a flashlight shines on the tape recorder) when the game begins:

> *"Attention all agents! Attention all agents! You are about to receive your 'Missions: Possible.' While playing your situation, at all times it is important to remember three things: 1) WHO you are 2) WHAT your goal is in the scene, and 3) WHERE you are. Repeat: who, what, where. This tape will self-destruct in five seconds. Good luck!"*

1. After the tape is heard, the lights go on and sealed envelopes (with the word "Secret" printed on them) are passed around to all the participants. Each player opens an envelope to find a slip of paper with a situation written on it: a character (*who*) and his or her goal in the scene (*what*). Some examples:
   - You are an escaped convict who must find a place to hide.
   - You are an ecology "freak" who sees pollution everywhere.
   - You are a newspaper reporter columnist looking for a juicy story.
2. Two players volunteer to do the scene. They step out of the room without discussing *who* they are and *what they want*. While they are out, the rest of the group decides *where* the scene could logically take place (e.g., the escaped convict and the heart surgeon *might* be in a deserted office building).
3. The two players come back in the room, receive their *wheres* privately then review their *whos* and *whats*. Then they begin the scene and passionately and honestly go after their goals — making sure that they do not directly verbalize to each other who they are and what they want.
4. The players proceed with the scene without interruption while the rest of the class observes the character interaction.
5. Each improv is followed by brief comments. What made the improv believable? How did the actors play their goals? What was the emotional relationship of one character to another? What did they want from each other as the situation developed? What made the actions clear?

This theatre game is an exciting way to discover spontaneously how a scene — or even a whole play — develops with complications and a climax that flow naturally from the interactions of the characters.

Write a series of note cards as an outline for your play. As you do, keep some important structural elements in mind. Why does your play start *now?* How is the past reflected in the present? What changes does the central character undergo? Think about such questions as you sort out and arrange your note cards to sequence your scenes. It's a good idea to tack the cards on a large bulletin board to help you easily shift them around and see the scenes' relationships to each other. Remember, as you work with the cards you can build up your sequence or pare it down until things begin to jell.

NOTEBOOK (JOURNAL) FEATURE

Write your reactions to these three expressions: "I write to understand as much to be understood." (Elie Wiesel) "Writing is an exploration. You start with nothing and learn as you go." (E. L. Doctorow) and "How do I know what I think until I see what I say?" (E. M. Forster). Jot down some thoughts concerning what you are learning so far about yourself, others, or some aspect of the playwriting topic you have chosen to explore. To get started, you might want to describe one new insight about yourself (or about any of the others in your group) which you have gotten so far through writing a play. How has writing about your particular subject matter changed your ideas or attitudes about the topic?

chapter VI

MORE ON PLOT — AND PLOTTING LESS

It is the supreme misfortune when theory outstrips performance.　　　— Leonardo da Vinci

Habits are first cobwebs, then cables.
　　　　　　　　　　　— Spanish proverb

The word "drama," as you know, means "to act or do." Now that you have a basic grasp of plotting theory, your job is, as always, to "to do the do" — write a play.

What will separate you from the "textbook theorist" is the advice offered throughout this book — to plunge in and write!

No need, however, no matter how inviting, to plunge into shallow or rocky waters. We trust that with a basic structural guide in hand, you will now have a clearer idea of where you are heading.

Remember, there are all kinds of ways to write. Guy de Maupassant once apologized to a friend, "sorry I have written such a long letter — I did not have the time to write a short one." Do you have the time to save time by taking the time to think through the plot of your play, or as much of it as you can? As you think, you can playfully write a sort of shorthand to yourself. Such devices as diagrams, outlines, and charts can sometimes save a lot of time in the long run.

Remember, you need not follow an outline slavishly. Rather than being carved in stone, an outline exists mainly to help you further to shape your work creatively.

If it is a good outline, its shape will change and grow, even as your play changes its shape until its final form jells (and that may change, too, during productions.)

As important as having some kind of working outline is developing good writing habits. Too many writers get into a rut because they do not have a working routine, whether it is writing 1,500 words a day as George Bernard Shaw faithfully did, or three hours a day, or even three pages or three lines of dialogue a day. Writing daily (or nightly) will keep your writing instrument — you — oiled, in tune, and ready for longer stints when you are so "hot" and energized that you cannot stop writing even if you wanted to.

If you get stuck writing dialogue or character sketches, a good way to keep your daily writing routine intact is to try your hand — and imagination — at some of the following plotting aids.

AIDS FOR PLOTTING

Scene and Scenery

Scenery is what the audience sees when the curtain goes up (or the lights come up), the setting of a play. A scene is the basic unit of the plot. It is the action that takes place within the setting. Think of one of your favorite stories. See if you can plot out in your mind or on paper its scenes in sequence. The next time you go to a play or watch a television play, see if you can identify its changing scenes. Jot them down on the program and later reflect about the dramatic effectiveness of the sequence.

Opening Scene

By establishing the proper mood or tone, the opening moments of a play can let an audience know or feel what they can expect to see. For example, the card game in *The Odd Couple* sets us up for an evening of comedy. *Hamlet*'s opening moments establish a mood of mystery and expectation. *My Fair Lady*'s opening outside the Royal Opera House in Covent Garden contrasts the richly tailored aristocrats who are leaving the building with the poor costermongers and street entertainers doing acrobatic tricks. This scene prepares the audience for the first encounter between Higgins and Eliza.

Cover Scene(s)

A character may have the need to go offstage for a very important action. On stage, the ongoing action "covers" the offstage action. For example, in Act I of *The Odd Couple*, Felix goes to the bathroom, and Oscar, Murray and the card players crowd around it, worried that Felix is going to kill himself. Felix, of course, is really throwing up while his friends think he is taking pills to commit suicide. Felix's offstage action is made believable by the realistic reactions of his friends onstage.

Obligatory Scene

Special thought should be given to those scenes in which central and opposing characters must confront each other as your play nears its resolution. For example, in *The Odd Couple* when Oscar kicks Felix out, Felix makes Oscar feel guilty. "I've been looking forward to throwing you out all day and now you even take the pleasure out of that," Oscar laments. Felix starts to leave. Then Oscar, concerned, quietly asks him back. After these closing scenes of oscillating emotions, Felix eventually goes, leaving Oscar saddened. The comedy of human feelings is enriched through the charaters' seriocomic confrontations. In *Death of a Salesman*, Biff confronts his father with the fact that he knows Willy has been taking gas through a rubber hose. In a stormy exchange of love-hate dialogue, Biff admits that he's a "bum" and tries to tell Willy who he is. Biff breaks down and cries, admits to Willy that he loves him. Willy is deeply touched and amazed.

The French Scene

The French scene is a scene marked by the entrances and exits of characters. A character enters, bringing with him or her a new want or desire. Sometimes a character may participate in the existing action. For example, in the first scene of *The Browning Version*, Taplow and Frank have a scene. Shortly thereafter, Frank leaves and Andrew and Millie have a scene. Each scene consists of characters bringing with them definite goals and objectives that somehow either get in the way of or aid the central character's long-range and immediate goals. (See page 85 for an example of a French scenes chart.)

Scenario

A number of playwrights find it useful to write a scene-by-scene breakdown of the actions (the "bare bones") as far as it is possible to project. In this way they are able to link scene to scene and see *concrete* relationships and interactions between characters. Some writers get started by jotting key scenes on 5 x 8 note cards. Then they lay out the cards and shift them around until a semblance of a plot gradually takes shape.

As you lay out your scenario, you will find it helpful to note any questions to yourself about plotting and characterization problems. You will probably discover that you have to leave spaces here and there because you simply do not have enough information at the time to complete the continuity. This is perfectly natural. One of the heartening things that will keep you returning to your writing desk is the wonderful sense of discovery that accompanies the closing of gaps and solving of creative problems. As a "drama detective" of sorts, you can look forward to discovering all the missing bodies in the world of the play *you* are creating.

A Note on Outlines

Even those who rebel against the general notion of outlines find them helpful in some way. For example, Nicholas Meyer, who wrote and directed the film *Time After Time*, thought it was "boring" to work from an outline when he was in college and a visiting writer explained how important it could be. Years later, when Meyer started directing a film, he hired an artist to sketch out a storyboard (frame-by-frame drawings of the action). Although the storyboard never was finished or even consulted, it proved helpful because Meyer was forced to explain his scenes to the artist, making them clearer in his own mind. In a way, a good outline should help you to visualize the action of your play from scene to scene and moment to moment.

Proportioning

What follows may seem a "mechanistic" way of looking at things, but beginning playwrights frequently ask, "What goes into each act, and how long does an act have to be?" As a way of getting started with proportioning your play, you may wish to plot the key incidents broadly. For example:

One-Act Play: The Browing Version

The action is tightly compressed into some fifty or so pages. the exposition and situation foreshadowing Andrew Crocker-Harris' loss of both his wife and his teaching position occur early in the play; the crisis of Andrew's revealing that he knows of his wife's affair with Frank Hunter occurs about halfway through; and the climax of Andrew's asserting himself to headmaster Frobisher transpires close to the end.

Two-Act Play: Death of a Salesman
Act I (about an hour)

   Willy's crackup
   Return of Biff
   Past — Biff flunks school
   Willy and woman in Boston
   Willy plays cards with Charlie
   Willy seeks support from Ben
   Linda seesk support from her boys
   Biff will see Oliver, finds rubber hose

Act II (forty minutes)

   Willy to seek New York job
   Willy is fired
   Past — Willy seeks support from Ben
   Willy borrows money from Charlie
   Willy informs sons he's been fired
   Biff tells Willy bad news
   Past — scene with woman in Boston
   Biff breaks down: Willy moved to destroy self

Three-Act Play: The Odd Couple
Exposition: Felix kicked out of his home
Situation: Oscar, not sure if Felix will take his life, ponders what to do with him.

Act I (thirty-five pages)
Felix finally believes his marriage is over. Oscar wants him to pick up clothes. At end of act Felix's wife cuts off communication; doesn't want to speak to him. Felix settling in for a couple of days; mistakenly calls Oscar by his wife's name, Frances.

Act II (16 pages)
Scene I
Oscar threatens the men's relationship by asking the sisters for a date. Felix responds that they all can have dinner in Oscar's apartment.

Scene II
Felix breaks down in front of dates. Felix refuses to go upstairs to see the sisters. Oscar feels like pushing Felix through the window.

Act III (18 pages)
Oscar threatens to throw Felix out of apartment. Felix "quits" Oscar. Felix leaves. Card game. Sisters

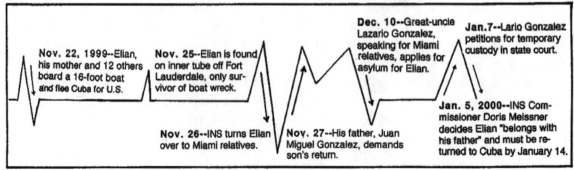

Emotional Ups and Downs of Elian Gonzales--Father's Point of View--First Months

Nov. 22, 1999--Elian, his mother and 12 others board a 16-foot boat and flee Cuba for U.S.

Nov. 25--Elian is found on inner tube off Fort Lauderdale, only survivor of boat wreck.

Nov. 26--INS turns Elian over to Miami relatives.

Nov. 27--His father, Juan Miguel Gonzalez, demands son's return.

Dec. 10--Great-uncle Lazarlo Gonzalez, speaking for Miami relatives, applies for asylum for Elian.

Jan.7--Larlo Gonzalez petitions for temporary custody in state court.

Jan. 5, 2000--INS Commissioner Doris Meissner decides Elian "belongs with his father" and must be returned to Cuba by January 14.

Chart of Elian Gonzales case, which gives you a good idea of the flow of conflicting events.

An "obligatory scene" comes toward the end of a play at a point where the central and opposing characters cannot avoid confronting each other. In *The Odd Couple*, Oscar laments to Felix: "I've been loking forward to throwing you out all day and now you even take the pleasure out of that."

return. Felix returns — the men make up.

The curtains of the first two acts must bring the audience back.

——————— JUST FOR YOU ———————

Plot out the key incidents in your script for either a one-act or a full-length play.

Graphs

You may have enough perspective on the forward movement of your play to chart a graph showing the ups and downs of your characters throughout the main line of action.

Such a graph — like the one on page 82 illustrating the events surrounding the Elian Gonzales case — may help you see changing character relationships and emotional turning points within the designated framework of your play.

If you have already written a draft of some of your play, a graph or chart may help you sharpen or clarify the focus of what you want to say and show structurally.

Diagrams

Shorthand, doodles, notes to yourself are all helpful. Whatever works for you, works.

Who-What-Where Chart

You may wish to make a Who-What-Where Chart which gives you a good idea of the flow of your scenes. The Who-What-Where chart may be looked upon as a blueprint from which the rest of the plot can be constructed.

WHO: Who is in the scene?

WHAT: What is happening in the scene? (Or what does each character want?)

WHERE: Where is this taking place?

See page 85 for the first seven French scenes of *The Browning Version*.

Remember — just as with a scenario — during the actual writing process there will be spaces that cannot be completed, simply because you cannot be expected to know everything during the conceptualization stages. The reality is that there will be considerable shifting of relationships and movements from space to space as you construct your plot. The actual writing of dialogue and scenes will further affect the shape of your plot and the spaces within it.

Structure and Texture

As you shape your plot, you will discover in your own way that structural problems and solutions may better help you hear how characters talk and get ideas for settings, music, and elements that

(continues on page 86)

OBJECTIVE-OBSTACLE-OUTCOME CHART

OBJECTIVE	OBSTACLE(S)	OUTCOME
Tragedy: *Hamlet:* Hamlet: to revenge the death of his father.	Claudius, the murderer of the father.	Tragic. Claudius is killed. Hamlet too.
Drama: *Death of a Salesman:* Willy Loman: to win success and direct Biff's life.	Biff Loman, who wants to lead his own life.	False victory; Willy gets Biff's love and commits suicide so that Biff can benefit from insurance money.
Comedy: *The Odd Couple:* Felix Unger and Oscar Madison: to change each other's lifestyles.	Each's obstinacy about preserving his way of life.	Felix kicked out of Oscar's apartment, but things turn out okay.
Drama: (and dark comedy) *The Homecoming* : The male family (esp. Max and Lenny) want to persuade Ruth to stay on their terms.	Ruth (to some extent, Teddy and Sam)	Ruth stays, but on her terms.
Musical: *My Fair Lady:* Higgins wants to control Eliza on his terms. Inner conflict: "Never let a woman in my life."	Eliza Doolittle wants to be treated as a woman, not as a wager.	Reconciliation: He's "become accustomed to her face."
One-Act *Browning Version* Andrew Crocker-Harris wants to retire with quiet dignity.	Boys in school (Taplow) Millie Frobisher	Millie put in place. Frank becomes friend. Andrew will appear at commencement.

A who-what-where chart (opposite page) will help you visualize real people in conflict-resolution situations in a specific place, as in *The Browning Version*: John Taplow and Frank Hunter (rear) and Andrew and Millie Crocker-Harris (front).

CHART SHOWING FRENCH SCENES: *THE BROWNING VERSION*

FRENCH SCENE	*WHO*	*WHAT*	*WHERE*
1	TAPLOW	Taplow coming in with book, last day of school . . .	Andrew Crocker-Harris's sitting room.
2	TAPLOW and FRANK	. . . to take test. Character exposition — of Andrew — "no feelings" — Taplow does not like him. Imitates and makes fun of "Crock" in front of Frank.	Same
3	TAPLOW, FRANK, and MILLIE	She overhears Taplow making fun of her husband. Taplow worried that he will not pass now. Millie sends Taplow away.	Same — upstage unseen by Andrew
4	MILLIE, FRANK	She's angry that Frank avoided her all week. Learns Andrew starts new job in September. Millie is having an affair with Frank. She wants him to come with her to summer place. Frank concerned about Andrew's finding out. Millie upset — won't see him for six weeks. She's in love with Frank. She knows Taplow was making fun of her husband. More exposition about Andrew — that he once had more gumption. Frank feels sorry for Andrew. Millie jealous of Frank's women acquaintances — she berates him for missing an appointment with her. She's hanging on to him desperately. Frank says he will visit her this summer.	Sitting room
5	ANDREW, FRANK, MILLIE	We learn that Andrew has drafted timetables for last fifteen years. Frank relates warmly to Andrew, asks about new job, school for backward boys.	Sitting room
6	TAPLOW, FRANK, MILLIE, beautiful connection	We learn Andrew has been sick. Taplow returns, Millie leaves. Andrew and Frank talk about Taplow.	Sitting room
7	ANDREW, TAPLOW	Frank exits. Andrew tests Taplow. Andrew revealed a scholar in exposition. Andrew reminisces that when he was Taplow's age he did a translation of *Agamemnon*.	Sitting room at desk

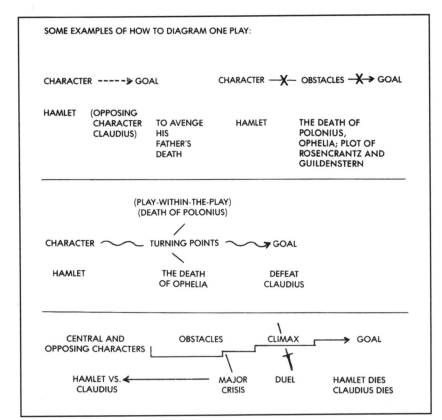

(See discussion on *visual stake* in Chapter IV, page 61.)

Exploring the "Where"

Some playwrights discover structural insights from the settings they envision for their plays. Laying out scenes with a good idea of how you feel about the atmosphere of a set or the kinds of things that go into a particular place can yield clues about the people who inhabit the place, as well as what happens to those people. You may wish to lay out the various "wheres" in your play and list the things that could happen during a specific time, paying attention to temperature and seasonal changes.

Another useful technique is to think of a particular place in your play as having six sides. [1] This "six-sided where," if it were a room, would include the four walls, ceiling, and floor: a fancy garden might include side of house, row of bushes, two sides of a pool, Japanese lanterns, and ground. Be as specific as possible when describing the "six-sided wheres" in your settings.

contribute in other ways to the mood of the play. In turn, the writing of actual dialogue will contribute to your structural ideas, which were difficult to formulate in your mind but now catch sparks when you put pen to paper.

Colors

Some writers think of scenes or bits of action as colors suggesting contrasting moods. For example, in *The Devil and Daniel Webster*, the mood switches from the rosy, happy wedding scene to the suddenly gloomy, gray second scene upon the arrival of the devil to collect his debt, the life of Jabez. A number of writers think visually in colors. Often a character "wears a mood" that can affect or control the direction of the entire scene. For now, you may wish to make a color collage of the dominant feeling each character or scene evokes in your play.

Objects

Once the central character, major goals, and opposing characters have been selected, some playwrights think of the scene-by-scene use of key objects (each having a dramatic function), which will figure prominently in the action of the play.

Music

Many plays can be thought of in terms of musical composition. Ionesco's *The Bald Soprano* runs in movements, perhaps a concerto; for example, there's the allegro-paced gibberish episode. If you think of the work as a concerto (solo piece sung by a soprano?) it concludes with its theme again picked up, though altered. (If minor key in first movement, it reappears as a major key in the last movement.)

Arthur Miller has referred to his play *The Price* in terms of "modulations" and as a "quartet." He comments on the exact nature of the "integrity of the parts" as very intense.

[1] Thanks to David Shepherd, founder of The Improvisational Olympic.

PLOT CONVENTIONS

A convention is an unspoken agreement the playwright has with the audience that it will make believe certain things are happening on stage although those things could never happen in a literal or real sense. In Coleridge's term, there is a "willing suspension of disbelief" on the part of an audience to accept an otherwise unconventional action. The actor's transformation into *The Elephant Man* and the stylized horses in *Equus* (see page 124) are theatrical conventions. The reappearance of the dead tech sergeant to replay the incidents leading to his murder in *A Soldier's Play* is another example. And so is Eliza Doolittle, every time she bursts into song to release her boiling emotions ("Just You Wait"). In fact, a play by its very nature of artistic selection is a convention. In plotting, we've already talked about a "covering scene," which gives the illusion of a long passage of time offstage through the occurrence of a shorter scene onstage. Here are some more conventions.

Subplot

A subplot is a related story thread that has a life of its own apart from the main line of action. Rosencrantz and Guildenstern in *Hamlet*, Millie and Frank Hunter in *The Browning Version*, and Freddie Eyensford-Hill in *My Fair Lady* strongly influence their plays' outcome. In strict terms, however, they are not subplots since, comparatively speaking, they have a "limited life" in the play. Subplots usually detract from the main action and very often distract the audience's attention from the play as a whole. But then, again, it is difficult to make rules, for a subplot skillfully interwoven into the main fabric of a play can add drama, color, or humor. For example, the subplot of the impending marriage of the peppery, lovable Alfred P. Doolittle adds a glow to *My Fair Lady*, and the character manages to steal the two scenes ("With a Little Bit of Luck" and "Get Me to the Church on Time") that feature him. In *The Homecoming*, the subplot of MacGregor's affair with Max's wife, Jennie, transpires in the past; yet the revelation of the affair adds a chilling twist to the play's ending.

Because subplots are difficult to manage, a beginning playwright would do well to concentrate on a structure that avoids them. Even so, you may wish to experiment with this convention in a longer play. Subplots rarely occur in one-act plays.

Stage Time vs. Real Time

In *The Browning Version*, Taplow's trip to pick up medicine for Andrew Crocker-Harris would take considerably longer than it does. Again, this instance of "stage time," which gives the illusion of "real time," is a convention. The collective mind of the audience adjusts to and accepts the convention if the spirit or essence of the incident or action touches a deeper reality than one that is literal and earthbound. As an example, Alan Jay Lerner uses an interesting technique to give the illusion *in My Fair Lady* that Professor Higgins and Eliza are working together through many, many nights. The reappearance of six servant-narrators in a pool light during a montage relating the progress of "Poor Professor Higgins slaving night and day" imaginatively and clearly establishes the convention. An audience sits two hours in a theatre and totally accepts the passage of several weeks in *The Odd Couple* because of the brilliant characterizations of the two men wreaking havoc on each other's lives. In *Death of a Salesman*, the whole life of Willy Loman is telescoped through the theatrical juxtaposition of past/present images filtered subjectively through his mind.

Frames

In this convention the action of the play is set up or triggered by a theatrical device, an event, or an image. *Sweeney Todd* is framed when the title character and his macabre victims ascend ashen-faced from a graveyard, and we flash back to find out what happened. In the opening of *Amadeus* we are presented with old Salieri as a wheelchair-bound, cranky lunatic who slowly transforms — via lighting, costuming, and acting — into the younger Salieri. The main action of the play then proceeds to show the court composer trying to sabotage young Mozart's career. Kevin Wade's *Key Exchange* is set in Central Park on a series of summer afternoons. At the top of each act the characters come in on bicycles because it's an effective way to get the characters on and off the stage (and an excellent frame). *The Diary of Anne Frank* is framed by the discovery of Anne's diary by her father. As the name implies, a frame encompasses the entire action of the play and usually ends where the play begins. Be wary of overusing (or even using) a narrator to frame your action. Too often a narrator (in spite of its effective use by Brecht, Wilder, and Shakespeare) becomes a cop-out when scenes should be dramatized instead of narrated.

FINDING A FORM FOR PLAYS THAT DO NOT STRESS PLOT (PLOTLESS PLAYS)

If you feel uncomfortable with elaborate plots, you are not the only one. Emile Zola, a nineteenth-century novelist and playwright, considered plotting "child's play," an infantile exercise in tying up complicated threads just so they could be untied again. Zola was objecting, of course, to the heavily melodramatic plays of his time whose plots were "crowded with incident." In this country, William Saroyan wondered why characters and plot had to be forced into preconceived visions when art is supposed to deal with "capturing and presenting" an aspect of life.

No one wants to force a plot or, for that matter, anything else. If you feel that constructing a plot — no matter how simple or complex — isn't your thing, you still have a number of options. You may wish to compose a series of vignettes or sketches, or find a form that presents a mosaic of theatrical images centered around a particular theme or concept.

The Dining Room by A. R. Gurney is a series of vignette still photos in which a dining table serves as a centerpiece for dozens of characters who flow in and out of scenes that feature holidays, birthday parties, and other family occasions of American middle-class life. Stephen Sondheim's musical *Company* is a succession of images — bittersweet encounters, actually — between lovers and other couples. These scenes flow out of the life of the central character without recourse to heavy plotting. The "concept" musical *A Chorus Line* hinges on a dance audition without much plot to speak of (many consider the director-lead dancer relationship to be an intrusion).

You may decide to write a play primarily evoking a strong mood, such as the feelings of dread and doom permeating John Millington Synge's *Riders to the Sea*. Rather than depending on external dramatic action, such plays are more concerned with internal "action of inaction" such as found in Beckett's stream-of-consciousness "monologue of the mind," *Krapp's Last Tape*.

Another good example of a mood play is *The Dance and the Railroad* by David Henry Hwang. Critic Mel Gussow of *The New York Times* has called this play a "poem of situation" rather than a play of action. The play is set in the pioneering American West in the 1850's. Two Chinese laborers carry on a conversation while one of them, Lone, performs Tai Chi and meditates. The other man, needing money, is eager for the workers to end their strike of the Transcontinental Railroad. The two men are in themselves striking contrasts of mood and thought. The theatrical blending of Eastern and Western dramatic conventions weave song, dance, and gymnastics into a rich tapestry of theatrical styles. Such a play is not conceived of or evaluated in terms of plot but rather in evocative colors, feelings, and esthetic performance values.

In discovering such a form, you may wish to have your characters relate more in apposition — side by side — than in direct conflict with each other; look for what makes you feel comfortable.

The form you devise may be a series of related monologues, Reader's Theatre, or poetic outpourings. An example of the latter is Ntozake Shange's *for colored girls who have considered suicide/when the rainbow is not enuf*, a choreopoem in which six actresses recount, through poetry and movement, a wide-ranging spectrum of emotions encompassing what it means to find oneself as a black woman: first love; the end of an affair; graduation; life in a new city; and other cameos depicting key moments of their lives as they discover options for expansiveness.

——————— JUST FOR YOU ———————

Ask yourself: If you don't wish to construct a play with strong central and opposing characters and strong conflict and crises developed in a linear progression, what can you offer instead—striking moods, vignettes, theatrical images, poetry held together by something else? What???

SOME MORE THOUGHTS ABOUT TIME

Most plays move forward in chronological time (linear), some within twenty-four hours like Greek classical plays. Others, like some of Shakespeare's plays or the plays of Bertolt Brecht, sprawl over time and are set in different places. Plays with a linear structure vary greatly. For example, in Thorton Wilder's *The Long Christmas Dinner*, characters age and die and are replaced in minutes.

Nonlinear plays (which do not move forward in a straightforward chronological line) also vary greatly. Most noteworthy, perhaps, is Luigi Pirandello's *Six Characters in Search of an Author*. In this play, a family (who may be real flesh and blood or mere fantasy characters) intrudes on the rehearsal of another Pirandello play and proceeds to enact scenes from their lives that flash backward and forward. They bare their souls and blur not only time, but also dreams, reality, and the artistic process itself.

The Bedbug, by the Russian playwright Vladimir Mayakovsky, has an epical flashforward, leaping ahead in time a half century after the play's unlikely hero is accidentally frozen with a bedbug in a block of ice. *Miss Saigon* has a big, famous flashback in the second act that shows how Chris and Kim were separated in the first act. Peter Schaffer's *Amadeus* begins with a double flashback into the title character's love-hate relationship with Salieri; and Harold Pinter's *Betrayal* starts at the end of a couple's emotional relationship and moves back in time, finally leading to the husband's discovery of her betrayal.

In some structures, the special use of time serves the play's theme in unique ways. For example, in Michael Frayn's *Copenhagen* two brilliant scientists — one German and one Danish — are lifelong friends who worked together on early phases of the atomic bomb, but now find themselves on opposite sides during World War II. The play juxtaposes the present with our knowledge of the destruction the bomb caused during the past, zeroing in on a secret meeting held in 1941 in which the two scientists confront each other's motivations and responsibilities.

You might be influenced by the ability of movies, television, MTV rock videos and the Internet to skip around with ease through time and space. Perhaps, having seen such movies as *Back to the Future, Field of Dreams,* and *The Sixth Sense,* you might wish to experiment with so-called virtual reality, time warps and mind games.

It is, of course, up to you to decide how to structure your play to best fit the story you want to tell in dramatic terms. However, do not let a fascination with time-bending cinematic techniques (that have their own frame of reference) dominate your play at the expense of character development. The plain truth is that time-jumps that appear so fluid on the screen because of film editing and special camera and lab optical effects are difficult and, most often, awkward to pull off on stage. To put it positively, in the medium of theatre, the story is most clear when time moves in a straightforward manner, or moderates the pace and scope of any variation, as befits the physical limitations of the stage. If you are writing stories for the stage that explore human emotional relationships, the way you do that within a linear or manageable nonlinear structure should be a major consideration as a beginning playwright.

IN SUM

Writing is rewriting. Bernard Slade relates how he started to write his comedy *Same Time, Next Year* in May on a plane ride from Los Angeles to Hawaii and had roughed out a draft of the first act by the time he landed. He finished the rest of the play by July.

Arthur Miller has described how he wrote three-quarters of the first draft of *Death of a Salesman* through one balmy spring night — and spent almost a year afterward finishing the play and rewriting it. Most writers go through a number of drafts of their work, rewriting lines, scenes, and acts.

Some playwrights write great characters and dialogue but discover, unfortunately, that they have

CONTRASTING TIME FRAMES

The dramatic action in William Inge's Pulitizer Prize-winning play, *Picnic,* set in a backyard of a small town, takes place during a twenty-four hour period.

In *Ty Cobb* by Lee Blessing, three actors representing Ty Cobb at different times in his life (young athlete; middle-aged businessman; aging cancer patient) unleash their memories and interact with each other, contributing to a dynamic understanding of the legendary baseball giant. Consider alternative forms for your play, to best fit the content you are dramatizing.

Form serves content. In Harold Pinter's *Betrayal,* Jerry and Emma's affair is revealed by progressing backward in time, depicting different levels of deceit and betrayal among wife, husband, and lover.

structurally reached a dead end for lack of adequate planning — i.e., plotting. Again, balance is important. Overplanning can kill the spontaneity and joy so crucial for creative discovery, whereas little or no planning can often lead to chaos.

We hope the aids offered in this chapter will prove useful for you to find your own technique and voice.

PLAYWRIGHT'S PAGE

1) If you are writing about the problems of people and how they face and overcome those problems, why is it important for you to have a crisis in your play? Diagram the crisis of your play in relation to the central conflict.

2) How is a play's climax related to a play's opening scene? Give an example from a play you have seen or read. Now give an example from your play.

3) Are you clear about your play's resolution? What are some of the ways to end your play? Which ending do you think is the most logical? The most honest? How

In Peter Shaffer's *Amadeus,* Salieri (as portrayed here in the movie version by F. Murray Abraham) is both the narrator of the stage play and also its central character. We see him first as a seventy-year-old man, then he transforms into a young man and relates, in flashbacks, the episodes of his love-hate battle with Mozart, himself, and with God.

NOTEBOOK (JOURNAL) FEATURE

Jot down some thoughts on the different forms for plays. (What are your favorite forms? Linear? Flashbacks? Play-within-a-play? Explain why.)

Save a space to write your feelings regarding the structure of a play that is scheduled for performance in your community. Make some notes on what you will be looking for regarding the play's dramatic structure.

For now, you might wish to take a break from your own play and diagram the structure of a play that you may wish to write in the future which contains a time warp, time travel, flash-forward, or other unusual form. How does its plot compare with the one you are structuring now?

would you "color" the scene?
4) What does your title have to do with your play?
5) What does your title not have to do with your play?

MORE **RAW** MATERIALS

Read . . . some of the scenes from your play to friends or family. Get some reactions. Take notes. But give yourself some time to decide what you want to do with the reactions you get if you see patterns developing.

Harper: " . . . My dreams are talking back to me." Tony Kushner's Pultizer Prize-winning play, *Angels in America*, moves forward in chronological time. Some characters have hallucinatory scenes that are timeless. The play uses "magical realism," a combination of realism with supernatural and surreal elements. It is an epic study of the grueling ordeal of a latent homosexual, from his guilt, contraction of AIDS, to final miraculous recovery by the intervention of a winged angel descended from above — all set within the socially turbulent 1950's, focusing on the character of the predatory Roy Cohn.

Act . . . Playwright Tom Stoppard has said that he enjoys being a playwright because writing dialogue is the only respectable way he has of contradicting himself. Double fun! Write a dialogue about this.

1) Enact a brief scene between two characters entitled, "To plot or not to plot!" Jot down a brief scenario or diagram of what you come up with.

2) Encore: Change this book into any other object that two people could want for whatever different reasons or motivations. Write a short dialogue showing this conflict in action, and act it out.

3) Create a character with a distinct personality from another place and time. Become a reporter and conduct an interview with this person. Make sure the character's lines bring out the time and place in which he or she lives.

4) List the "wheres" in your play and have them describe themselves.

Write . . .

1) As a variation of the above exercise transform this book into another book that will suggest a new set of characters and situation (Bible, textbook, UN guidebook, celebrity mag, and so forth). Devise an Objective-Obstacle-Outcome Chart for the situation. (See page 84.)

2) Think of an interesting incident that happened to you, a friend, or a family member. Was there anything important at stake? Draw a picture or describe a *visible stake* involved if there was one.

3) Devise a Who-What-Where chart (see page 85) for the idea of your play. Don't worry if there are holes or vague spots in the chart; these can always be filled in later.

4) With a friend or classmate improvise a short dramatic scene. Give each of you a strong goal that is in opposition to the other. At some time during the improvisation, bring in a third character who adds a *complication* to the ongoing conflict; i.e., blocks the central character's goals. *Outline* the scene that develops.

5) Think of someone you really admire or respect. Conduct an interview between a reporter and your "idol" as dialogue. When you enact this with a friend, play your "idol's" role (If you don't have an "idol," make one up or create a villain instead), using some of his or her personality quirks or mannerisms. *Chart a graph of what happened.* (See the graph on page 82.)

—— SUGGESTIONS FOR CLASSROOM ACTIVITIES ——

These exercises are designed to explore the important aspects of form. Again, choose those that you feel the most comfortable with. You may wish to try another form at a later time.

Discuss . . . Form a Playwrights Discussion Panel and talk about the various kinds of dramatic structures that appeal to you, using as examples plays you have read, seen, or are writing. Points to cover might include:

- how a great variety of linear plays that move straightforward in chronological time may differ markedly in form (such as the tight, forward-moving structure of Jean-Paul Sartre's one-act play *No Exit*; the back and forth expressionistic movement in Arthur Miller's *Death of a Salesman*; and the zig-zag movement of Eugene Ionesco's Theatre of the Absurd one-acter, *The Bald Soprano*). Review some examples offered in this chapter and share examples from plays you are familiar with.
- the role of flashbacks in plays. Share examples of how flashbacks work well. How can they also get in the way of the dramatic structure, even confusing an audience? Share some examples.
- how plays with a strong element of fantasy are best served by a linear structure (such as Jean Giraudoux's *The Madwoman of Chaillot*) or by a nonlinear structure (such as Tennessee Williams' *Camino Real*). Share some examples.

Read . . . some plays or scenes from plays that were mentioned during your Playwrights Discussion Panel.

- Look in the local newspaper for reviews or descriptions of plays being presented in your community. Perhaps there is a play that fits a description of a dramatic structure that has not been touched on in this chapter. See the play if you can. Do you agree or not agree with the reviewer? *

Act out with your group a short-short scene that is presented in straightforward linear fashion and then do it with a flashback. Remember, a flashback is a memory device that cuts into the flow of chronological time order to show what happened at some time in the past. It may come at a moment of present high tension to show what happened before, and then continue in chronological order to the resolution (e.g., in Act Two of *Miss Saigon*). Use the following structure for the flashback:

present — past — present.
(flashback)

How do you think the way in which the story is told will affect the audience's reactions and emotions?

Write . . . with a partner or in a group, some additional dialogue in the form of a flashback for the play you just acted out. File it in your notebook, journal, or mind. You never know when you will come back to it (or it to you).

* Thanks to playwright Elana Gartner for this very useful idea.

chapter VII

CREATING YOUR CHARACTERS

A walking contradiction partly truth and partly fiction …   — Kris Kristofferson

"What a character!"
      — Ferrari (Sydney Greenstreet) in *Casablanca*

How many times have you heard someone say about another person, "Wow, what a character!" But when you think about it, you, too, have been a character all your life, with a unique set of fingerprints and a special way of looking at and living in the world. Though you share a lot of characteristics with other people — country, color, sex, age, beliefs, and so on — it is how you specifically act and feel in relationship with others that makes you unique. You've been evolving all your life. As you're discovering while writing, it also takes quite a bit of growth to become a character in a play.

You, as the playwright, are in the first position to see how the *separate* selves of a character fit into each other; and how the whole character, in turn, fits into a pattern of relationships with others. In this chapter, we help you create characters and deepen characterization by asking:

• What are the differences between a role, a character, and a personality?

• What are some aids that can help you create your characters?

• How can you deepen the characterization in your play?

CHARACTER TERMS

Social role is a person's place or position in the community.

Examples
Henry Higgins is a bachelor phonetics professor living in London.
Dorothy Gale is a teenage schoolgirl who lives on a farm in Kansas.
Willy Loman is a father and salesman who lives in Brooklyn, New York.

Character is the fleshing out of the details of a social role.
Examples
Henry Higgins is a handsome, suave, middle-aged bachelor phonetics professor who always must have his way. (This is what the author intended and what the audience perceives. Higgins himself may feel differently: that instead of being arrogant, he's really self-assured and self-reliant.)
Dorothy Gale is a sensitive, vulnerable, but assertive orphan schoolgirl who daydreams and fights to make her dreams come true.
Willy Loman is an insecure salesman in his 60's who loses his job and fights to hold onto his family.

Personality traits are those special little idiosyncrasies that etch a character into the memories of an audience. Have you wondered why a man would mutter to himself as he walked down the street? (Willy Loman in *Death of a Salesman*). Why a young man would feel sorry for a man he once despised?

(Andrew Taplow in *The Browning Version.*) Why a young girl would suddenly break into song? (Dorothy in *The Wizard of Oz.*) Perhaps these things have happened to you. Empathy is sharing to the point where an audience cares deeply what happens to a character.

Examples

Henry Higgins is a moody, vain, conceited, handsome, suave, middle-aged bachelor phonetics professor, who seesaws between moods of elation (when he's winning) and depression (when he doesn't get his own way). Both moods often contradict his outwardly generous air.

Dorothy Gale is a sweet, vulnerable, moody, deeply emotional girl who can be assertive to the point of "liquidating" her enemy and feeling sorry about it.

Willy Loman is a romantic, selfish, loving man who talks to himself, lives in a dream world, imagines people are out to destroy him, and finally destroys himself to help someone else he deeply loves.

All these characters fight for their goals, live in a dream world, talk to themselves, and speak (or sing) out. Yet each one is markedly different. Personality traits deepen what a character does and what he or she thinks and feels — often a maze of contradictions and mixed emotions at different times.

The "BIG" particular goals of a character will move your play ahead. "Little" personality quirks and traits contribute to the richness of human feelings, giving your play density and veracity. Drama consists of *specifics*. The more finely etched the character traits are in *real* speech and actions (and inaction when required), the more believable your characters will be.

By becoming involved with the characters of the play — as the details of each scene accumulate — an audience obtains insight into human behavior. The audience perceives how characters strive to be basically true to themselves, yet often, unknown to them, are affected by the actions of other characters.

——————— JUST FOR YOU ———————

"Wow, what a character!" Here are three variations of an exciting exercise [1] that shows how any role can be deepened through the addition of *specific* personality traits.

1) *Emotional Hurdles:* With a partner pick two roles that are reciprocal; that is, mother/daughter; boss/worker; teacher/student. Decide on a very specific place, say, a school classroom. Devise a conflict or problem in which the roles will interact; e.g., teacher wants student to turn in homework but the student objects. Enact the scene for three minutes. The *first* minute should be "colored" by the same emotion for both characters (say, jealousy); the *second* minute, a different emotion (hatred); and the *third* minute, still a different emotion.

2) *Time Dash:* Pick roles as above. Add an incident that has a conflict. The *first* minute should be some set time before confrontation; the *second* minute, during the actual confrontation; the *third* minute, some specific time after the confrontation. For example, the roles might be a boyfriend and girlfriend who have been invited to a party. During the *first* minute they might be on the way to the party; the *second* minute takes place in the middle of an uptight situation during the party; the *third* minute comes right after the party, having it all out.

3) *Space Jump:* Pick roles and incidents as above. This time, for each minute of the total three minutes, provide a *different, specific* locale. For example, the roles might be father and son debating about "bad" friends. (Whose — father's or son's?) The three places might be a deserted beach; a crowded shoe store; and home (specifically the kitchen). Vary roles, times, places. Add other characters when appropriate. The important thing to notice is how the "little" things — slips of speech, emotional colors, gestures, nonverbal cues, and hesitations — turn the role into a character, making things fresh and alive. As in life — as in this exercise — when you write, take chances to improvise, and "let your-

[1] Thanks to David Shepherd, founder of the Improvisational Olympic.

self go" within the structure; break out of the structure when you feel the urge.

CHARACTER AIDS

Conceiving Characters

Professional playwrights vary markedly when it comes to creating their characters. Some writers never embark on the actual writing of a play until they perceive the full "offstage" lives of their characters. That is, they want to know as much about their brainchildren as humanly possible. Other playwrights like to discover what their characters do, think, and feel during the actual process of dialogue writing and rewriting.

Most playwrights prefer to *model* their characters, at least during the beginning writing stages, on people they know in real life. For example, take the social role of the Willy Loman character. It was patterned somewhat on Miller's father-in-law, who was a salesman. Neil Simon used his own brother (and his brother's roommate) as the original models for Oscar Madison and Felix Unger in *The Odd Couple*. Some of the characters in Lanford Wilson's plays are based on real people he knew well in his native town of Lebanon, Missouri. August Wilson's cycle of plays all take place in the Hill District of Pittsburgh. Other characters are *composites*; that is, some traits were drawn from one person and other traits were extracted from another person. Some characters were created entirely from the imagination.

As novelist and playwright W. Somerset Maugham observed:

> The writer does not copy his originals, he takes what he wants from them, a few traits that have caught his attention, a turn of mind that has fixed his imagination, and constructs his characters. [2]

It's not uncommon for a playwright to say, "There is a little part of me in each of the characters I imagine." After a draft or two, characters' traits that have been only sketched in will gradually assume a fuller dimension as pieces of the human puzzle come together. To a large extent, that's why you write — to puzzle out who your characters really are, what they do, and why and how they feel. During the beginning stages of writing, most playwrights tend not to rely on elaborate sketches or outlines of characters. Insight and intuition are the guides.

Regardless of how you conceive your characters, strive to make the role, character, and personality quirks work off each other, combining them in ways that are fresh and original. As a way of getting started, think about images and events in your own life that integrate role, character, and personality.

For example, the summer I was working on this book, I was on one of my perpetual diets. Thus, physically, you could say I'm sort of a heavyset person. Emotionally, I can be short-tempered under pressure. Mentally, I'm rather quick to jump to conclusions when rattled. In my role as a writer, I was putting in my usual one thousand words a day. On this particular afternoon I was scribbling in a restaurant located in a shopping mall in upstate New York. Next to the restaurant there was a department store where I went daily to weigh myself on one of the scales in the housewares department. To eliminate every ounce of excessive weight, I emptied all my pockets. I then went to do my writing stint in the restaurant. After that I ambled over to my car to go home, but to my horror I couldn't find my keys. Expectantly, I ran back to the restaurant, but the keys were not there. This greatly depressed me. Suddenly, I remembered emptying my pockets when I weighed myself earlier. Elation! The keys must still be on the floor. Thank God! 1 ran back to the housewares department and found the keys. I promised myself to include this incident in a play someday, or at least to remember it as one important key to *character*.

———————— JUST FOR YOU ————————

As you go through your drafts of writing, ask yourself: Have I integrated a character's social role, personality traits, and quirks in the most honest and believable ways possible? Think of one example of how you did — or can.

_____

[2] W. Somerset Maugham, *The Summing Up*, p. 68.

The motivations of your characters should be sufficiently clear to make their beliefs and behavior convincing. Even an out-and-out villain such as Claudius manages to gain our sympathy in one scene.

More Things to Think About When Drafting

By this time you are probably well into scripting your play. So the following guidelines and hints may also serve as a useful checklist. We will discuss a character's dramatic purpose; objectives/obstacles; scope of play; kind of play; and life-style.

I. DRAMATIC PURPOSE

Make a list of all characters in your play and ones you may include later. Ask yourself if the character is a *central character* (either keeps the play moving forward or is the character around whom the dramatic actions evolve); an *opposing character* (attempts consciously or unconsciously to block the central character's major goal; at times can even be the central character); or a *contributing character* (lines up somehow, at one time or another, with central or opposing character, sometimes with both). In as few words as possible, jot down the relationship each of these characters has to the other. If you like, you can make a "flow chart" or a "match 'em up chart." (See page 86.)

A. Central and Opposing Characters

It is important to reiterate that opposing characters are not necessarily villains or "heavies." Far from it, an opposing character may be a deeply loved and loving person, a positive life-giver. Central and opposing characters should not be thought of in rigid terms. As in life, there is often a noticeable ambivalent blurring between them.

For example, in Lorraine Hansberry's poignant drama *A Raisin in the Sun*, the central character, Walter Lee Younger, is opposed by his mother, Mama Lena Younger, a decent, churchgoing woman. (See page 111.) She deeply loves her children, wants the best for them, is proud of her black heritage, and is extremely fair-minded. She has her dream (moving her family to a good neighborhood); Walter Lee has his (buying a liquor business and getting ahead). Their values clash, their actions clash. There is anguish and pain when Walter is cheated by a "friend" out of the insurance money he has put into a fledgling business.

At this point, Mama lashes out at him, but she is patiently understanding as well. She feels her son will eventually find himself and reassert his dignity and pride. And Walter Lee does come to clarify his sense of values when he tells off Linder, the man who has been denying the house to the Youngers because of racial prejudice. In short, Walter grows emotionally as a character. His true values are tested in action. There is a constant stripping away of false values until his true underlying character stands clearly revealed, a man of dignity and worth. Thus, Mama Lena is the opposing character in the dramatic and not in the characterlogical sense.

Biff Loman in *Death of a Salesman* is considered an opposing character because he challenges Willy's sense of values and major goal of pursuing false dreams. Yet Biff is searching for meaning in his life, just as Willy is searching (pathetically, it turns out) for what his life has meant to him.

Even central characters who, on the surface, are actually cruel or appear despotic have reasons or motivations for doing what they do. For example, in *Hamlet*, an out-and-out villain like Claudius receives the audience's sympathy as he tries to atone for his crime. For most of the drama we have seen the play develop through Hamlet's eyes. Now, in Act III Scene iii, we see Claudius alone presented as a rather harmless, actually helpless, creature who must be forgiven if he is to escape eternal damnation. He is sincere and atoning. He realizes there is joy in heaven for sinners who repent (for being a Christian). We have not expected to see the cunning lion presented as a lost sheep, and that is why the scene is so powerful.

KING

O, my offence is rank, it smells to heaven;
It hath a primal eldest curse upon 't,
A brother's murder, Pray can I not . . .
My fault is past. But O, what form of prayer
Can serve my turn? "Forgive me my foul murder?"
That can not be, since I am still possess'd
Of those effects for which I did murder,
My crown, mine own ambition and my queen.
May one be pardon'd and retain the offence?
In the corrupted currents of this world
Offence's gilded hand may shove by justice
And oft 'tis seen the wicked prize itself
Buys out law: but 'tis not so above; . . .

Hamlet, overhearing Claudius at prayer, feels he cannot be a true "father's son" if he permits the possibility of Claudius' soul receiving a better destiny than the man he has murdered. We now begin to question Hamlet's motives. Can we identify with the actions of a man who desires the eternal damnation of a soul that sues for "grace in a time of need"? Can we feel sympathy for a man who believes that "revenge should have no bounds"?

Unwilling to forgive his uncle after hearing Claudius' confession, Hamlet resolves to become a killer, just as Claudius has been. The act at this specific point probably gives Claudius more sympathy than he deserves. [3]

We can often better understand a potentially unsympathetic character's current goals when his or her background is dramatically illuminated. Sweeney Todd, the infamous villain of Fleet Street, is a victim of harsh circumstances. A barber by trade, he was sent abroad after being convicted by a corrupt judge of a petty crime. Sweeney eventually finds his way back to London, where he discovers that the same judge who sentenced him also had seduced his wife, who is now apparently dead; the judge is at this very minute coveting Sweeney's daughter! Bitter Sweeney swears revenge against all enemies of decency. With the delightfully gregarious Ms. Lovett, he slices heads off all manner of hypocrites and turns out meat pies from their ground-up bodies. We may not admire Sweeney's actions, but we can certainly sympathize with his motivation.

Contrast is another key to think about. Central and opposing characters who find themselves with opposing values and outlooks usually show marked contrast in roles, character traits, and personality quirks. Higgins, the pedantic, arrogant professor, mellows as Eliza makes miraculous progress shown in elegant detail. Eliza, the "guttersnipe" flower girl, softens, then toughens in relationship to Higgins' newfound regard for her. Quiet, reserved Andrew Crocker-Harris stands and grows in strong contrast to the aggressively shrewd Millie who slowly — again, we experience the dramatic details from scene

[3] John F. Andrews, "The Purpose of Playing: Catharsis in *Hamlet*" in *Poetry and Drama in the English Renaissance in Honor of Professor Jiro Ozu* (Tokyo: Kinokuniya, 1980), pp. 1-19.

Combining characters may play an important role in a script as ally or foe of the central or opposing character. In *Annie*, the orphans' attitudes and actions towards Miss Hannigan help us to accept Annie's eventual escape. Miss Hannigan, though a delightful adversary, is a good example of a static character; that is, one who does not change or grow during the course of the play.

to scene — cracks up.

In Lanford Wilson's comedy *Talley's Folly*, the romantic couple consists of a German immigrant with a sharp sense of wit who loves his sweetheart but somehow can't let his true feelings show, and the girl who, by contrast, brims over with feeling for him but is never quite sure she really loves him. In Shelagh Delaney's *A Taste of Honey*, the central character, Jo, is illegitimate and lonely; and her mother, hard-drinking and sociable.

Internal Contrasts

Also observe how contrasts dramatically occur *within* a character. Iago, the crafty manipulator who uses others as pawns in his own Machiavellian game of chess, sets the *Othello* plot in motion. Othello is a man of extreme outward action, but inwardly romantically charming. But, overwhelmed by his frenzied jealousy, he rises in passion in stark contrast to Iago's spidery craftiness. Iago's is a double-edged personality: he prides himself on his brilliant craftsmanship even as he feels contempt for what will come from it. Like what may happen to many of us, each loss of familiar, safe ground forces him to risk the alienation of others. He undergoes a graphically detailed identity crisis in which the ambivalence of love and hate produces self-doubt and anguish. The complexity of mixed and often warring emotions gives the character dramatic depth.

In plays such as *The Homecoming*, where the fear or threat of conflict is more implied than externalized, characters such as Ruth and Max act more in apposition with each other than in opposition to each other. But the contrast still exists. Without contrast, art is static and plays are boring. Characterizations must be especially sharp in relatively plotless plays. Ma and Lone in *The Dance and the Railroad* are two contradictory characters on the surface; but in effect, they beautifully complement each other in their contrasting representations of Western and Eastern influences.

B. Contributing Characters

No matter what dramatic function these characters perform in relationship to central and opposing characters, they should all have their own reasons (motivations) for being, feeling, acting, and reacting. Here are some examples of different kinds of contributing characters.

1) *Confidants:* When central or opposing characters have the need to share thoughts and feelings, they may confide in a friend or family member: Hamlet, for example, with Horatio; Willy Loman with his neighbor, Charley; Higgins with Colonel Pickering. Be careful not to use *confidants* merely for the sake of dispensing information (to your audience) that can be better conveyed through dramatic interaction. In any play, all characters should have a life of their own and not exist merely as "crutches" for the playwright to lean on. A confidant can even

be an animal; for example, *Gigi* soulfully sings "Say a Prayer" to her cuddly cat.

2) *Foils* help bring out traits of another character. A foil may be a "straight man" to a humorous character, such as the card players in *The Odd Couple* who act as comic foils to Oscar Madison and Felix Unger. On the other hand, Polonius is a doddering, foolish, and sometimes wise foil to the razor-sharp Hamlet. Ma is the foil to Lone in David Henry Hwang's *The Dance and the Railroad*.

3) *Minor* characters are usually not crucial for a play's dramatic development. Examples include the card players in *The Odd Couple;* the gravedigger in *Hamlet*. Yet minor characters, skillfully introduced and developed, can add color, human interest, and dramatic excitement. Fortinbras, for example, is a relatively minor character with only a few lines, yet he is indispensable to enlarging and elucidating Hamlet's story. The waiter is a minor character in *Death of a Salesman*, yet he is an important link to establish the reality leading to Willy's stormy scene with Biff, which, in turn, triggers Willy's revelation of the past events in Boston that crucially influence the present moment. Henry's mother, Mrs. Higgins, is a relatively minor character in *My Fair Lady*, yet she has charm galore and fulfills one important role of testing Eliza's transformation.

4) *Walk-on* characters provide local color, take part in crowds, act as messengers, or perhaps just carry spears in classical plays. They usually double as other characters. Ask yourself if such a character is really needed in your play. Be aware of just who really is needed to tell your story most dramatically and truthfully; and beware of "wasted" characters who serve no dramatic function. William Saroyan comments on the use of extraneous characters in the cast description of his one-act play *The Man With His Heart in the Highlands*. After listing the relatively small cast, he goes on to state there are eighteen neighbors. How is this mystical figure arrived at? Most likely that was a deep secret of the whimsical playwright. The neighbors "appear" only once in the play when they gather in front of the house to cheer MacGregor after he finishes his horn solo. No doubt Saroyan was poking fun at plays that feature large casts in place of large hearts. Some walk-ons, run-ons, or stand-ons create atmosphere for the audience to absorb. If their use is judicious and fits into the total artistic design, they, too, can have their day on stage. For example, the blind children of the Perkins Institute who help to establish a sympathetic attitude toward Helen in *The Miracle Worker*, or the orphans in *Annie*. Some contributing characters may never appear on stage, but their presence may nevertheless be strongly felt. For example, Old Grandaddy in *Crimes of the Heart* deeply affects the fates of the three sisters even though he is never seen.

Cast Size

In school productions, a large cast is often desirable to give more students an opportunity to play parts.

Professional productions, in which actors are paid, may require smaller casts for budgetary reasons.[4] In effect, this means that cast size may depend on the pocketbook of the people producing the show. There are shows with relatively large casts, with parts that can be doubled. For instance, in *The Devil and Daniel Webster*, the actor who plays a wedding guest also portrays one of the members of the jury. As a general guideline, the size of your cast should depend on what you are trying to say in the most artistic yet most economical way possible.

Playwright and critic Walter Kerr once made the point that some large-cast dramas are "public plays" set on a street or other public place in full view of people. For example, tenement conditions and oppressive heat force people to congregate outside in Elmer Rice's 1929 Pulitzer Prize-winning play *Street Scene* (45 characters on stage).[5] But even then, cast size for "public plays" primarily depends on artistic choices. For example, the cast size of *Joseph and the Amazing Technicolor Dreamcoat* is conditioned by the fact that the playwright has chosen to show all eleven of Joseph's brothers in action (the brothers play other roles as Egyptian characters of Pharaoh's court). Another "public play" set out-

---

[4] Not always. The Royal Shakespeare Company's production of *Nicholas Nickleby* has an ensemble of 41 gifted actors portraying over 119 roles among them. (Of course, the actors do everything from becoming the scenery, to making the wind and other sounds).

[5] Walter Kerr, "Two on the Stage — Much Too Often?" *The New York Times*. January 10, 1982.

doors, *Waiting for Godot,* requires only three actors. Thus, there are no hard and fast rules about cast size. It is always wise to recall that the Greek playwright Aeschylus skillfully told his stories with only two actors. (Some plays may require only one; see Chapter X and Appendix E.)

II. OBJECTIVES/OBSTACLES

Every character in a play, whether major or minor, has *an overall objective* that is revealed through consistently motivated and detailed dramatic actions. For example, the strong-willed Dorothy Gale's overall objective in *The Wizard of Oz* is to return to Kansas. In every scene she has a subgoal that somehow relates to her larger objective. Whether or not this goal is blocked or further realized hinges on (1) the innate character of the role (weak, strong, both), and (2) the goals and countergoals of the opposing or contributing characters (ditto). Ideally, the short-term goals add up, leaving a total impression on the emotional expectations of the audience. We, in the audience, want to connect with a character's stake through what he or she says, feels, or does, expressed in the richness of vocal and visual *details.* We are also interested in what a character may *not do* because of a limited awareness that is intended by the author.

Levels of Awareness

Imagine that you are caught in a swirling, almost dreamlike drama in which *you* are the central character. In the dream, you are in a school or community situation: you are a person of integrity and independence surrounded by a bunch of clique members. You have not been asked to join the clique. You may be truly troubled that cliques exist; or deep down, you may be upset that you have not been asked to join one. In either case, you are miserable. Your feelings are a jumbled, tangled mess. You manage to talk to some of the other people about the situation and gradually discover, to your amazement, that a lot of people in the clique are not really happy about being in one. Over a period of active searching, you discover that many of the people you thought had "superior" images of themselves

really may feel insecure on a deeper level. To a great extent, it is the fear of being alienated, rather than common interests, that curiously unites the members of the cliques.

Your level of awareness (the reason or motivations for *inner* actions) will greatly influence your behavioral choices and the consequences of those actions. *Actions produce reactions.* Let's get back to that dream. No doubt while you are searching out reasons why you have not been accepted into the cliques, the cliques are reacting to your actions and reactions. The dream can turn into a nightmare, depending on how much and in what ways you become involved and the ways the others respond.

So too in a play. A character's level of awareness concerning the rest of the characters may impinge or intrude on the intervening dramatic action. The audience has a more comprehensive awareness (like a split-screen) denied to certain characters on stage. For example, Maria in *West Side Story* is denied contact with the Jets until it is tragically too late. She is aware that the Jets and the Sharks may never reconcile their differences peacefully. But her love for Tony transcends the growing animosity between the two conflicting cultures. Her limited awareness of what *could* really be, in turn, prompts Tony to try to make peace with the Sharks or at least attempt to have a fair fight. We in the audience, too, are aware of what will result from spiraling alienation — tragic misunderstandings and death.

Hamlet is highly conscious of what he stands to win or lose in roles that he finds progressively difficult to handle. From orphaned son he becomes detective, then avenger when he becomes convincingly aware of his uncle's bloody role through the play-within-a-play, "The Mousetrap." His stage of super-awareness and concentrated action touches off a frenzied reversal of revelatory incidents implicating Rosencrantz and Guildenstern in Hamlet's aborted death.

On the other hand, Willy Loman in *Death of a Salesman* has virtually no awareness of what is really happening to him; or you could say he has too much awareness of what falsely constitutes success in America (materialism). At the end of the play, Biff breaks down and relates how much he does, in fact, love his father. But Willy's awareness is distorted. In the next scene he interprets Biff's loving actions to mean that his son also craves material success, when human understanding and communication are what Biff really wants. Willy destroys himself so that his son can use the insurance money for material gain and success in the business world. Because of his relatively limited awareness of what is happening to him, Willy's choices are short-changed, too. Inner violence is his only way out. Though the consequences of Hamlet's actions are tragic, his choices are more open because of his high level of consciousness. Tragically, awareness alone won't help him against a corrupt court.

─────────── JUST FOR YOU ───────────

To what degree are your characters aware of their feelings and actions? Do they know as much as you do about them? If you know more about them than they do, do you let them know? (In other words, don't become a mouthpiece for your characters. Let them be what they have to be.)

What key choices are available to your central characters? What choices are blocked? Think about the major consequences of each choice and alternative avenues of action.

III. SCOPE OF PLAY

A play dynamically highlights a character during a very specific segment of his or her life. What particular part of that life you choose will markedly affect how you develop your characters and the quality of details you may wish to impart to any one character.

For example, if the characters are nearing the end of their lives, as are King Lear or Willy Loman, you must find ways to compress those events leading to the play's dramatic climax. Arthur Miller does it by letting the audience see the key events of Willy's past unfold into the present. Shakespeare telescopes the end of King Lear's long life through skillful exposition and characterization. Hamlet's short life is presented through fast-moving scenes that establish an exciting rhythm. What he thinks, sees, does, and how he reacts to evolving events is compressed into a year or so of time. On the other hand, some plays lend themselves to a multiscenic development of character at different points in their lives; e.g., over a year or sometimes a whole lifetime, as in *Barnum* (twenty-five years).

Faye Dunaway in the Broadway production of William Alfred's *The Curse of an Aching Heart* spanned twenty-three years in her portrayal of Frances Anna Duffy Walsh, starting out as a thirty-three-year-old divorcee; then back-flashing to a roller-skating fourteen-year-old schoolgirl in Brooklyn; then flashing forward to her married years; then as a 1920's flapper. The form of the play, of course, is a memory play. Such a form artistically enables those backward and forward leaps covering the years 1923-42, revealing Frances as a true survivor.

Paddy Chayefsky remarked that his characters are caught "in the decline of their society," a concept that was the essence of almost everything he wrote. Whether the scope is epic or compact, a person's life in a play is coalesced into compact periods of crisis. All the characters' revelations leading to and away from the central crisis should be *truthful* during any moment they occur. The accumulation of funny, serious, absurd, or whatever moments add up to the total portrait of the character — believable actions and dialogue that always ring true.

IV. KIND OF PLAY

Playwrights forget it too easily from time to time, but the *kind* of play you write affects the kind of characters you'll have in it. Say you are working on a comedy. But what kind? There is a vast difference between the slapstick tomfoolery of Bud Abbott and Lou Costello, the farcical maneuvers of the Marx Brothers, and the elegant wit of Oscar Wilde's characters. In these three examples, various degrees of exaggerated comedic actions are all built on the bedrock of truthfully observed behavior.

In some "Theatre of the Absurd" plays, characters are stripped to their essentials. Some characters are literally unable to move, as in Beckett's *Endgame*. They are truly stuck. Yet even though they are distant and of another world, we somehow can relate to

Complex characterization is based on the wide range of human emotions. Though his deformity makes John Merrick an object of pity, his wit and understanding in *The Elephant Man* make him a character of startling beauty and compassion. He is a good example of a dynamic character that is, one who changes and grows during the course of the play.

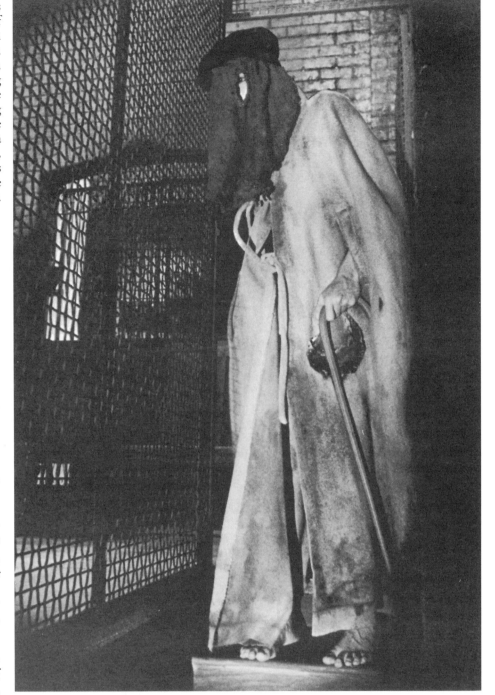

them. In this play, the central character, Hamm, is leglessly confined to a wheelchair while his parents inhabit ashcans. Underneath the grim surface, truisms about life's absurdities find expression in theatrical metaphor.

Humor in serious plays can shake up complacency or give vent to the expression of normally forbidden urges. In the Seventies there were a number of plays expressing the breakdown of society in the aftermath of a brutal war in Vietnam and a failing economy at home. Moral themes are reflected in the bittersweet comedy of Brian Clark's *Whose Life Is It Anyway?*, the poignant *The Elephant Man* by Bernard Pomerance, and Edward Albee's *The Little Old Lady from Dubuque*. The central characters are either sick, maimed, or dying. Yet, though each is basically immobile, their outlook and sense of inner freedom are tempered by a chilling wit that permeates the plays.

This point vividly came home for me when I saw a production of *Joe Egg* by the British playwright Peter Nichols. The drama concerns two par-

ents, Bri and Sheila, and their attempt to keep their marriage intact in light of the fact that their ten-year-old daughter, Josephine, is a brain-damaged "vegetable." Joe sits quivering in a chair, her body immobile — not a pleasant sight. Nichols simultaneously involves the audience and makes it squirm, too, in his imaginative use of black humor and theatrical "distancing" devices. For example, the father burlesques doctors and nurses in English music-hall style as he directly addresses the audience from time to time about his plight. In the first scene, the audience even becomes a "class," which Bri lectures. In addition to these sketches and bold black humor (which still manages to be refreshingly upbeat), there is one heartbreaking surprise for the audience that enables them to feel the pain the couple is going through. At the first-act curtain, Joe suddenly springs from her wheelchair and acts out her mother's sunny fantasy of what could have been if Joe were normal instead of . . . The audience is shocked, moved, shattered.

A fresh layer of characterization and feeling has been added to the parents' roles through a brilliant and believable stroke of theatricality. But the theatricality would be worthless without a strong foundation of truthful characterization and minute realistic details that build to the incident.

--------- JUST FOR YOU ---------
"Look-Walk-Talk"

Up to now, many of the examples in this chapter have been of characters who are immobilized to varying degrees. Limited choices, you say? Now let yourself go! Create a character, first visually. Add *one* feature at a time. Now add a *walk*. How does the character *talk*? Develop the look, walk, and talk and think about *specific* gestures the character might make under specific circumstances.

In addition to "surface" characteristics — looks, walk, talk, gestures —be mindful of the *inner* qualities of characterization, those innate and often difficult emotional traits that are so lifelike that they will spill from your gut into the very souls of your characters, animating images into real people: a chance remark, an offhand gesture, a telltale look, and so forth.

_____

You may have such a natural sense of who your characters are that they will write themselves. No need for charts, character sketches or the like; the "character" will just happen.

Plays So Lifelike, Funny and Sad

If you sense while writing that you are giving birth to a funny play, the audience may also feel underneath the humor the wellspring of pain hidden in your unconscious. Delight and despair often share the same stalk.

As an example, consider how tragedy and comedy are magically blended in Beth Henley's Pulitzer Prize-winning play *Crimes of the Heart.*

The three MaGrath sisters are going through an incredible string of tragic coincidences. The time is five years after Hurricane Camille. The place is Hazelburst, Mississippi, specifically a kitchen, pervaded by a genteel shabbiness but tidy and bright, somewhat eccentric (a couch in the kitchen is a prominent fixture). The youngest of the zany trio, Babe, is naive and desperate. She has just shot her husband. Why? "I didn't like his stinking looks!" Why did she make herself a pitcher of lemonade before calling the police? "I was just thirsty." (We find out later that her husband was a bastard.)

Meg, twenty-seven, is excitable and promiscuous, selfish and generous. She sought stardom as a singer but now admits it was all a fabrication, a bad dream, and that she's been recently released from a mental institution.

Lenny is a warm-hearted, timid fussbudget whose misfortune it is to have a shrunken ovary. Her horse has just been killed by a lightning bolt. When the play opens she is celebrating her thirtieth birthday, which everyone else has evidently forgotten. She is still forlornly looking for a man.

The three MaGrath sisters share a father who ran out on them, a mother who committed double suicide with a pet cat, and an old granddaddy family patriarch who lies in the hospital with "blood vessels popping in his brain."

Sound like a soap opera? Not the way Ms. Henley, with her sharp Southern Gothic sense of humor and incredible sense of how real people behave, has written it.

From this rich tapestry of eccentrics, the playwright spins a world an audience may enter so freely that the laughs come naturally and consistently. Ms. Henley does not tell jokes as such. The characters stick pretty much to telling the truth as they see it — with all the dreadful and honest details. Again, the details add up.

Humor Springs from Life

The "jokes" evolve from truthful experiences.

Every character is an individual, yet fits into a larger design. In *Crimes of the Heart*, the three MaGrath sisters are united by past actions and present insights, though each is unique and has her own distinctive voice.

For example, a running motif in the play is the sisters' dying grandfather, whom Lenny had been faithfully caring for until he was hospitalized. When the news that he has just had a stroke comes in, Lenny and Babe start laughing hysterically, and the audience joins right in. It is one of those times when tension is so unbearable that you must break into laughter to relieve the strain. When Meg enters, she has no awareness of what's going on, so intent is she to bring in her own problems. But soon she is an insider and shares in the laughter of her sisters.

The gradual disclosures of truthful insight about the past also help to bring the sisters together. Babe, for example, realizes that her mother hanged herself along with a cat because she was afraid of dying alone. United by such past actions and present insights, the sisters come even more and more to look and sound like a family, as when Meg finally discards her frowzy wig toward the end of the play to reveal her natural blond hair (like her sisters'). Are Ms. Henley's characters wacky? Not really, according to the playwright, "just vivid." Ms. Henley has remarked that she loves to "keep people off balance." (That the characters are all somehow "imbalanced" — like most of us — no doubt also helps.) Perhaps what happens on stage is funny because all these tragic things are happening to *other* people.

What helps is that things happen in the most believable way, with small actions building skillfully on previous actions, almost like musical refrains adding up to a rich harmony of bittersweet feeling.

It is as if the MaGrath sisters flow in and out of each other's scenes, each bringing in a limited perception of what's going on in the larger picture. The audience's awareness of what has happened in previous scenes fills in the gaps. The partial bits of character awareness are then counter-orchestrated and blended in such a way that what one character is experiencing slowly dawns upon each of the others.

For example, when Meg makes her first entrance, she begins to chat first with Babe and nervously devours tiny squirrellike bites of Lenny's birthday present, a box of candy. Later in the play, Lenny discovers the eaten-into candies and explodes at Meg. (The subtext is that Lenny is really angry at Meg because Meg has been bugging Lenny about her lack of assertiveness with an old boyfriend.) Lenny demands to know why Meg bit into every one of the candies, her birthday present. Meg offhandedly remarks that she was looking for the nuts, a statement that defuses Lenny's anger, and everyone breaks into laughter. This is thrilling characterization.

Unlike *Joe Egg*, which uses a surrealistic style to

convey strong inner feelings of the characters, *Crimes of the Heart* is a heightened form of realism, outrageously larger than life, to be sure. But like *Joe Egg* and other tragic comedies, the laughter is wrung from pain. Behind all the zany improbabilities lies a basic, universal truth about the dark secrets and little crimes of the heart: envy, neglect, quiet despair, and gentle hope that not only exist in little towns across the land but inhabit the very landscape of all our hearts.

What's Funny?

The presence of an audience connects with a play's comic intent even though the characters are unaware that they are in a comedy. For example, while rehearsing for *The Odd Couple*, Art Carney and Walter Matthau as Oscar Madison and Felix Unger were crying about their divorces. The actors thought the scene would be greeted with sympathetic silence. Yet live audiences seeing and hearing the same scene couldn't stop laughing. Yes, there was sympathy, the sympathy of recognition and empathy.

You, as the author, will develop a sixth sense of what is potentially funny and serious on stage. Sometimes a particular line or passage may not read funny but will play very funny (with the live actors, pacing, pauses, and presence of an audience). (This is why it is so important to test your plays in some kind of workshop situation.) You can talk about and dissect humor, but as E. B. White said, if you do it at great length, the thing will gradually die like a frog under dissection. Through writing, hearing, and seeing your work performed you will build up your own sense of what is incongruously funny, outrageous, or worth a smile. You will intuit (in the wise words of Arthur Schopenhauer) how "humor overthrows logical expectations," as in Innuarto's *Gemini* when Bunny Weinberger stuffs her mouth full of spaghetti and mutters, "I'll just pick a little."

V. CHARACTER LIFE-STYLE

People's life-styles are reflected by their ages, where they live and why; what they do; their choice of friends and families; their feelings, thoughts, work, leisure activities — or lack of same — and the times they live in. Aim to be as *specific* as possible when exploring the life-styles of your characters, even if you wind up using only a fraction of the data stored in your subconscious. Little things may open up larger possibilities for dramatic action and insight. Be mindful of the way small details can change character dramatically. Even with a particular age group — say, junior high school age — vast differences among individuals are commonplace. Physically, most girls finish their growth spurt by the end of junior high. Boys, on the other hand, don't grow as much as half a foot and thirty pounds during this period.

Variations in Individuals

Both boys and girls of this age group are affected by psychological characteristics associated with puberty: awkwardness, preoccupation with appearance, diet (often poor), and irregular sleeping habits (usually inadequate). Most youngsters are drained by the emotional process of growth. This is the age of intense friendships and quarrels and confusion over whether one is an adult, a child, or somewhere in between. Yet there is tremendous variation in *individuals*. Some early maturing ninth-grade girls look as if they might be the mothers of the late-maturing youngsters. These are physiological matters. When one considers a youngster's social setting, family upbringing, and background, his or her life-style becomes even more evident. The same with any age. Such plays as Coburn's *The Gin Game* and Thompson's *On Golden Pond* explode stereotyped notions of old age when they focus on the individualized personalities of older adults.

Isolated Facts

With so much to know about so many characteristics, a single fact or factor may often help you bring a character into sharper focus.

Social Fact: Anne Frank, age thirteen, a Jew. *Circumstances:* July 6, 1942, enters an attic to hide, with her family, from Germans in World War II. Best friends often replace parents as confidants during the teen years. Usually, an adolescent's peer group is the primary source for general rules of behavior.

Inner Feelings: But Anne is living exclusively with adults, except for Peter. Two years later she blossoms into a young woman, expresses the pangs of adolescence, first love, sexual awakening. Soon there are stirrings of deeper love.

Social Fact: Maria, born in Puerto Rico, emigrates to America as a teenager. She wants to "break out" and explore womanhood.
Circumstances: In America falls in love with Tony, who is from a different culture.
Inner Feelings: Grows stronger about feelings toward Tony, but outward social violence complicates her single-minded vision of love and peace.
Social Facts: Annie, age nine, *orphan . . .* wants to find parents. Helen Keller, age six and a half . . . *unable to see, talk, hear* ; social prejudice; spoiled . . . resists learning. Two characters, both very young, but affected by different facts, personal, and social conditions.

—————— JUST FOR YOU ——————

List some of the characters in your play and the special facts and factors that affect their lives. What are some of the feelings associated with those factors? Jot them down.

B. Animal Image

Sometimes you will be able to envision your character as an animal that captures the essence of the personality: for example, in Anton Chekhov's *Marriage Proposal,* a one-act comedy about mistaken intentions:

Father: boorish bear, protects his darling cub
Suitor: wounded puppy, constantly licking his wounds
Girl: henpecking away for "principles"

In *Crimes of the Heart:*
Lenny: ostrich (at beginning)
Meg: squirrel (when first enters)
Babe: scared rabbit (last scenes)

In *Amadeus:*

Salieri: wounded lion, licking scars
Mozart: strutting peacock

In production, some animal images actually materialize: Rooster moves like one in *Annie;* Tybalt, like a cat in *Romeo and Juliet.*

A single fact or factor may often bring a character into sharper focus. as in this scene from *West Side Story* when social prejudice comes in the way of love.

C. Adjective/Adverb

Think of a few adjectives to describe your characters. These adjectives may change, of course, but the exercise will help you focus some of your feelings about "your creations."

Henry Higgins: conceited, brilliant, rash, talkative, sensitive, arrogant

Eliza Doolittle: sassy, bright, boldly assertive, resourceful, remorseful

Hamlet: thoughtful, rash, crafty, sensitive, loving, hateful, childish, rational

Claudius: crafty, thoughtful, rash, loving, hateful, sensitive (prayer scene)

The MaGrath sisters in *Crimes of the Heart*:

Lenny: timid, hysterical. compulsive, assertive

Meg: promiscuous. selfish, caring, generous, untruthful, truth-seeking

Babe: naive, thick-headed, desperate, exasperating, lovable

Emotions suggested by these adjectives occur at different times in the play, of course; that's why it's a good idea to describe the character only briefly when he or she is first introduced. The character will be undergoing changes (subtle as they are) through most of the play: additional character, stage, and vocal directions can be added when they occur in the play.

D. Colors

Remember, always, that the other characters will perceive a character differently than would you or I. A useful technique is to color the dominant emotion of a scene *as the character would see it*.
For example: In *Death of a Salesman*, from the point of Willy, *Act I*:

French Scene 1: Blue (melancholy) with tinges of red (hope)

French Scene 2: Rosy (scene in past, Willy and boys Simonizing the car)

French Scene 3: Gray (scene in past, Willy with woman buyer in Boston)

The colors chosen in your scenes should have personal meaning for yourself, as well as to the characters.

E. Names

Names often impart a sense or essence of who the character is or what he or she represents.

Willy Loman (Willy Low-man)
Biff (American pizazz)
Doolittle (just that)
Felix (easy)
Oscar (harder sound)
Higgins (he can)
Eliza (life)

————————— JUST FOR YOU —————————

Review the names of your characters. Has each name jelled for you, or do you feel the names can still be changed? How? Sit down with your characters for a chat. Get to know them better — ask them if you can ask them some questions, at least ten:

Name of the character
1) Who are you?

_____

2) What do you think you want most? (in play)

_____

3) Why do you want what you want?

_____

4) Under what circumstances do you want what you want? (plot)

_____

5) When? (specifically)

_____

6) Where? (specifically)

_____

7) Describe your most immediate environment(s).

_____

8) Who gets in the way of achieving your objectives in each scene? (perhaps you don't know) Why do you say this?

_____

CHARACTER CHECKLIST CARD (longer form)

Character:

Nickname: _ Height: _ _ _ _ _ _ _ _ _ _ _ _ _

Age: _ Weight: _ _ _ _ _ _ _ _ _ _ _ _ _

Where character lives currently (be as specific as possible): _ _ _ _ _ _ _ _ _ _ _ _ _ _ _ _ _ _

Where character used to live (again, be specific): _

Members of the family (whether seen in play or not), and how character feels about relatives: _ _ _

_ _

Whom character likes (in play): _

Whom character dislikes: _

Whom character loves (when and why?): _

Whom character hates (when and why?): _

Whom character has mixed feelings about (why?): _

Who gets in the character's way? (why?): _

Who helps character? (why?): _

What does character look like? (include "public" and "private" look; clothes, costume, adornments,

height, weight): _

Does character have an animal image? (what?): _

Physical traits?: _

Mental traits?: _

Life-style: Note character's school, background, current job, feelings toward society, beliefs, hobbies, interests, how sleeps, what likes to eat, pet expressions. Write a bio or character capsule.

Dramatic function: What character's role is in the play (central character, opposing character, contributing character; what kind?)

Remember that getting to know your characters is often like meeting friends (and also enemies) and getting to know them. Ask your characters the same questions you would ask a friend.

9) How do you feel about the obstacles in your way?

_____

10) What do you have to do to get what you want? List at least five specific things:

_____

Duplicate this list for your other characters.

_____

———————— JUST FOR YOU ————————

How do other characters perceive your central character and opposing characters? Take any of the above characters and change "I" to "you." Is your character strong, weak, or what? When specifically? Why? How is strength/weakness revealed, concealed, or set aside? For how long? What happens next?

IN SUM

Characterization is the fleshing out of a social role. Personality traits and idiosyncrasies help give a special in-depth flavor to characterization.

Some playwrights like to know as much as possible about the "offstage" life of their characters before writing, whereas most discover who their characters are through the actual writing process. Some of the ways playwrights conceive their characters are through modeling real people; through basing characters on composites of people; or through completely concocting a character from imagination. Creation of characters usually combines all these processes.

Some techniques for deepening characterization include thinking about and investigating

Good, bad or a combination, the motivations of a central characters (as Macbeth) must be clear to an audience, even if they are not clear to the character. Who is really your central character? What does he or she want? Who gets in the way?

the hardest time writing? Why do you think this is so?

3) "The best plot is a human being." Reevaluate: Do you think this is so? Why or why not?

4) What do you think is the correlation between plot and character?

5) Do you think your characters are as believable as possible (even if they happen to be fantasy characters)?

MORE **RAW** MATERIALS

Read . . . and reread any of the plays you've read so far. As you do so, focus on how real the characters are, what makes you believe in the characters? Listen to your play being read *aloud*. Then ask yourself (and the actors) if the characters still feel consistent and real.

your characters according to their (1) dramatic purpose; (2) objectives and obstacles; (3) scope of play; (4) kind of play; and (5) lifestyles.

Useful aids to investigate your characters' lifestyle include asking how they look, talk, walk; examining their social factors and inner feelings; and thinking in terms of adjectives, colors, animal images, and musical contrasts.

Act . . . Play "Keep in Character." With a partner carry on a two-way conversation while wearing "character glasses" made from colored construction paper. These glasses should evoke different mood — sad, happy, pessimistic. As a variation, the dominant mood can be taken from the color or design of the shirt you or your partner is wearing. *Stay in character* suggested by the mood as you enact a scene of conflict.

PLAYWRIGHT'S PAGE

1) Which characters in your play are you having the easiest time writing? Why do you think this is so?

2) Which characters in your play are you having

Write . . . a brief character sketch for each of the characters in your play, clarifying their dominant traits. Make sure you see the world, fears, prejudices, hopes, memories, and opinions through the eyes of the character.

——— SUGGESTIONS FOR CLASSROOM ACTIVITIES ———

Choose from these exercises designed to help bring your characters to life.

Discuss . . . in small groups, traits of the characters in your plays that you think bring them (and the play) alive. (For example, smoking, cheating, biting fingernails, brushing hair, singing on the street.) Share how *specific* circumstances in the play bring out these characteristics and how they affect the circumstances of the play.

Read . . . aloud some of the character bios and monologues written in class. What do you like about them? In a positive manner, explain how you reacted and why.

Write . . . a "name story" * about how some of the characters in your play got their names. These can include nicknames and personal names that reflect inner hidden qualities and ancestral/cultural/family backgrounds. Was the name chosen for the character or was it self-created (by whom and how)? What is special about the name? Perhaps it's a name that only a celebrity might have. It might be a disguised name or a shortened one.

*Thanks to Alistair Martin-Smith and Maya Ishiura for the suggestion, which is based on their work in native mythology of Canadian aboriginal peoples, the names being revealed through dreams and special events.

In A *Raisin in the Sun*, Walter Younger pursues his dream to be somebody, even if it means jeopardizing his sister's education by giving her share of the insurance money to a con man. Opposing Walter is his mother who wants him to succeed with integrity and pride, to be "the head of the family . . . like you supposed to be." Hers is an adversary-advocate role.

Act . . . Play "Character Tag" to discover the feeling of becoming a variety of characters and speaking *naturally* as they might.
1. Players stand in a circle. Two are asked to go into the center of the circle and quickly become any contrasting characters (e.g. a mother and daughter) and enact a very short scene with a conflict.
2. After 30 seconds or so, a player on the outer circle taps one of the actors on the shoulder and picks up his or her last line of dialogue and repeats it, only this time as a totally different character in an entire-

ly different set of circumstances (e.g. if the mother's last line in the previous scene was "The wash needs to be carried up," the player might quickly make the new character an art critic who says, "The wash needs to be carried up — more towards the top of your painting." The other player, then becoming the artist, might say: "No, no that wash would weaken the colors of my painting!" and the scene would continue.

3. After another 20 seconds or so, a new player taps the other actor and repeats his or her line as a new character in totally different circumstances, and actions.

ONGOING CLASS PROJECT

Work on your group play. Is every character in the play needed? Does each one fufill some dramatic need? How many unneeded characters can be cut? Why do you think a character should be cut? Is there contrast between characters? What are you trying to say about some aspect of the human condition in your play? Is it being said *dramatically* through the distinct voices and specific intentions, actions, and feelings of the characters?

Minor characters must also be given distinct character traits as the mechanicals all have in *A Midsummer Night's Dream*, two of whom are seen here performing their play-within-a-play at the end of the play. Do your characters have specific, individual character traits that help to delineate who they are?

NOTEBOOK (JOURNAL) FEATURE

Look over your own play carefully. Read it aloud by yourself or with someone else. Jot down some feedback (See Appendix B, Giving and Receiving Feedback, pages 174-176) and ideas you get concerning your characters. For example, review what each ones' overall objectives is. What is it in each scene (scene objective)? What feelings are your characters experiencing at *specific* times? WHY do they do what they do (intentions)? What do they want — or think they want in different scenes? Why? How can characters be made (or do they need to be made) more real — even if they are fantasy characters? Author Toni Morrison has said what most writers learn through the experience, "… a good writer revises so much and seldom finds the first try satisfactory." Ask yourself: What aspects of the characters do I still need to work on? Make notes. You can always select which of the notes you have to work on — now or later.

chapter VIII

THE ART OF SOUNDS AND SILENCES

Upon my knees, what does your speech import?
I understand a fury in your words,
But not the words.   — *Othello*

Suit the action to the word, the word to the action.
                                        — *Hamlet*

Chances are that of all the parts of a play—character, plot, music, visual elements, theme, and dialogue — the least troublesome so far has been dialogue.

It is likely, in fact, that your apparent ease with dialogue prompted you to write a play in the first place. Why, then, do playwrights still have difficulty writing really good dialogue? We further ask:

- What are some of the differences between "real-life" and stage dialogue?
- What are some helpful hints for writing effective dialogue?
- How do the uses of silence complement speech?
- What are some of the things we should know about visual elements?

"REAL" VS. IMAGINARY DIALOGUE

The dialogue of John Millington Synge, author of the one-act *Riders to the Sea*, was considered so "real" and "true to life" that he was actually accused of hiding in inns so that he could put his ear to the attic floor and eavesdrop on the people below. Then all he had to do was put down exactly what he heard and his play practically wrote itself! How else could he so realistically capture the speech patterns, rhythms, and flavor of his Irish compatriots? In this country, Paddy Chayefsky wrote so naturally that he too was sometimes accused of writing dialogue by tape-recording people's speech and transcribing it on paper. The same has been said of August Wilson.

The reality is that for most professional playwrights writing dialogue is an art — that is, highly selective. Dialogue on stage is no less "real" than painted flats of scenery that may seem real even though we know they're not. In fact, dialogue that pours from the mouths of people without some kind of "lifelike" artistic editing and rearrangement suffers from the theatre's most deadly sin — boredom.

The art of playwriting is an extremely concentrated enterprise. An actor playing a boring character still manages to infuse his or her body with the required energy and imagination to make the character come alive. So, too, with dialogue. Even the language of a dull character must somehow show liveliness (in its artistic choices and arrangement of sounds). Listen to Hamlet describe boredom — but without a boring line:

How weary, stale, flat, and unprofitable seem to
me all the uses of this world.

In Picasso's phrase, art is a "lie like truth." To reach a deeper level of reality, we often have to distort life (like perspective in drawing) to make it seem more real. No matter how spontaneous your writing, a careful process of selection continually takes place. Utterances, words, phrases, pauses, and sentences must match what the character would say (or not say) at a precise moment in the play and also fit esthetically into the entire pattern of the work. Quite a mouthful! Here are some helpful "do's and don'ts" for writing (and rewriting) effective dialogue.

A HANDFUL OF DIALOGUE HINTS

1) *Keep It Natural*

A surprisingly large number of beginning playwrights (advanced ones, too) think that because they are actually writing something — that is, committing an idea to paper — they have to wax literary and always have their characters speak complete, straightforward, and all too logical sentences. (We're not talking here about Henry Higgins and other truly literate characters.) So-called literary dialogue sounds as stilted as an old-fashioned butler announcing "Tea is served, madame." A small sampling:

Guy: Hello. What are you doing here?
Gal: I don't know. What do you think?
Guy: I do not know, but it is something about which I intend to find out.

Do you know people who really talk like that? The characters may have something like that in mind. From their mouths, however, the following dialogue is more likely:

Guy: Hi, there. What're you doing?
Gal: There? What do you mean there? How should I know? (Lost in her thoughts.) Hmmm?
Guy: I said, what do — oh, c'mon, you know what I said . . .
Gal: (Still in a daze.)
Guy: Well, what d'you think —?
Gal: About what?

Have you ever wondered why it takes so long for people to say good-bye on the phone? David Mamet, author of *American Buffalo* and a playwright who writes beautifully natural dialogue, asked himself the same question. His answer was that two people on the phone really *can't* say good-bye. The dialogue goes on and on and on (and on). Stage dialogue, of course, cannot go on and on

unless it befits a character to do so. An example is the pompous, garrulous mayor in Gogol's *The Inspector General.* You can think of others. In the theatre a "rounding off" of life occurs, making dialogue appear real but not so real that it is dull. The net effect of good dialogue is that it conveys the essence of whatever you want your character to convey in both a truthful and a theatrical manner.

Dialogue, Both Truthful and Theatrical

Being an actor helped Kevin Wade to develop his "ear" as a playwright. When Wade was writing *Key Exchange*, he was able to say lines out loud and make sure they sounded "human." For him, dialogue had to be natural, but he also knew that natural dialogue was not necessarily theatrical. Thus, he had to create the illusion of natural speech rhythms to conform to the energy and pacing within and between characters.

Anton Chekhov was a master of raising common vernacular speech to a delicate poetry of the theatre. So is August Wilson today. Notice that in the writings of these and other "natural" playwrights a common technique is the inversion of words. Thus, instead of "do you know that?" it's more natural to write, "you know that, don't you?"

A question answered by a question is another familiar form of repartee in life, as well as on the stage. An excellent example of how silence and speech complement each other through questions and answers is found in *Crimes of the Heart.* There is a simultaneously sad and funny exchange between Babe (who had earlier shot her husband) and her newly acquired attorney.

As Babe describes it, immediately after she shot her husband she fixed a pitcher of lemonade and shouted out if her wounded husband wanted some.

The perplexed attorney asks Babe how her husband answered. (In an earlier scene we have seen Babe, with great gusto, make a pitcher of lemonade for her sister and herself, so we know the great fondness she has for a cold glass of lemonade.)

Now the lawyer wants to know if Babe called the police after shooting her husband. No, Babe replies. Why, the attorney wants to know. I made a pitcher of lemonade, Babe replies. Why, the lawyer asks again. I was dying of thirst, she answers. These

Whether your dialogue is street slang or the literate language of Henry Higgins in *My Fair Lady*, keep it real.

responses are funny because the audience has a strong, specific, visual picture of the previous lemonade-making to match the present verbal exchange.

You will also notice from reading and seeing (and writing!) plays that natural dialogue frequently takes the form of rhetorical repetition: Again, from *Crimes of the Heart*. (one sister trying to help another):

MEG: Calm down —
you wanna coke, you
wanna coke. Let me
get you a coke.

When playwright Clifford Odets listened to people's speech around him, he observed that there was something wonderfully heightened and poetic about the way the "ordinary" person spoke. David Mamet has correctly observed that the way people speak is interconnected with the way they act. In its own way, then, dynamic dialogue is dramatic action. One of the best ways to get in tune with natural dialogue is to listen carefully to the way people from all walks of life speak (eavesdrop in restaurants, movie lines, bus stops, etc.) and not through words alone.

It's especially important to observe body language in its myriad shapes and essences. Think about the marvelously varied ways people talk nonverbally and try to communicate with each other, avoid contact, or even cover up or contradict the words spoken. A nervous person may talk in a steady stream, stammer, or clam up altogether. But when that person clams up, notice how loudly the body speaks, with perhaps hand-wringing or fidgeting fingers or a subtle cough accompanying those empty silent gulfs.

———————— JUST FOR YOU ————————

Let's get physical . . .
Spend several hours observing people's body language in different situations. Do they touch each other? How? When? What are the relationships?

Can you tell without their words? How? Make mental notes or written notes on what you observe. How does this exercise especially apply to your play?

---

2) *Dialogue Grows Out of Character*

The eminent psychologist Otto Rank observed that "speech creates the soul." Speech also soulfully reflects the *inner* life of a character. In life, have you noticed the little pet phrases your family and friends use repeatedly in their speech, familiar pauses or unique rhythms of talking? By the same token, can you think of ways to flavor your characters with *real* speech?

Another important practical question you can ask is, "Would my character really say this under these particular circumstances?" You will often be tempted to have the character convey something "profound," perhaps something *you* really want to say. Avoid the temptation. Playwrights who permit characters to become mouthpieces for their ideologies are better suited to write tracts or newspaper editorials. (Joseph Conrad aptly said trust the tale, not the storyteller.) Even among the most accomplished playwrights, there is a tendency from time to time to moralize or interject extraneous philosophy.

Some playwrights have good-natured fun creating characters. who may speak for their point of view. Sean O'Casey gently pokes fun at Jack Clitheroe and by extension at himself in *The Plough and the Stars*; as does Chekhov with the sensitive Trofimov in *The Cherry Orchard*; and Lorraine Hansberry with Benetha (her younger self) in *A Raisin in the Sun*. When characters do become raisonneurs (or rational voices for the playwright), like the poet in Miguel Pinero's *Short Eyes* and Tom in *The Glass Menagerie*, the dialogue must still grow out of character actions and feelings.

Sometimes you will be tempted to get in a clever (or even honest) line of dialogue even though you know the line is premature: the character would simply not say the line at this time. I'm guilty of this, and so are many playwrights I know. Such extraneous claptrap should be eliminated like so many weeds in a garden. Usually, this kind of editorial pruning occurs during a second or even later draft. When you have more objective distance .and

are more willing to surrender your precious "gems of wisdom," you can cut those words and actions a character simply would not say, do, or feel.

In sum, it's important to remember that if you want your point of view to be known, let it emerge from the dramatic interaction. Keep your dialogue personal, particular, and above all, honest and natural.

Stage Idiom

The question often arises how speech of historical characters should be handled. Shakespeare has Romans in *Julius Caesar* speak excellent English, and so do the Danes in *Hamlet*. If you want to give a hint of period or local color, most professional playwrights agree that a balance between modern speech and the idiom of the period is the desired aim. You can get a feel for the period through the rhythm of words and pauses. Historical plays (Maxwell Anderson's *Valley Forge* is an excellent example) retain certain phrases, words, and rhythms of earlier times. We can never know exactly how people from the past conversed, but the important point is that the dialogue should sound plausible enough, have the ring of truth, so that a member of the audience doesn't jump up and cry, "People would not say that then!" Most playwrights line up strongly against the use of "campy" anachronistic slang, which may be fun for today's audiences but is totally out of phase with the historical period written about. Yet one never knows. Theatre is magic and the magical takes place all the time. Anything can and does happen. Thus, within the Biblical setting *of Joseph and the Amazing Technicolor Dreamcoat*, Pharaoh breaks into a zippy Elvis Presley character jazzing up the lyrics and singing up a storm. In Charles Ludlum's Ridiculous Theatre Company's zany production of *Camille*, the title figure was played by a man in high camp gear who spoke fractured dialogue to match.

Song Lyrics

The idea for a song can start with a character trait (Tevye, the weary milkman in *Fiddler on the Roof*, talks with God: "If I Were a Rich Man"); with an emotion (Jewish people have to leave "Anatevka"); a character twist, or dramatic development

The lyrics of a song in a musical, like good dialogue. spring from inner character and specific circumstances. Young Harry Houdini's solo, "I'm Gonna Fly" in the author's musical *The King of Escapes* flows from his father's disapproval of Harry's aspirations.

in the story.

Although the convention of character bursting into song is larger than life, most song lyrics are squarely rooted in life and grow from character. Therefore, the lyrics should sound like dialogue the character would say under the *particular* circumstance when the welling up of emotion is so strong that the character — like a dam bursting — must break into song.

In the collaborative process, lyricist and composer teams vary markedly. For example, Richard Rodgers gave Lorenz Hart the tunes first. With his second collaborator, Oscar Hammerstein, Rodgers often worked from already supplied lyrics. For *Fiddler on the Roof*, the music by Jerry Bock was written first, and Sheldon Harnick set the lyrics to the music he felt most strongly about. Then gradually Harnick began writing the lyrics first, which Bock set to music. Once the concept and character of the show came to be known intimately, the idea behind the lyrics — the idea — became the propelling force. [1] As Arthur Laurents, who wrote the book for *West Side Story*, advises, think of universal characters or themes. Make sure there is an emotional underpinning. Outline where you think the songs should go.

[1] Richard Altman (with Mervyn Kaufman), *The Making of a Musical* (New York: Crown, 1971), p. 24.

Here is how the lyrics of one of my musicals came to be written. *The King of Escapes*, a musical play about the life of young Harry Houdini, called for a song to convey the troubled inner feelings of the main character in Act I, Scene 5. Composer and lyricist Jaimey Steele explains how she wrote the lyrics for "I'm Gonna Fly."

I set to work in the following manner. I read the script carefully, paying close attention to the circumstances that lead up to the song. From the script I discerned that Harry was feeling insecure and unsure of himself, that he was having second thoughts about pursuing his dream of becoming a magician, and that these feelings had been brought about by his father's lack of approval and understanding. Yet it was clear that the way he was feeling was temporary and that the character possessed great confidence and strength.

Once the material has been gathered, a metamorphosis must take place. *The composer must become the character.* He or she must put himself into the character's shoes, see what he sees, feel what he feels and think what he thinks. Thus transformed, I decided to combine what Harry (I) was thinking and feeling with his (my) physical location.

In this case, it was the rooftop of a New York City tenement building. [The play takes place during the early 1900's.] It took only a little imagination to see "the sky above the street below" and to have Harry say "here I stand all alone." With a touch more imagination, I could visualize pigeons "soaring wide over the rooftops so high." From there, it seemed natural to tie Harry's dreams and aspirations to the image of the birds in flight. Hence, "I'm Gonna Fly."

I tried not to say too many things. I tried to keep the lyrics clear and simple. I used the technique of stating Harry's concerns in each verse and then resolving those concerns in each chorus. Musically, through the melody and the tempo, I worked to reinforce the feelings I had tried to convey in my lyrics.

Notice, I chose short intervals between notes and a flat rhyme for each verse with no emphasis on any particular note. For the chorus, on the other hand, I changed to larger intervals and to a more uplifting, driving rhythm, with strong emphasis on some notes to achieve an expansive feeling of flight.

The lyrics:

PAPA: Well, these people won't be there to applaud you. Good luck, anyway. (He leaves.)
MAMA: It's not your fault, Eric. It's this house, this city, so many people living under one rooftop . . . how's it possible — you look and so much clear sky, it's a wonder... (She exits.)
(He is alone.)

HARRY:
(Sings.)
    The sky above
    The streets below
    Here I stand
    All alone
    Those I love
    Don't understand
    Have no faith
    In my dreams
    And plans.

    But I'm gonna fly
    Like the pigeons circling wide
    O'er the rooftops so high
    I'm gonna fly, I'm gonna fly.

    Now I'm wondering
    Deep inside
    If perhaps I shouldn't try
    If I'm aiming way too high
    Out of misplaced foolish pride.

    But I'm gonna fly
    Like the pigeons circling wide
    O'er the rooftops so high
    I'm gonna fly
    I'm gonna fly (x 2)

(Blackout, as he exits.)

Subtext

People don't always say what they mean. They often speak underneath and between the lines. For example, "Don't worry about me, dear!" may be a subtle signal that admits a failure before it actually happens. Many nonverbal cues — gestures, posture, use of spatial environment — are unconscious behavior. These nonverbal cues can fill in missed connections in dialogue such as a misunderstanding arising from a lack of personal awareness or from cultural differences.

Show me a person who communicates by words alone, and I will show you a rather dull being. Unless the person is somehow frozen, spoken language is normally complemented by some kind of periodic gesture, facial expression, body movement, varied postures, eye contact (or lack of eye contact), and pertinent spatial positions in relationship to other characters. The hands especially are telling indicators of feeling. Recall Walter Younger's fingers tapping on the table from sheer boredom (and suppressed rage) in *A Raisin in the Sun*, lashing out at his bad luck with outstretched fists, or saying hello to Agasi with a "manly" bone-crushing handshake, or gently stroking his wife's hair in loving affection.

Just as words can speak and bespeak confidence, frustration, rejection, love, so can subtle characteristics be revealed through a minute scratch of an ear, systematic rubbing of eyeglasses, or touching one's hair haphazardly. In fact, it was Sir Cedric Hardwicke who observed that he could tell how good actors were by the things they could say without speaking.

But be careful of stereotyping. Those tapping fingers could be an energizing motion instead of saying "boredom." The sense of gesturing must be interpreted in light of the total social setting and the particular circumstances at hand.

When they are important to delineate character or advance the story, include gestures and other physicalization as stage directions.

You may indicate in stage directions important "business" that advances the plot, establishes a mood, or delineates a character's action or motivation.

For example, during the opening moments of *Crimes of the Heart*, Cousin Chick — who is prone to gossip — fusses with fixing her pantyhose while telling Lenny the latest news about Meg. The very funny panty business breaks up the monologue, reveals Chick's snoopy character, and advances the plot.

The play itself starts with a marvelous bit of nonverbal business. Lenny lights a solitary birthday candle on a cookie, an action that vividly suggests how alone she is feeling. At the end of the play, the three sisters gather around the table and share with Lenny a cake topped with lots of candles and practically the size of the table. This action visually and touchingly reestablishes the sisters back together again.

——————— WHAT IF ———————

the characters in your play were incapable of speaking? Think about the most significant gestures or physical movements peculiar to each of them. When you think such a brief description is important to help establish and deepen characterization, feel free to include it as a stage direction.

For example, from *The Browning Version*:

MILLIE: I had a letter from your father today in which he says he once had the pleasure of meeting your mother.

TAPLOW: (Uninterested but polite.) Oh, really.

Very often, an action described in a stage direction will ironically and humorously contradict the verbal message. From *West Side Story*:

SCHRANK: All right: kill each other . . . But not on my beat.

RIFF: (Such innocence.) Why if it isn't Lieutenant Schrank.

Vocal Directions

Turn back to the Introduction. This is the way the first two lines read now:

MEP: Hi. (Seeing YOU holding this book.) Have you read it yet?

YOU: No, I haven't . . . (Looks through the book.)

But what if you respond as follows:

YOU: (Annoyed.) No, I haven't . . . (Looks through book.)

or

YOU: (Excitedly.) No, I haven't . . . (Looks through book.)

Obviously, vocal directions can change the immediate intent of a character's speech and the mood of the play. If the line is said excitedly, the action of looking through the book will match the words (or contradict it for comic effect). Directors and actors (as well as readers) essentially get an idea of vocal inflection and emotional coloring through the sense of the scene. However, if a direction is vitally important to delineate character, move the plot, or establish a mood, indicate it as such in a stage or speech direction.

3) *Dialogue Has Its Own Character*

In addition to springing from character, good dialogue usually has the stamp of its own character, capturing the unique flavor of the speaking character. Good dialogue inherently has *universal* appeal, which can be *felt* by almost any individual in the audience. This means that even though the dialogue has its own distinctiveness and nuances in a dramatic context, it can also be *emotionally understood* by people from a variety of backgrounds and cultures.

The resonantly dense dramatic poetry in Samuel Beckett's *Waiting for Godot* expresses a bleakly desperate world where characters face a vast void: the play is performed all over the world from Alaska to Japan in places as diverse as universities and prisons, testifying to its timely universality. The dialogue is unmistakably Beckett.

When Gaston sings the title song of *Gigi*, and Higgins sings "I've Grown Accustomed to Her Face," the unmistakable stamp of Lerner and Loewe's speaking-singing patter permeates the songs.

David Mamet's dialogue has been referred to as a "symphony of slang" because of the way he adroitly captures the flavor of inverted syntax, including words that don't belong filling in for adjectives that should belong, the mixture of the profane and the profound, missing words, elliptical and unfinished phrases. For example, from, *American Buffalo*, the Al Pacino character comments on the futility of life: "Some guys are gonna flip a coin always called heads. You ever notice this?" Pure Mamet!

Harold Pinter is well known for the pauses and silences that permeate his dialogue. Pinter's distinctive style of writing dialogue and indicating pauses is carefully thought out. The playwright is careful to point out that what appear as pauses in print are really what happens in the mind and gut of the characters.

In certain plays (Pinter comes to mind again) in which overt action does not play a major role, it is especially important that dialogue be emotionally stimulating. The uniquely characteristic dialogue found in the simultaneously realistic and lyrical language of August Wilson; the use of musical overlapping voices in Michael Christopher's *The Shadow Box* and in Albert Immaturo's *Gemini*; the uncanny way characters speak past each other in Chekhov; the witty repartee of Shaw and Pinter, all are stylistic trademarks, culminations of dramatic instinct and the cultivated, well tuned, and trained ear of the experienced playwright. Are you reflecting your own style, your own sense of being?

4) *Dialogue Should Be Easily Spoken*

Good dialogue springs from inside the character, but technical considerations — especially clarity — are important too. Actors, after all, do not relish (to paraphrase the Bard) speaking muddled speech "trippingly on their tongues." The vexing problem of "line stumblers" can be handled during rewriting. A director may also point out specific line changes or suggest cutting or fixing a particular line that is technically out of place. But in the meantime, give your cast (not to mention your audience) a break and write sayable, playable dialogue. Here is an example of how one such "line stumbler" cropped up and how my partner, Joe Lesser, and I handled it (John is speaking):

Sarah, can you send your brother, Stevie, to the stones [quarry] sometime tonight?

The old "Peter Piper" syndrome, you ask? Possibly, but examples like that are not uncommon. Here's how the dialogue was rewritten:

JOHN: Sarah, I'm running over to the quarry.

SARAH: Steven — did you forget?

JOHN: Your brother? (She nods "yes.") He can go to the "stones" too. Tonight.

In sum, ask yourself such questions as:

- Do all my characters sound alike? Are they supposed to?
- If I am writing a comedy, why are there long, arid, humorless patches?
- If this is supposed to be dramatic, why is there a curious lack of tension and give-and-take in the dialogue? Why are there dull passages and pauses?

5) *Dialogue Is Economical*

What if you had to pay a dollar for every unnecessary word appearing in the first drafts of your play? You would think hard about putting some of the words there in the first place. In the memorable words of Queen Gertrude, the prescription often calls for "more matter, with less art."

LISTEN TO YOUR VOICE AS IT DEVELOPS

But here's the catch: By and large, playwrights intentionally overwrite in their early scribblings, preferring to rewrite, edit, and polish during successive drafts. Remember the ACES BASIS (Chapter III, page 51)? They apply to writing dialogue, too:

Amplify
— How can I get all the dialogue out whether it makes sense or not? If you keep on writing you will *have* to come up with something good. You might write nine bad drafts, but the tenth will be dynamite, so patience to keep reworking is important. And do *not* censor yourself when trying to get ideas out — just *do it.* Then you can think about it later.

Clarify
— How can I make clear to myself what the character is trying to say?

Edify
— How can I make clear to the audience what the character is trying to say?

Simplify
— How can I keep the dialogue theatrical and true?

Samuel Beckett has spent weeks polishing a single phrase. David Mamet has evolved whole plays starting with small conversations between offbeat characters. When it comes to polishing dialogue, remember that if speech really can be thought of as action, you will most likely develop a fine sensitivity to how rewriting a line can dig deeper into characterization. On the other hand, a line might be so perfect the first time out that "Striving to better, oft we mar what's well" (*King Lear*, I, 4).

SILENCE ON STAGE

An awareness of the various ways silent action can be effective on the stage helps you treat your own material more imaginatively and truthfully. According to scenic designer Lee Simonson, " . . . stagecraft at best is nothing more than the tail to the poet's kite . . . Playwriting is not based on architecture . . . . [2] While this may or not be true, many playwrights throughout theatre history have been involved onstage and backstage in some way or other. Ibsen, Shaw, Pirandello, Brecht, and Pinter all have written plays with particular kinds of theatre styles in mind. You too should be familiar with a variety of theatre styles. The best way to do so is to read plays, go to plays, and, if possible, act in plays.

STAGE GEOGRAPHY

The general stage areas of a proscenium type theatre can be depicted as follows:

(from point of view of actor facing audience)

U, upstage

R, right   C, center   L, left

D, downstage

[2] Lee Simonson, *The Stage Is Set* (New York: Theatre Arts Books, 1963), p. 39.

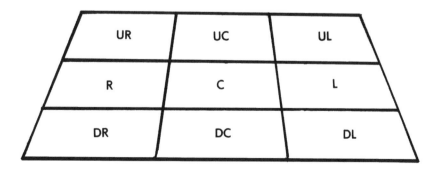

Relative areas of strength on stage:

5	2	6
3	1	4

You should be familiar with other types of staging as well:

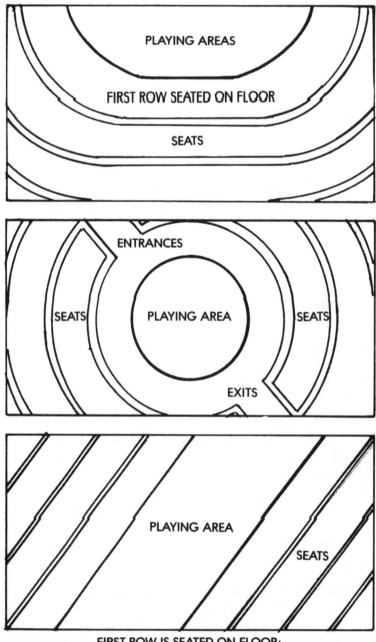

FIRST ROW IS SEATED ON FLOOR:
STAGGERED ROWS OF SEATS CAN BE PLACED BEHIND

"Stage as Platform": This expressionistic setting for *Death of a Salesman* enables the characters to move in and out of the past just as the images occur on the landscape of Willy Loman's tortured mind.

Importance of Stage Geography

An understanding of stage geography is important because characters often find themselves gravitating to specific areas on stage that have strong psychological associations. For example, in *Crimes of the Heart*, the three sisters lovingly huddle with each other on the seedy kitchen couch downstage left; in contrast, Babe pathetically tries to commit suicide in the gas stove located horizontally directly opposite (psychologically, too) from the cozy feeling associated with the couch. These are just two examples of the kinds of space — intimate and social — and how they complement spoken action. The use of space offers nonverbal cues and clues about the characters' behavior and attitudes. In Lillian Hellman's *The Little Foxes*, Birdie has her little alcove area where she plays the piano, retreats from life's harshness, and licks her wounds.

In *American Buffalo*, the cluttered table in an even more cluttered pawnshop almost center stage becomes an important fixture where the men plot (ineptly) the theft of a rare coin.

STYLES OF SETTINGS

There are two broad styles or conventions of settings for the theatre: 1) theatre as "picture," and 2) theatre a "platform."

A. Theatre as Picture: How "Real" Is Real?

This type of setting is not conceived as "real life," but as an illusion or a picture of life. It is almost as if the "fourth wall" of the stage were removed and you were peeping into the setting. We know the sets on stage cannot be real. What they offer is the "illusion" of reality.

1) Naturalism

In this most extreme form we find on stage an almost exact replica of a living room or other kind of interior setting.

Producer David Belasco in the late nineteenth century put a real grill (with real pancakes) on stage to represent a restaurant. Today a painted flat or a few stools and a mimed counter will do the trick,

The stylized use of mime, movement, and masks creates the illusion of horses in the theatrical production of *Equus*. Often a simple design stroke will suggest a larger reality.

reflected along the painted flats of riverbank docks. His central character wittily explains that the starlight on the rippling waters is electrically controlled and proceeds to catalogue how the backstage scenery works, thus purposefully undercutting anticipated romantic effects. He is showing us that nature will not be reproduced on stage. Art will.

As a reaction to naturalism, in the last century it was recognized by many directors, scenic designers, and playwrights that "realism" could be more effective if it were suggested on stage. What we are talking about is the use of dramatic metaphor, which compresses the essential meaning of the play's environment into practical, workable stage terms. A significant part of the whole is offered to suggest the dramatic atmos-

and that's called "suggested realism."

2) Suggested Realism

In *Talley's Folly*, Lanford Wilson beautifully demystifies the romantic shadows and moonlight phere pervading the play or scenes from the play. For example, a few painted flats or set pieces of trees might represent a whole forest.

B. Theatre as Platform

In the words of Emerson, "Art teaches to convey a larger sense by simpler symbols." [3] Theatre as platform attempts to *present* life rather than representing a "realistic" illusion of life.

Ancient Greek theatre was presented mostly on a bare playing space in large amphitheatres. The actors wore high cothurni (boots) and masks that amplified their speech. There was no pretense at realism, no eavesdropping or peeping into realistic living rooms. Tragic and comic emotions were presented larger than life. Likewise, on the Shakespearean stage, theatrical multiscenic pageants were presented on an essentially bare platform with levels. With a quick change of characterization and inventive language, the scene was easily shifted from place to place or literally around the world without moving a prop.

In the 1920's in Europe, there was a strong reaction to naturalism, and artistic revolts against representationalism (including "suggested realism") mushroomed. The new idea was to convey the essence of the scene through the esthetic interpretation of the stage environment. Thus, in symbolism, the imaginative use of lighting and space design can create a mood that evokes the essential metaphor of the play. A single stylized tree might say "forest." A coat of arms projected on a backdrop might be the one artistic stroke needed to suggest a royal throne room.

An effective presentational dramatic metaphor is the use of unreal doors and walls through which characters move to express the mobile concurrence of past and present time in *Death of a Salesman*. Another example is the image of a prize ring to convey the spirit of struggle in the original production of Clifford Odets' *Golden Boy*. *Barnum* uses platforms and a variety of curtains, which speedily and imaginatively turn into all kinds of settings spanning twenty-five years of the title character's life.

[3] Quoted in Robert Edmond Jones, *The Dramatic Imagination* (New York: Routledge Books, 1987). p. 23.

A simple screen-flat painted to indicate a stained-glass window and a few benches suggest a church for the setting of *Martin Luther King, Jr.* by Alice Childress and Nathan Woodward. The playwright, director, and designer try to find a symbolic or suggestive theatrical stroke that will evoke the larger details of a more realistic setting.

Some plays require little or no setting. A bare stage and simple lighting effectively complement the storytelling dramatic metaphor in Thornton Wilder's *Our Town* and Paul Sills' *Story Theatre*. Platforms and multimedia slide projections convey the metaphor of big-city ambience in the musicals *Your Own Thing* by Donald Driver, Hal Hester, and Danny Apolinar and *The Me Nobody Knows* by Gary William Freedman and Will Holt based on an idea by Herb Schapiro.

Frankly, many playwrights today do not wish to expend the energy to convince an audience that they are looking at something they know is not real to begin with, when a single design stroke can account for more truthful feeling for the same place. Some additional forms of "stage as platform":

1) *Constructivism:* "Biomechanical" utilizes a series of ramps, levels, constructivist built-up sets, best represented by Meyerhold in the Soviet Union and Richard Schechner's Performing Garage in this country. The Broadway set of *Sweeney Todd* is a another striking example.

2) *Theatricalism* admits openly that theatre is theatre. Scenery changes in front of one's eyes. Scenery is stylized. The tastefully artificial becomes a natural thing. For examples, *My Fair Lady, Barnum*, most musicals.

3) *Epic* — multiscenic; use of character devices that distance emotion; nonrealistic; direct address. Examples: Bertolt Brecht, Piscator, certain docudramas.

4) *Formalism* — theatrical moods created through lighting and geometric abstraction. Examples: Richard Foreman's *OntologicalHysteric* theatre pieces with string bisecting the stage; electronic effects; sculptural acting formations; other dreamlike effects.

5) *Expressionism* — purposeful inversion of realism to express or capture the subjective. interior feelings of the central character. Thus, in Elmer

In *Jitney,* the first full-length play that August Wilson wrote, the author's voice is already fully evident. His dialogue has the feeling of the poetry of everyday life. It has been compared to an "urban symphony" of music, in which all the characters express their unique voices. In a tense scene between father and son, set in the storefront of a gypsy cab company, an undercurrent beneath the dialogue bristles with poetic pungence.

In *Dancing at Lughnasa,* a moving play by Brian Friel, the poetic language soars, yet is grounded in rich Irish folk images and idioms reminiscient of the playwright Sean O'Casey.

Rice's *The Adding Machine,* the scenery looks distorted because that's the way Mr. Zero sees life. In *Death of a Salesman,* expressionistic techniques such as Willy Loman stepping through imaginary walls into the past of his tortured inner soul combine with the power of realistic characters and speech to produce provocative theatre.

Join the Scene!

You may be asking, "Doesn't all this discussion fall under the province of the scenic designer and the stage director?" Yes, it does, but an image of how you, as creator, "see" your play as you write it might affect the creation of other elements of the play. For example, overly realistic dialogue might be seen as out of place in an expressionistic or symbolic setting.

A variety of settings can complement what is being said and acted on stage . . .

. . . A collage setting for musical revue of Hot Headlines from Hunter College

. . . Simple scenery for classroom production

Lofty, poetic dialogue may be more suitable in an open, theatrical or symbolic, or expressionistic environment. If the setting is in a living room, one is less likely to hear heightened poetry in a closed-in interior setting, although to be sure the dialogue could still be witty and articulate as in Albee's *Who's Afraid of Virginia Woolf,* which is set in a living room, or the witty repartee heard at 27A Wimpole Street (where Henry Higgins resides). Again it depends on the specific nature of the room. T. S. Eliot's poetic *Cocktail Party* takes place in a drawing room, and so do many of Noël Coward's comedies.

Again, there are no hard and fast rules, but more open, expansive sets lend themselves to more open, lyrical dialogue. In a theatrical or symbolic setting, you might also have the stylized mime, movement, and expressive sounds found in Peter Brook's *The Conference of the Birds*; although to be sure, the racy, Runyonesque dialogue heard in *Guys and Dolls* could fit that kind of open setting as well. The point is that out of specific scenic images (the "stage of your mind") may come valuable ideas for character and dialogue.

Set Directions

Some playwrights love to write elaborate stage directions, the best known being George Bernard Shaw. Shakespearean plays have very sparse stage directions. When you read plays now, be aware of the description of the scene at the beginning of the

. . . Shadow theatre for children's theatre production.

play and the changes of setting. Does the description capture the mood of the opening moments? Is the description functional? Does it give insight into chararacter or story? A play like *The Miracle Worker* can sometimes do all three. What about your play?

27 WAGONS FULL OF COTTON

The scene for this lively one-acter by Tennessee Williams is the front porch of a cottage near Blue Mountain, Mississippi. Williams evocatively describes the porch roof and the doors of Gothic design, rich stained glass of azure, crimson, emerald, and gold. The details include fluffy white curtains and baby-blue satin bows. The whole effect conjures up a doll's house existence. In this way, Williams says a lot about the characters who live in the cottage and sets up a mood that will soon be contradicted by violence.

WAITING FOR GODOT

This beautiful poetic drama by Samuel Beckett calls for a country road and a tree. It's evening. The first stage direction describes Estragon sitting on a low mound attempting to take off his boot. (See page 38.)

THE ZOO STORY

Edward Albee's compassionate one-acter is set in Central Park on a Sunday in summer. The set calls for a couple of benches, behind which are trees. sky, and foliage.

Three one-acters all set outdoors — two representational (to different degrees) and one presentationalr — reflect the atmosphere and flavor of the plays' styles and content. Compare these plays with the interior settings of *The Homecoming, The Odd Couple,* and *A Raisin in the Sun;* and with some plays that combine indoor and outdoor locales, such as *Death of a Salesman, West Side Story, The Miracle Worker,* and August Wilson's *Joe Turner's Come and Gone.*

——————— JUST FOR YOU ———————

How did you describe the setting or scene of your play? is there any way you can further clarify and/or simplify the setting?

_____

. . . . Using an Open Theatre technique, actors create the scenery with their own bodies: Puff the Magic Dragon meeting Jackie Paper

An awareness of the various forms of theatrical style such as expressionism, selected realism, theatricalism, and symbolism will help you either to choose a highly distilled reality or to eliminate altogether any pretense of verisimilitude for your play's setting.

IN SUM

Dialogue aims to:

- be true to character
- move the action along
- be specific and economical
- be believable

Additionally, visual action on stage should be all of the above as well as honestly complement the spoken action.

In keeping with the trend of playwriting today,

a presentational style of production is used in which the stage is frankly admitted as being a stage, as opposed to representational styles of production that attempt (in varying degrees) to create the illusion of reality. Dialogue, by the same token, should *fit naturally into* and *complement* the visual environment. How your characters go about getting or not getting what they want is greatly influenced by where they are and when they are there. In this sense, a sense of key visual elements (be they gestures, costumes, hair style, adornments, or settings) should be indicated in your script when they are vital to clarifying plot, theme, or characterization.

PLAYWRIGHT'S PAGE

1) What have you learned about writing dialogue? Write a short dialogue about it.

2) Do you have an easier time writing dialogue spoken by men or women? Why is this?

. . . . Blue fabric imaginatively evokes the ocean in Coleman A. Jennings' *The Honorable Urashima Taro,* which is based on two Japanese folk tales.

3) What difficulties have you had in writing dialogue? What do you find easy about writing dialogue?

4) Have you gotten any ideas for your plays from the discussion of visual elements?

5) How do speech and silence complement each other? Give an example or two from your play.

MORE **RAW** MATERIALS

Read . . . as many plays as possible. Listen to plays on recordings. See as many plays as you can. Listen to the dialogue. Let it soak in. When it comes to writing your own dialogue, learn to trust your own "ear." Be especially sensitive to stage directions when you read scripts.

Act . . . out situations controlled by one dominant emotion, then change the dominant emotion for a full moment of the action. For example, the first scene could be controlled by anger, the second scene by ecstasy. Let the dialogue pour out. Don't plan it.

Write . . . and rewrite a page of dialogue inspired by the scene suggested above. What key differences do you discern between spoken and written dialogue?

—— SUGGESTIONS FOR CLASSROOM ACTIVITIES ——

Time to zero in on dialogue!

Discuss . . . You and a partner assume the voice and mannerisms of two characters in the plays you are writing. As those characters, carry on a conversation about the importance of writing good dialogue.

Record* . . .
• Spend some hours traveling to various locations, overhearing how people talk (note accents and dialogues, too). At home, jot down lines from conversations that could inspire your own writing.

• When this part of the exercise is done, take one line and start a dialogue through either acting or writing. Notice how the voices sound, especially dialects and intonations, as well as how words and phrases are emphasized.

• Imagine what people are physically doing as they are speaking.

Read . . .

• aloud a scene from your classmates' plays or from the play the class is writing together. Do you feel that the dialogue is true to character? Why or why not? How can you distinguish which character is speaking? Give some examples.

• body language of people you come into contact with. What specific gestures, postures or touches do you notice that shed light on what the person is saying, thinking, feeling, or doing?

View a play or movie of interest to you on TV — with the sound off. Can you follow the action? Why or why not?

Act . . . Play "Dial-log": Using real phone receivers or mimed ones, set up some circumstances and carry on a conversation with another very different character. Then change the circumstances so that a confrontation takes place between the two. Log down some of the words and expressions that were heard. As a variation, run through the scene with both characters talking only in clichés and trite language. Then, during the second run-through, they are to use dialogue that is real.

NOTEBOOK (JOURNAL) FEATURE
• Write about/draw the setting of your play. Is there a particular object in it that is important? Have the object speak in a monologue about its importance or relevance to your play. How does the object look, feel, and taste?
• Revise any dialogue or monologues in your play. Be prepared to justify why the dialogue needs to be revised. At the same time, remember that sometimes you can have good dialogue but it belongs in another play you may write.

ONGOING GROUP PROJECT
Revise any dialogue or monologue in your group play. Be prepared to justify why any dialogue needs to be revised, especially in light of the discussion of subtext.

Write . . .

• Someone starts writing a bit of dialogue on a sheet of paper and then hands it to someone else to continue. The sheet is passed on, and on, and on. Fun and surprises await you as this "chain of dialogue" reaches its climax! Then take one of the lines, write it on the chalkboard and write a vocal direction that goes with it (e.g., Jo: [*Hollering.*] I need some money!) and then say the line. Have others come to the chalkboard, change the vocal direction (e.g., Jo: [*Fearfully.*] I need some money!) Discuss the variations.

• Explore and experiment with subtext. This is, you remember, what is said, but not directly stated. Something else is going on under the line. Example: Boss: You're late! [Your job's in jeopardy!]. Look at the dialogue you have written for the Record exercise on page 130 or use dialogue you have written for your own play or for the group play. Ready for the challenging part? First, write your dialogue. Then cut out 50 percent of the words — yet still get the point across in the scene. Then ask yourself, "What must be said out loud, and what can the actor communicate with his or her body and voice without using all these words?" This kind of exercise ** is an excellent way to help you heighten your dialogue without losing meaning, flavor, or clarity.

*Thanks to Elana Gartner for the suggestion.
** Thanks for the exercise to John Fredricksen, stage director.

chapter IX

TO ADAPT OR NOT TO ADAPT

Good words are like a string of pearls.
> — Chinese proverb

You should learn to sail in all winds.
> — Italian proverb

At some time during your playwriting experience, you may wish to try your hand at adapting one of your favorite stories or a portion of a novel.

If the original source is in the public domain, you may proceed with your adaptation without clearance from the publisher. However, if the work is not in the public domain, you will have to obtain permission, in writing, to adapt the original source. This is true especially if you plan on selling your product or having it produced commercially at a later time.

CHOOSING A SOURCE

As we discovered in Chapter II, the very same elements that may make a story or a novel fascinating — such as vivid and poetical description, numerous minor incidents, subplots, and lengthy character discourses — tend to make a play talky and undramatic. A story or novel, in addition to freely skipping around in time, can also make use of many locales and may include dozens, even hundreds, of characters. Drama, on the other hand — especially a one-act play — generally fares better within a structured unity of time, place, and action. Stream-of-consciousness techniques highly successful in some novels and stories must therefore be sacrificed to dramatic elements. Compactness, immediacy, and clarity are needed if the work is to be transformed effectively to the stage.

For these reasons, only a few narrative works can be successfully transferred to the stage without some modification. In this chapter, we ask:

- What are the various transformation options?
- What are some of the major problems concerned with transforming narrative sources into plays?

TYPES OF TRANSFORMATIONS

One area of confusion arises from the terms used to describe how closely to adhere to the original source. For example, Joe McGinnis, the author of the book *The Selling of the President*, filed complaints against the producer of the musical version of his work. The author questioned the show's artistic integrity, even though the play only used the book's title and theme.

Transformations are generally designated dramatizations; adaptations; or "based on" or "suggested by."

Dramatization — close fidelity to the story, theme, and characters of the original source. If the material lends itself to literal transformation, you can almost completely accept the theme, plot, and characters and breathe dramatic life into the work.

Adaptation — intent of the playwright takes preference over the purpose of the author. A story rarely lends itself to literal transformation. An adaptation is close to the original material, but you can take greater dramatic liberties with theme, plot, and character than you would with a dramatization.

An adaptation should remain true to the spirit of the original source but still maintain its own integrity in form and feeling. *Raisin*, the adaptation of *A Raisin in the Sun*, effectively utilizes conventions of musical theatre to tell the story of the Younger family.

Based on or suggested by — terms applied by the playwright to a work that takes as its basis only fragmentary elements of the original story and its characters. More radical changes in plot, characters, and theme can be made in line with your intent. [1]

JUST FOR YOU

In your notebook label a page "Story to Stage," or something else you think appropriate. To start, list some of your favorite stories that you think could be transformed to the stage. Is the work in the public domain or will you need permission to transform it? Divide one page in your notebook into three vertical columns: (1) *Dramatization*, (2) *Adaptation*, and (3) *Based On* or *Suggested By*. Which type best lends itself to your needs? Why?

PROBLEMS IN TRANSFORMING NARRATIVE MATERiAL

I. PLOT

Narrative forms are unlimited by time or geographical space. Drama is a time art that deals with the "here and now." The plot of a play may begin long after the beginning of the story. Information regarding the past is told dramatically through exposition, flashback, or other structural devices. In drama, the incidents of the story must be so selected and rearranged as to produce the proper emotional

[1] Thanks to Roger Busfield, *The Playwright's Art* (New York: Harper and Bros., 1958), p. 199.

conflict and maximum dramatic impact. Plot, the interweaving of dramatic situations, is what actually makes the story happen in the "here and now."

In other words, the play transformed from a narrative — as we have seen with *The Devil and Daniel Webster* — should leave a unified impression and be consistent and plausible on its own terms. Work out a related chain of incidents that can focus on a limited aspect of a character's life. The playwright has the responsibility and challenge of sorting out an enormous amount of details and making them clear enough to an audience that may know almost nothing about the original source.

Example of Plot Adjustments for a Dramatization: The Courtship of Miles Standish:

When I was commissioned by Scholastic to turn the narrative poem "The Courtship of Miles Standish" into a play, I decided it would be a dramatization. That is, I stuck fairly well to the original. The one major plot change I made concerned the central character. I felt that the central character was John Alden, not Miles Standish. John has the dominant goal and inherent dramatic developmental action — his unstated love for Priscilla. The question was how this fact could be revealed to the audience. After all, as the poem makes clear, John would never confide his love to Priscilla as long as his close friend Miles Standish was living. To solve this problem I revived a character who precisely might know the little secrets of the small community (through making his daily rounds of Plymouth). This was the Reverend Brewster, and I made him a fully fleshed character.

I took the liberty of starting the play just before the wedding of Priscilla (in the narrative the wedding comes at the end), while she is waiting for her husband-to-be to arrive. We do not yet know who this is. The incidents in the dramatization then continue pretty much as they do in the poem, except for one key scene. Early in the play John Alden is on the way to Priscilla's house to propose on behalf of Miles Standish. The Reverend Brewster, whom I made a sort of well-intentioned busybody, suspects John's strong romantic interest in Priscilla. Through him, the audience is able to connect with John's tortured emotional bind (loyalty vs. love). Otherwise, the events in the poem are dramatized fairly straightforwardly. The elements of war referred to in the poem were stylized on stage through mime and movement.

Example of Plot Adjustment for Based Upon or Suggested By: The Bet

An editor at *Scholastic* suggested that my colleague, Joseph Lesser, and I write a one-act play based on a W. Somerset Maugham short story, "Mr. Know-All." The story's narrator is taking a fourteen-day ocean cruise from San Francisco to Yokohama. He runs into a conceited know-it-all type who tries to bring everyone around to his way of thinking.

Also on board are Mr. Ramsey, who is in the Foreign Service, and his wife, a sweet, modest young woman. Mr. Know-All guesses that Mrs. Ramsey's cultured pearls are worth around $15,000. Mr. Ramsey replies that Mrs. Ramsey bought the pearls for a mere $18 before leaving New York. Mr. Know-All insists that the pearls are expensive and asks to see them up close. Mr. Ramsey emphatically replies that the pearls are only imitation.

Mr. Know-All gets Mrs. Ramsey to take off the pearls: he looks at them through a magnifying glass and is about to speak, but she is about to faint. Mr. Know-All suddenly backs down and admits he was mistaken about the pearls. She is greatly relieved. The men chide Mr. Know-All for having been so cocksure about the worth of the pearls.

Mr. Know-All whispers to the narrator that if he had a pretty little wife he wouldn't let her spend a year in New York while he was abroad —implying that Mrs. Ramsey had an admirer who bought her nice things. Mrs. Ramsey, of course, is indebted to Mr. Know-All for saving her from the embarrassment of having her husband discover the affair she had while he was gone.

The *Scholastic* editor wanted this basic idea transformed into some kind of contemporary school setting. Therefore, Joe and I had to find an equivalent plot structure to convey the essence of the theme — a person who must swallow his pride in order to save another's reputation. The plot structure was modified so that it is the first day of school. Noah (the equivalent of Mr. Know-All, a braggart who can never be wrong) bets a friend of Laurie's that he knows the new girl from somewhere. How could this be, the others ask, when Laurie is from out of town? It turns out that Laurie's father had made headlines in another town as an embezzler. Noah had remembered reading the newspaper story. Noah preserves Laurie's reputation by losing his bet, but he has gained a friend.

Example of Plot Adjustment for an Adaptation: The Ballad of Box Brown

Because *The Narrative of Box Brown* — about a slave's daring escape to the North — is tightly constructed, it was relatively easy to locate a dramatic focus for the musical play. I decided that the play would concentrate on a few days in the life of the central character, Henry Brown, and trace the incidents leading to his decision to escape in a box.

The dramatic question clearly emerged as: "Will Henry be able to escape from slavery?" The central crisis leading to Henry's decision to escape is the selling of his wife, Nancy. If Henry can make it to the North, perhaps he can raise enough money to buy his wife back. This is his driving motivation.

To prepare the audience for the resolution of the dramatic question, it was necessary to create an interpersonal conflict, the seeds of which were already planted in the book. In the narrative, the actual relationship of John Allen, the foreman of the factory where Henry works, is barely explored. In the book, Henry makes a comment regarding Allen's

In adapting a story or novel into a play, artistic liberties may be taken. In *The Ballad of Box Brown*, the author added a dream sequence of Henry's entire family escaping to the North that did not appear in the narrative.

cruelty toward the other slaves; in the musical, the Allen-Brown relationship is greatly expanded in terms of specific actions. Allen is Brown's constant threat. Nancy, who is deeply worried about being separated from her husband, pleads with him not to provoke Allen. Throughout the musical, just the reverse happens: Allen provokes and intimidates Henry to the point where the latter's pride is challenged, and he finally strikes back.

A number of alterations regarding source material were made in order to tighten the dramatic focus of the play. For example, Allen is given specific motivations for his stealing. He attempts to get enough money to go out West and prospect for gold. The character of the abolitionist Samuel Smith (who is only briefly mentioned in the narrative) was given a number of significant actions as an agent trying to help Henry escape. Several of these actions involve the use of disguises, which add excitement and humor to the plot.

I found myself introducing specific complications to show the box continually in danger of being either detected or turned over, wrong side up. The scene aboard the boat is basically taken from the narrative, with the element of the irate husband being added. Also wholly invented is the scene of Allen turning up in Washington, D.C. and almost stealing the box until he is stopped by an agent of the URR (Underground Railroad); invented, too, is the scene in which William Still knocks out the Man-in-Cape when the box arrives in Philadelphia. I was basically faithful to thematic considerations of the original story. But since I took greater liberties

with plot in terms of its dramatic feasibility, *The Ballad of Box Brown* is clearly an adaptation.

———————— JUST FOR YOU ————————

Jot down in your notebook some key plot elements in your story transformation. Note the main interpersonal conflicts between characters in the stage adaptation. What is the major crisis and climax? Will you have a "dramatic clock"? What is the major dramatic question? How will the play end? Can you block out or diagram the scenes leading to and from the crisis? Remember, you don't have to know all the answers at this time. Thinking about the possibilities can be helpful.

———————————————————————————————

According to Kenneth MacGowan, "Characters must be so selected and developed that they include people who are bound to react upon each other, bound to clash, as well as lesser characters who by intervening may heighten the clash or perhaps help finally resolve it." [2] In transforming the narrative material into drama, a process similar to plot adjustments also occurs in character selection.

In the writing of historical novels there is ample critical support that the writer can take artistic liberty with the characters. Harold Cruse, regarding the various fictional interpretations of Nat Turner,

[2] MacGowan, *A Primer of Playwriting*, p. 62.

observes: " . . . I maintain that in dealing with a work of art the writer does have a certain license in depicting historical events. I don't happen to believe that in writing historical novels one is bound by every aspect and every fact of the character's life. The author chooses certain highlights of this character and molds them into a work of art." [3]

Character development should be geared toward the dramatic. That is, characters may or may not be in harmony with the essence of the story or novel; it is imperative that they carry the story through conflict, crises, and climax. For this to happen, you may find it necessary at times to add characters who do not appear in the original source. The use of fictional characters is sometimes needed to hold together a dramatic development or to flesh out other characters.

If an audience is free of any preconceived ideas, you, in turn, can enjoy an even greater freedom in your conception of characters. This is especially true in biography-drama. For example, Robert Sherwood in *Abe Lincoln in Illinois* created the wholly fictitious character of an old Revolutionary War soldier solely to demonstrate that the President knew men who fought in the Revolutionary War. Joanna Halpert Kraus acknowledges that some of her characters in *Mean to Be Free* are fictitious, but says they are typical of the more than three hundred runaway slaves — including children and babies — who risked capture during the course of Harriet Tubman's nineteen trips north to freedom.

Example of Character Adjustment in a Dramatization: The Courtship of Miles Standish

In my dramatization of *The Courtship of Miles Standish* for *Scholastic* it was necessary to delete certain characters, add several others, and deepen characterization in a number of instances. I have already mentioned the Reverend Brewster, who was included to objectify John Alden's ambivalent feelings of love and loyalty. I also created several characters who could be confidants of Priscilla. These friends try to persuade her to forget the bitterness of the New

World. There are enough clues in the narrative poem to indicate the tough-minded assertiveness of the maiden whose family had been wiped out by the previous harsh winter. In the play, I built up this aspect of characterization. From the narrative poem:

She, the Puritan girl, in the solitude of the forest,/Making the humble house and the modest apparel of homespun/Beautiful with her beauty, and rich with the welfare of her being.

John and Priscilla sit down and talk of the birds and the beautiful springtime, and Priscilla remarks:

Kind are the people I live with, and dear to me my religion;/Still my heart is so sad, that I wish myself back in Old England./You will say it is wrong, but I cannot help it: I almost/Wish myself back in Old England, I feel so lonely and wretched.

John answered: Indeed I do not condemn you:/Stouter hearts than a woman's have quailed in this terrible winter./Yours is tender and trusting, and needs a stronger to lean on;/So I have come to you now, with an offer and proffer of marriage/Made by a good man and true, Miles Standish the Captain of Plymouth!

Even the Captain himself could hardly have said it more bluntly./Mute with amazement and sorrow, Priscilla the Puritan maiden/Looked into Alden's face, her eyes dilated with wonder,/Feeling his words like a blow, that stunned her and rendered her speechless: Till at length she exclaimed, interrupting the ominous silence/ "If the great Captain of Plymouth is so very eager to wed me,/Why does he not come himself, and take the trouble to woo me?/If I am not worth the wooing, I surely am not worth the winning!"

I transformed the essence of the above section of the narrative poem as follows (it's the tail end of her friends' visit):

PRISCILLA: Friends, you all mean well — and while I do think of the pretty flowers that bloom in old England, the

---

[3] Harold Cruse, "The Integrationist Ethic as Basis for Scholarly Endeavors," in *Black Studies in the University: A Symposium*, eds. Armisted L. Robinson, Chester Foster, and Donald H. Ogilive (New Haven: Yale University Press, 1969), p. 24.

winding village streets, the familiar faces of those I've lived with —

BETH: Well, then —

PRISCILLA: While I *think* of old England, Beth, I *know* I will stay here in New England . . . to carry on the work of building a place in the New World. Did we sail 65 days across the sea enduring great hardship and pain to leave? After only one year of settlement? Did we?

ANNE: (*Her FRIENDS start to rise and exit.*) Still . . . we wish you'd reconsider. . .

PRISCILLA: Have a good day, my friends — the sun shines — all is well.

BETH: Yes, Priscilla. It's spring now — but don't forget another cruel winter to come —
(*As they exit, JOHN ALDEN comes in. The women nod "good day" to him and exit.*)

PRISCILLA: Hello, John . . . please sit.

JOHN: (*Uncomfortable.*) I'll stand, if you don't mind — All is not well, Priscilla. I do not mean to alarm you. But there may be another attack soon. You'll need protection.

PRISCILLA: We all need that, John —

JOHN: You are a good woman, Priscilla. Stouter hearts than yours have trembled during our terrible winter — so I come to you now with an offer of marriage . . .

PRISCILLA: (*Looking up from her weaving.*) Yes, John?

JOHN: (*Blurting it out.*) An offer made by a good man and true — Miles Standish, the Captain of Plymouth Colony!

PRISCILLA: (*Stunned.*) Oh? If the great Captain of Plymouth is so very eager to wed me, why does he not come himself and take the trouble to woo me?

JOHN: He did not say. He — I mean— I—

In any kind of transformation, character changes are inevitable. For example, in my dramatized play *The Bet*, high school students were substituted for the ship passengers in the original story. These characters included George, a practical joker, and Ellen, friend of Laurie, the central character. These characters, though minor, do a great deal to establish the fun and banter between the high school kids on the opening day of school.

Example of Character Adjustment in an Adaptation: The Ballad of Box Brown:

It became necessary to add several characters not found in the original source. In fact, over half of the main characters in *The Ballad of Box Brown* are invented. Three-quarters of the invented characters are indispensable for the development of conflict and complications.

For example, the part of Caleph (Nancy's brother) was created to show how the tension generated by slavery was felt within Henry's own family. Caleph's distrust of all white men deflects into anger at Henry when the latter decides to take the advice of Samuel Smith, the white abolitionist. Later in the play, Caleph slowly begins to trust Smith. Caleph, a carpenter, then is able to help Henry by building his means of escape — the box.

It was also necessary to invent characters who would round out and tie together various strands of the dramatic action. The chorus, for example, plays a variety of roles needed to advance the dramatic progression of the play and add atmosphere: Underground Railroad agents, workers in the tobacco factory, and neighbors who live near Henry.

Several invented characters are young people. The play was written for a family audience. Jonah, a nine-year-old boy, is a major character and a source of direct identification for the audience. And Laura, although in only two scenes, is integral to the plot. (In fact, her quick wit saves Jonah's life.)

The complex question of how one must sometimes compromise his dignity in order to play the "game of survival" is a very real one for today's youngsters. In the play, Jonah sees that his uncle loves him even though Henry, in frustration, explodes at the boy. Jonah, therefore, accepts his uncle as a man with human weaknesses and strengths rather than as a superhuman hero.

─────── JUST FOR YOU ───────

Continue to work in your notebook. What characters from the original source will you keep? Which ones will you delete? Of the characters you decide to keep, how will they change in the stage transformation?

Note possible transformations re: Central Character/Opposing Character(s)/Contributing Characters (and dramatic function).

─────────────────────────────

II. DIALOGUE/SONG

One school of thought encourages the playwright to use as much dialogue from the original source as possible to ensure that a large part of the play will be true to character. Then, only when necessary would you create your own dialogue and match it as closely to the spirit of the original source as possible.

However, it is not always possible to use dialogue intact from the narrative source. According to the eminent critic and theatre historian John Gassner: "Dialogue in the drama is more self-sufficient than in a novel; it is impossible to resort to prefatory remarks explaining the nature of a speech. Consequently, good dialogue must be written not for mere beauty of sound and imagery but for expressiveness." [4]

Arthur Miller offers a fundamental reason why it is difficult to lift scenes of dialogue directly from novels and put them on stage:

[Novels] may seem perfectly stageworthy on paper, and on occasion they really are, but for the most part, the novelist's dialogue is pitched toward the eye rather than the ear and falls flat when heard. Conversely, the dialogue in a story needs to sacrifice its sound in order to be convincing to the eye. And this is another enticement stories have for playwrights — as one writes dialogue the thirst returns for playwriting and the "right" to tell a story through sounds once more. [5]

[4] John Gassner, "The Nature of Drama," *Producing the Play* (New York: The Dryden Press, 1953), p. 27.

[5] Arthur Miller, "Foreword: About Distances," *I Don't Need You Anymore* (New York: Bantam Books, 1968), p. xi.

A sound middle ground concerning the problems of incorporating or rejecting dialogue from the original source is to blend the dramatist's dialogue with that of the narrative. A point would be reached where the theatre audience would have a difficult time discerning where the novelist's words leave off and the playwright's dialogue begins.

If your narrative source does not contain that much dialogue, you might either have to reject the narrative as a source or be prepared to reconstruct the speech of the characters in particular situations. This is what Edward Albee had to do when he adapted Carson McCuller's *The Ballad of the Sad Cafe*, which contains only a few lines of dialogue.

Altering Dialogue

In a number of instances, you will discover dialogue in the narrative source that is verbose, extraneously philosophical, or poetic (without being dramatic). The words may be written in a forced style or with frills better suited to the eye than to the ear.

Here, a process of alteration similar to that found in plotting and characterization will hold true. Much of the original dialogue will have to be removed completely or changed to conform to sound principles of writing for the theatre. Dialogue, after all, should accomplish a number of functions: delineate character, move the plot along, and illuminate the dramatic action and major dramatic problem. Dialogue aims for directness and dynamism, except when specifically intended for another purpose.

Verbose, long speeches in the original novel should be used sparingly in the play, if at all, unless truly befitting a particular character. Even if your dialogue is poetic or lyrical, it should also strive to be dramatic and vital.

The question of how closely you should adhere to well-known passages, such as famous historical speeches or monologues, deserves some comment. Some writers insist on using the exact dialogue, whereas others seek to enhance a familiar line or passage because a sense of drama is needed. Most likely, you wouldn't consider "improving" on a well-known speech by Abraham Lincoln. On the other hand, always to use the exact dialogue, when it may be wordy for example, is to limit your selective process as an artist and to do possible injustice to the dramatic treatment.

Any quotes from the source should be unnoticeably interwoven with your created dialogue. Again, quoted excerpts may have to be cut and edited with clarity. You can tell if a famous quote has been edited effectively if it doesn't stick out too boldly. Some famous quotes from the original can call attention to the fact that the play is based on another source.

Example of Dialogue Adjustment for an Adaptation: The Ballad of Box Brown:

Because very little dialogue appears in *The Narrative of Box Brown*, it was necessary to invent most of the language eventually heard in the play. To be sure, in isolated instances a line or two served as the basis for dialogue. For example, in the narrative, Brown refers to two passengers aboard ship arguing about whether the box they are sitting on has come with the mail. Recalling the incident, Brown remarks that it was a male all right, "but not the mail of the United States." This casual remark was transformed into an actual interchange of dialogue in the play.

Several song lyrics were inspired by incidents recalled by Brown. For example, the bittersweet song "Like Leaves" developed from Brown's memory of his mother taking him on her knee and saying: "My son, as yonder leaves are stripped from off the trees of the forest, so are the children of slaves swept away from them by the hands of cruel tyrants." When the show's lyricist, Emme Kemp, wrote "Like Leaves," she had to adjust the tone and texture of the narrative words to make them more sayable.

During rehearsals of the musical, actors at times would offer (often unconsciously) suggestions of idiomatic speech, which were incorporated directly into the dialogue. Such line changes and additions of words or phrases are not uncommon during rehearsals and even during the run of a show.

For example, during the rehearsals of the videotape version of "The Ballad of Box Brown," the actor (George Tipton) portraying Henry Brown changed the playwright's line, "A man's pride can stand so much," to "A man's pride can stand so much puttin' down." The actress (Lorice Stevens) playing Nancy confided to Henry that she was worried about being "sold down river" rather than "down South" (as I had written the line). Many of the song lyrics in the play also conveyed the essence of the period (e.g., "The Cow" and "Wake up, Jonah"). In instances where the lyrics were invented, they were written in modern speech with a hint of local color.

Adaptations from two different sources: *Fiddler on the Roof,* based on the stories of Sholom Aleichem, and *Oliver!,* based on the novel by Charles Dickens.

─────── JUST FOR YOU ───────

In your notebook — or wherever — start scribbling or reworking some dialogue from a beginning scene, from somewhere at the end, or from anywhere. Write as much as you want — or can; refine whatever you like. Surprise yourself. Write!

─────────────────────────

III. VISUAL ELEMENTS

The problem also arises of how to transform to the stage settings referred to in the narrative.

Friedrich Dürrenmatt, author of *The Visit*, offers a representative solution to the problem. Describing the genesis of *The Visit*, he writes:

> . . . how can I show a small town on the stage? At that time I was frequently traveling from Nüremberg, where I lived, to Berne. The express train always stops once or twice at little tiny stations. Next to those little buildings, there's a small comfort station. It was very typical sight as a small railroad then: it can be used very well as a stage picture. Now, the railroad station is the first place you see when you come into a town, that's where you have to arrive. The spectator comes into Güllen with the railroad station, so to speak. [6]

Dürrenmatt is alluding to the use of dramatic metaphor, which compresses the essential meaning of the play's environment into practical, workable stage terms. A significant part of the whole is offered to suggest the dramatic atmosphere pervading the play or scenes from the play. According to stage designer Mordecai Gorelik:

> Thus, the attic bedroom of *The Three Sisters* is not only an attic, not only a bedroom, not only a girl's room, not only a room of the period of 1901, not only a room belonging to the gentle folk whom Chekhov wrote about . . . it may be . . . the scene of a raging fever. There is a fire going on outside. The whole house is restless, tossing about out in this fire-atmosphere, unable to sleep.

People wander about dumbly or blurt out sudden confidences, as if they were lightheaded . . . [7]

Other examples of scenic metaphor include the four movable benches and a chalkboard that fluidly convey the essence of a classroom, a restaurant, a courthouse, and various living rooms in the multi-scenic *Children of a Lesser God* by Mark Medoff. A white line and black rear panels that turn around to reveal mirrors ingeniously capture the metaphor of dance, permitting the actors to spin out their dreams on an essentially bare stage in *A Chorus Line*, which grew out of the Public Theatre's workshops of Joseph Papp's New York Shakespeare Festival. You, too, can utilize a presentational style of production in which the stage is frankly admitted to be a stage, as opposed to using a representational style of production that attempts (in varying degrees) to create the illusion of reality.

Obviously, for example, one cannot put a whole cafeteria on stage. So in our play *The Bet*, Joe Lesser and I called for just one table to be set under the ever-present loudspeaker as a symbolic reminder of the hustle-bustle of a modern school.

The trick for *The Courtship of Miles Standish* was to find a dramatic symbol or metaphor that would not only suggest the community of Plymouth but also evoke the specific atmosphere of those who lived and worked in it. Rather than use a realistic setting, we left the stage essentially bare except for some chairs and tables. Much of the action was mimed for greater mobility from scene to scene. A cyclorama of flowers in the back evoked the feeling of growth and love, as well as pinpointing the spring-like atmosphere of the play.

Example of Visual Adjustments for an Adaptation: The Ballad of Box Brown

The problem of discovering the right metaphor for *The Ballad of Box Brown* was difficult. In the early drafts, I felt that because of the play's form — essentially a flashback in which Brown's story is acted out while he tells it to a young agent of the URR — the visual sense of the production would

─────────────────────────

[6] Interviewed in *The Playwrights Speak*, ed. Walter Wager (New York: Hill and Wang, 1969), p. 82.

[7] Mordecai Gorelik, "Designing the Play" in *Producing the Play*, by John Gassner (New York: The Dryden Press, 1953), p. 314.

lend itself to a storylike theatrical quality. Written into the first draft, therefore, was the direction that the scenery (such as Brown's house and the tobacco factory) be suggested through spiraling levels, much as was done in the Broadway production of *The Me Nobody Knows*. I also suggested in the script that the chorus could make "human" representations of the various modes of transportation that would carry Brown to his destination. The chorus would become the moving wheels of the train, the waves upon which the ship travels, the ramps down which the box is rolled, and so forth. Thus, no clear-cut dramatic metaphor was evident during the first draft; rather, there was an eclectic potpourri of unified multimedia and "Open Theatre" devices.

While writing the second draft of the play, Fred Morsell (the director of the videotape based on the stage play) suggested a presentational style of staging reminiscent of the Broadway production of *Purlie Victorious* by Ossie Davis Jr., Gary Geld, and Peter Udell. The play would open in a Baptist church as choir members take off their robes and are transformed into characters from the past. The minister would become the Reverend William Still, the "conductor" of the Underground Railroad. All the props and costumes in the play would be stored in the pulpit to be used by the characters when the occasion arose. Furthermore, the pulpit itself would transform into the box in which Brown travels on his journey North.

As fascinating as I found this idea as a workable stage metaphor (Brown's transformation from slave to abolitionist expressed through the transformation of various scenic elements), the metaphor had to be abandoned in the third draft of the play. In fact, in this draft Brown's adventures continue beyond Richmond (where they had terminated in the second draft). It would be confusing for a child audience to see the pulpit transformed into the box and then again become the pulpit behind which Jonah and Henry ride during the final scene of the play. There would be too much blurring for a young audience of what is real and what is the fantasy application of reality.

The audience enjoyed seeing the actors transform their bodies into various modes of transportation during the URR song-and-dance sequence.

Because children enjoy seeing actors become "human" machines (such as giant computers, typewriters, and pencil sharpeners), the actors suggested the modes of transportation through movement and mime. This idea supports the metaphor that the Underground Railroad was not necessarily made up of real trains that traveled underground, but was composed of a network of human beings who risked great danger to help slaves to escape.

———————— JUST FOR YOU ————————

In your notebook or in your script, jot down some dramatic metaphors for your play. Describe them in stage directions or even draw them, no matter how rough the idea is. Jot down other ideas for finding story/stage visual equivalents.

IV. THEME

If you stick too closely to the original source you may not be able to express your own vision fully and create your own characters. Instead, you may find yourself reflecting the opinions, characters, and dialogue of the story's author.

A crucial question always is how closely one should adhere thematically to the original source.

I share Lehman Engel's beliefs concerning thematic fidelity to the original source. Referring to musical adaptation, Engel remarks that he is not necessarily in favor of using all the characters from the source in the new treatment; nor is he against adding nonexistent characters or making "changes in plot or structure." He continues: "To the contrary, these two latter procedures are often necessary. But I do object to discarding elements of the original which define the core of its idea, without which little or nothing remains . . . "[8]

Workers in the theatre generally agree that an author's idea (or an interpretation of that idea) behind the story should be reflected in the play's "theme." You can ask if you've retained the essential elements of the source material so that the audience

[8] Lehman Engel, *Words and Music* (New York: The Macmillan Co., 1972), p. 273.

will not be offended by the change (unless you intend the audience to be offended, startled, or aroused by the change).

In order to reflect the essence of the story's themes, you should be familiar with all you can about what is implied as well as written in the narrative source. What was the author's purpose in writing the original work? Was it the character development of a central character such as Oliver Twist, or to present a picture of a Biblical event as portrayed in *Joseph and the Amazing Technicolor Dreamcoat*, or a socially involving adventure tale such as *Nicholas Nickleby*? Many playwrights contend that whatever is felt to be the thematic core may be emphasized in the dramatic work.

On the other hand. there are playwrights who acknowledge that their responsibility to the original source ends with the adoption of the plot and chief character. From then on they think their main responsibility is to fashion a work of theatre that must be judged on its own merits as a play and not on its allegiance to the source. Especially if the source is biographical, the material will vary greatly according to the beliefs and attitudes and the style of writing of the playwright. Thus, the thematic interpretation of Joan of Arc as portrayed by Maxwell Anderson, Jean Anouilh, and George Bernard Shaw varies in accordance with the playwrights' personal style, country, religion, and moral beliefs.

The play will also be influenced by the form of play and theatrical image desired. Different works transformed from the same fictional material will naturally provide different theatrical effects.

It thus appears reasonable to assume that you can alter the narrative source as you interpret the material, yet still retain the essential theme of the work.

Though most often you will depict a theme that has universal content, it is equally true that you may attempt (consciously or unconsciously) to deflect some of this meaning onto the needs and desires of your audience. For example, the Tevye stories by Sholom Aleichem served as the basis from which Joseph Stein and the lyricist and composer created the book of *Fiddler on the Roof*. Like most playwrights working from derivative sources, Stein attempted in his own way to capture the essential theme and essence of the original work. Stein has

remarked that the adaptation problem was to be true to the spirit, the feeling of Sholom Aleichem and "transmute it for a contemporary audience . . . to relate the story of Tevye, his family, and his community in terms which would have relevance for today." One of the major themes of the original stories — the crumbling of tradition — is the one developed in the musical. [9]

How you treat your theme will be mostly affected by your vision and artistic choices. The adaptation of *Nicholas Nickleby* transferred the spirit of the novel onto a stage peopled with a large but imaginative cast. *The Brothers Karamazov*, with a large set of characters in the novel, only uses four actors in its stage version. The four actors play the brothers, and, because the action of the play is seen through their perspective, they also play their father as well as many other characters. Thus, the thematic spirit of the novel lives in an imaginative stage treatment. So, too, with *Strider*. The beautiful stage production is based on a story by Leo Tolstoy and was first adapted by Mark Rozovsky, keeping intact the story and theme of man's inhumanity to man and how humanity can soar in the face of cruelty and adversity. The story of how an old brokendown piebald workhorse keeps his spirit high has also been captured in the new English version by Robert Kalfin and Steve Brown, and the theme has been brought to life with an inventive presentational setting and staging encompassing mime, movement, and dance.

IN SUM

In this chapter we have discussed specific problems and solutions that occur during the transformation of story to stage including the alteration, addition, and deletion of material in the original source.

If a sufficient and significant number of incidents from the narrative source are kept essentially intact, the play can be considered a dramatization. The terms "based on" or "suggested by" involve more radical changes of plot or characterization. An

[9] Stanley Richards, ed., *Best Plays of the Sixties* (Garden City: Doubleday and Company, 1970), p. 242.

adaptation is somewhat closer to the original material, but it can take greater liberties with character, plot, and theme than does a dramatization.

In all three transformation processes, judicious selection and arrangement of incidents and characters present the primary challenge to the playwright.

Your dramatization will most often start near a point of conflict, move progressively forward, and result in a climax developed through well-motivated characterizations.

Dialogue may have to be adjusted or wholly invented, yet it should retain the flavor of the narrative unless the story is updated or contemporized. Setting and locales found in the narrative should be transformed into a suitable stage metaphor.

Examples were offered from some of my repertory to show the kinds of problems that may come up during the transformation process in the areas of plotting, characterization, dialogue, and settings. Though a play may retain the essence of the narrative's theme, it ultimately must be viewed on its own merits as a play and not as a story or novel.

The Emcee with two Kit Kat Kittens in *Cabaret* (book by Joe Masteroff; music and lyrics by Kander and Ebb). See Research, page 144.

PLAYWRIGHT'S PAGE

1) Who is your favorite character in your stage transformation? How does he or she differ from the character in the original source?

2) Do you think you have enough plot to carry forward the progression of dramatic action? Is there too little plot? Too much? How can you make the adjustments?

3) What dialogue adjustments did you have to make from story to stage?

4) After a first draft of your script, can you state what its theme is? How does this differ from the theme — as you interpret it — in the original source?

5) In the future, what other stories would you like to transform to the stage?

MORE **RAW** MATERIALS

Read . . . Encore: According to the critic, playwright, and director Walter Kerr, if a novel is a "grand tour," then a play is like a "mine shaft." Do you agree? Why or why not? Think of a novel you have read. Do you think it could make a play? Why or why not?

Act . . . Select a short story. With a group of friends/colleagues act some of it out. Break the story down into scenes. Then assign characters. When you enact the scenes, be mindful of:

- Who you are (physical and vocal traits)
- What you want (character goal)
- Where you are (environment)
- The beginning, middle, and end

Write . . . Individually or together, write out the scenes that emerged from the story. Another way is to audiotape the scenes and write out the dialogue.

After reading this chapter, take another look at the comparisons of the story and play versions of "The Devil and Daniel Webster" in Chapter Two.

——— SUGGESTIONS FOR CLASSROOM ACTIVITIES ———

Discuss . . . in small groups or with a partner
- plays and movies you have seen which are based on novels or stories. What do you think worked in the adaptation? What did *not* work and why? What are some of the factors that go into a stage or movie adaptation? For example: How the number of characters, or actors needed to play them, affects the choices a writer has to make; consideration of settings and the cost to reproduce them in a film; amount of time that can be given in the drama to plot elements in the novel or story. What happens when a narrative form is transformed into a dramatic form? What may be lost? Gained? Changed? Give some examples from stage and movie adaptations you have seen or read.
- your ideas about a favorite story, novel, song, poem could be adapted for a staged play. How would you try to best convey in dramatic terms what the theme of the novel or story is trying to say?

Read . . .
- aloud some of the group's ideas for an adaptation. Perhaps one of these ideas might make a good basis for a group-written play.
- how playwrights have adapted novels and stories, such as Arthur Laurents' account of how he adapted *Romeo and Juliet* into *West Side Story* in his autobiography *Original Story By*. Why is the music important?
- plays that have been adapted from stories and novels such as *The Grapes of Wrath, Les Miserables, Of Mice and Men, Pride and Prejudice* and *Showboat*.

> NOTEBOOK (OR JOURNAL) FEATURE
> Jot down your ideas and bits of dialogue for an adaptation you might like to do some day. Why do you think the story, novel, poem, or song that you have chosen would be good for this? Would you still call it by its original title? What characters would you cut, change, combine or even add? Why?

Research . . . the transformation of *Cabaret* from the John van Druten stage play *I Am a Camera,* which, in turn, was adapted from "The Berlin Stories" by Christopher Isherwood. You may wish to use the jigsaw technique. Divide the group into three subgroups (the musical version, stage play, and short story) to research and report on the process of adaptation. (Future screenwriters, check out the film adaptation and report on the process.)

Act . . . out different versions of the same scene of a novel or story. How do they differ? How are they the same?

Write, with a partner or by yourself, the improvised scene you acted out. At a later time, you and some partners may wish to adapt some short stories (possibly by the same author) and string them together to make an evening of theatre. The actors can play multiple roles, perhaps one being the author who would tie the stories together with a narrative or comment, as does Anton Chekhov in *The Good Doctor* in Neil Simon's stage adapation of a number of Chekhov's short stories.

chapter X

OPPORTUNITIES IN THE THEATRE

The reward of a thing well done is to have done it. — Emerson

Writing is rewriting. — Everyone

Now that you have finished your play (with the above thought about rewriting in mind) you can begin exploring production and market possibilities. You may also wish to investigate other kinds of writing. In this chapter, we ask:

- What are some specific workshop, production, and market opportunities for your play?
- In addition to the more traditional forms of playwriting, what are some other kinds of dramatic writing you can explore? These forms include revues, one-person shows, docudramas, story theatre, and multimedia possibilities.

PRODUCTION POSSIBILITIES

Workshops

If your play has been read by friends or in a classroom setting with an eye to steady improvement, you may feel ready for some kind of production. The best place to start is right in your community, perhaps in your school or community center with a workshop production.

Many fine productions have started as workshops. Probably one of the most famous of these is *A Chorus Line*, which kicked off with a group of actors experimenting over a long period of time in workshops sponsored by the New York Shakespeare Festival. *Nicholas Nickleby* (dramatized by David Edgar) began its successful history in a workshop in Stratford, England. *Joseph and the Amazing Technicolor Dreamcoat* got its start in a boys' school in England and developed over the years into its present form.

Check with the production facility in your school or community on the possibility of having your play done in a workshop. Perhaps with some actor friends you can first get a public staged reading or a public performance that goes beyond a reading.

Public Staged Reading

By way of example, one of my playwriting students, Martha Santer, had her play *Office Work* (which explores interpersonal relationships in an insurance office as six co-workers vie for much more than self-esteem and promotion) done in a public staged reading at the Impossible Ragtime Theatre as pan of their TNT series.

Although actors hold scripts in a staged reading, an artistic attempt at characterization is valid. Actors may occasionally "drop script" and interact in certain scenes or have exchanges of memorized dialogue.

According to Ms. Santer:

Many good things come out of this experience. Through hearing *Office Work* read aloud by a full cast, I caught dull spots and repetitions, plus I experienced an audience's reaction to my work.

I immediately learned many things. For example, I realized that I'd underestimated the significance of Thomas, the corporate spy, to the plot. Katherine was too innocent for what she had to do. And Suzanne was sometimes too mysterious when directness would be more effective.

The director and audience gave me specific feedback and asked me many questions. The responses included: the end came too fast; there's too much telephone ringing; when are we supposed to realize that Thomas is a spy?

I was forced to think about and articulate what the central conflict is; what story do I really want to tell? What do I want the audience to get? More specifically, what was really happening between Dougherty and his wife, and why can't I give him a name the actors can pronounce?

Although *Office Work* was underwritten, TNT showed me the play's potential and gave me plenty to go on. In addition, other theatres showed interest in my work; and the attention, in general, boosted my confidence.

Public Performances

Jean Reynolds, who had been my student at Hunter College, wrote the play *Matches* with Peter Schumann.

According to the authors, *Matches* is a six-character comedy about three marriages (or one). The action takes place in the lounge of a tennis club. All six characters are on stage throughout the action. The couples, all dressed in tennis attire, are: Mary-Ellen and Jean-Luc, married approximately ten years, who engage in sophisticated game-playing (we do not mean this negatively): Lois and Hank, married approximately five years, who are having growing pains: and Betty and Frank, who meet and marry during the course of the play and enjoy the first blush of love.

Many of the group scenes have overlapping realities, which can be carefully choreographed for a delightful effect. *Matches* contains many "private moments in public." During rehearsals, the actors and director discovered which of those moments are heard by characters involved in the moment and which are not. Here is how that process evolved. The play was developed over the year in a series of actor workshops and then had a public performance directed by Alan Wynroth. Ms. Reynolds continues:

Peter and I were part of a play-reading group that met regularly at my apartment. Members were actors, writers, directors, and interested parties we had known and/or worked with. *Matches* came from this group. Peter and I wrote the scenes, had them read, discussed them, and then rewrote. Eventually, the play became part of the Open Eye's New Stagings Lab. It was also performed as a workshop production at the Williamstown Summer Theatre Festival.

We were particularly interested in overlapping realities and the use of contrapuntal voices. In workshop situations, these elements could be tested and reworked.

As a result of the stagings at The Open Eye, *Matches* is now being considered for Cable TV production.

We might mention that a cable television outlet in your community may be in the market for a good script. This possibility is definitely worth checking in your community or college.

Musical Productions

The musical is an exciting form because it involves the widest use of theatre convention: bold and quick-cutting leaps through space and time, expressionistic or theatrical settings, dynamism of rhythm in music and dance. Direct contact with audiences is exciting as the stage comes alive with transformational surprises. With all this freedom, you still need a solid structure, as we have shown with examples from *My Fair Lady* and other musicals. According to Lehman Engel, musical stage works cannot exist without feeling as one of the most basic elements. [1]

Paul Golob, one of my students in the Hunter College Gifted Youth Drama Program, wrote a musical that was performed at Stuyvesant High School when he was a student there.

According to Golob:

---

[1] Lehman Engel, *Words and Music*, p. 58.

I'd like to discuss one particular piece of dialogue in the play's first scene that illustrates our creative process. But first a little background information on the plot of *To Hell With Heaven*. The play is the story of two young professional people, George Atrick and Geraldine Simmons. Finding themselves in a hospital, they independentally recount the last thing they remember driving along the highway before getting into a car crash. After their attendants leave, George and Geri meet and get to know each other without discovering that they had crashed into each other earlier in the day, and there were no survivors. George and Geri are not in a hospital after all; they are in a checkpoint station between heaven and hell. The stage partition takes on a new importance when it is revealed that it divides those persons bound for heaven from those hell-ward bound.

The couple's hostility is complicated by the appearance of two new characters, George's mother, who died the minute she heard about George's accident and proceeds to subject her son to an unmitigated barrage of nagging; and Geri's fiance, a rock guitarist who took an overdose of cocaine upon hearing the news of Geri's death and becomes obsessed with crossing the uncrossable barrier and breaking George's skull as retribution for causing the accident.

I asked Paul to talk about some of the problems he had writing the script. He continues:

One of the first problems we encountered was to present the car crash to the audience in a way that was dramatically feasible and entertaining. Just having George and Geri talk about the accident would become boring after a while. We decided to tell the story musically, with George and Geri alternating stanzas: and the attendants punctuating the melody with half-sung questions and exclamations. We were also able to add a touch of comedy by having the crash occur as the two characters rush to appointments with their respective analysts. This system seemed to work well, and Steve [co-author Steve Newman] and I were able to write the first two verses of "To My

Analyst" very quickly.

The problem of dramatically representing the crash, however, persisted. The verses we wrote merely set the scene but could not convey the necessary drama and tension of the actual crash. To remedy the situation, we decided to insert about a minute of spoken dialogue between the second and third verses of the song. In this way, we were able to switch back and forth between George's and Geri's version of the story while the piano dramatically underscored the dialogue. We could then write a third verse (sung by the attendants), which sort of summed up the predicament. We finished the song a couple of days later and proceeded to work on the interior dialogue. I really didn't know the best way to go about writing dialogue (we hadn't written any yet) so we relied on a method we were both familiar with — improvisation. We would sing through the song, with Steve and me taking either George's or the attendants' part; my sister Stephanie sang Geri's part. When we reached the dialogue, the two actors playing George would improvise a "dialogue." (Actually, George and Geri are interrupting each other's monologue to his or her respective attendants). We tape-recorded each of these improvisations, weeded out the lines that didn't work, and made a note to keep those that did.

We used this process of improvising, editing, and rerecording for about a month, composing two other songs during that time. Only after we finished those songs did we begin to write dialogue in earnest. At this time, I listened to the extant recordings, put in some ideas of my own, and transcribed this new version of the dialogue onto paper. After some editing and revising by both Steve and myself, the dialogue took shape as a dramatically effective portrayal of the car crash. The background music complements the words perfectly, pushing the audience to the edge of their seats by the time George's line "Oh no! We're going to . . . !" brings back the regular music and lyrics for the third verse.

"To My Analyst" [lyrics by Paul Golob, music by Steve Newman], complete with the interior dialogue, was the product of a process that proves not only that good acting in a play can be a result of good writing, but also that good writing can be a result of the versatile acting abilities of the writers.

Experimental Drama Workshops

You may decide on your own method of working, which may develop through research and improvisation.

The play *My Immediate Intensity*, for example, was not written in the conventional sense. My colleague Roberto Monticello, an accomplished and prolific playwright, had conducted drama workshops in a mental institution. Audiotapes were made of some of these sessions. Later, Monticello worked with professional actresses who at one time or another had been institutionalized. These actresses listened to the audiotapes and, together with Monticello, worked out a dramatic format based on but not limited to the audiotapes. In this way, they artistically "treated" the source material. The "text" was composed out of transcripts from actual drama workshops conducted by Monticello.

According to Monticello: "In using the 'script,' the task was to find the irrational logical that opens up into a veritable explosion of revelations about the true nature of the characters. The play was a recreation—a vision reenacted—with very few allowances made for conventional performances/audience relationship purposes." Monticello continues:

The patients in the mental institutions had a tendency to overact, underact, change their roles throughout the plays, refuse to go on with it, establish relationships that they "forget" later, forget what was happening and start the play over and over again, dealing with each other from different levels of reality, at the same time revealing deeply felt sentiments of love, need, loneliness, desire and, ultimately, the state of the human condition.

The process which the actors recreated has been remarkable. We've been exalted, scared, desperately cynical. conciliatory, idealistic, threatened, hateful . . . but somehow, always hopeful and conscious of how lucky we are to have each other m this terribly difficult and demanding work. This is

not a finished product. There could never be a finished product. Artists can create from a sense of indignation.

Additional Workshops

Even when your play has had a production, you may wish to continue working on it. The initial reviews of *Annie* were dismal when it was first tried out at the Goodspeed Opera House. But with additional long, hard work of testing and reshaping the show, the rough edges were worked out. Michael Weller's off-Broadway play *Split*, after its first run, was redone at The Second Stage in New York for further reevaluation and reworking.

After reworking your play you may wish to try it at still another workshop and get additional perspective on it. Many theatre companies, such as Playwrights Horizon, at 416 West 42nd Street, New York, NY 10036 and others in your area may have workshop facilities. You may wish to send them your script. Martha Santer's *Office Work* was rejected by over twenty production companies before it was finally accepted for a reading by TNT at The Impossible Ragtime Theatre. One open door can lead to many other possibilities. Keep trying!

MARKET POSSIBILITIES

After you have had a successful workshop, staged reading, or public performance, you can attempt to market your script. It is always preferable to submit a manuscript through a recognized agent. Usually, agents will look only at scripts that have had some kind of production. Scripts must be submitted to agents in the acceptable script form (see, for example, Appendix A) and be accompanied by a self-addressed stamped envelope (SASE). For a list of recognized play agents consult *The Literary Market Place*. The following are excellent sources of play publishers as well as play contests:

1) *Literary Market Place*, R. R. Bowker Company, 1180 Avenue of the Americas, New York, NY 10036.
2) *Dramatists Source Book,* eds. Kathy Sova, Samantha R. Healy, Jenifer Sokolof, New York:

Theatre Communications Group, 2001
3) *Playwright's Companion*, ed. Molie Ann Meserve. New York: Feedback Theatrebooks, 1998.
4) *Writer's Digest* & *Writer's Market*, 9933 Alliance Road, Cincinnati, OH 45242.
5) *Writer*, 8 Arlington Street, Boston, MA 02116.

Make sure you first write to the publisher regarding the suitability of your script. Most publishers have specific needs at specific times. For example, publishers such as Samuel French avoid large-cast plays. This publisher considers ten or more actors a large cast. Large-cast plays suitable for junior and senior high school production are sought by Plays, Inc. and The Dramatic Publishing Company.

Contact Theatre Communications Group (T.C.G., 355 Lexington Avenue, New York, NY 10017) about their publication Information for Playwrights. The Dramatists Guild of America also has valuable information for members. Their address is 1501 Broadway, New York, NY 10036. Also check New Dramatists, 424 West 44th Street, New York, NY 10036 for valuable information.

If you are serious about the theatre, you should consider joining The American Alliance for Theatre and Education, c/o Dept. of Theatre, Arizona State University, Tempe, AZ 85287, and the Educational Theatre Association, 2343 Auburn Avenue, Cincinnatti, OH 45219. Also seek information concerning the Eugene O'Neill Memorial Theatre Center, 305 Great Neck Road, Waterford, CT 06385, and the National Playwrights Conference, 1680 Broadway, Suite 601, New York, NY 10023; the Williamstown Theatre Festival at Williams College, Williamstown, Mass. 11267 (403-597-3131). Also look into the Center for Creative Youth at Wesleyan College: The Russell House, 350 High Street, Middletown, CT 06454 (860-685-3307). Please consult the Internet for additional summer stock opportunities. A theatre in your community may have a mentoring program, in which professional playwrights, directors, or dramaturgs guide new playwrights.

Contests

Scripts for playwriting contests do not have to be submitted through agents. There are numerous contests both for one-act and full-length plays. I broke into the field of playwriting through entering a national contest, which I won. Seeing my first play performed was truly an exciting experience. Probably the best-known contest is the annual Great American Play Contest sponsored by the Actors Theatre of Louisville. Scripts must be unproduced and unpublished. Send your script (with SASE), to Contest, Actors Theater, 316 West Main Street, Louisville, KT 40202.

Also check out the exciting Young Playwrights, Inc., which was founded by Stephen Sondheim in 1981. Young Playwrights, Inc. sponsors playwriting contests for young people, a Young Playwrights Festival in New York, and playwriting instruction. For more information on Young Playwrights, Inc., call 212-307-1140, or write to them at 306 West 38th Street, Suite 300, New York, N.Y. 10018. E-mail: writeaplay@aol.com. The Young Playwrights website address is: www.youngplaywrights.org.

Announcements of playwriting contests regularly appear in *The Writer* magazine, *Writers Market*, *Literary Market*, and *Backstage* (330 West 42nd Street, New York, NY 10036). If you have home or school access to the Internet, feel free to search the Web for playwriting contests information. However, before entering any contest, write to the theatre or sponsor for the contest guidelines and enclose a SASE (self-addressed stamped envelope). Some contests charge a fee. Always make sure a contest is legitimate before submitting your play — and money.

REVUES

If you are in between plays, you might consider writing shorter pieces with some collaborators.

Revues have always been a popular form of theatre in England and in this country. A revue is a series of skits, sketches, and songs that hinge on a particular theme. The New Faces series, produced by Leonard Sillman, consisted of satirical sketches, energetic dances, and new songs. They were popular from 1934 to 1968, with perhaps the most successful year being New Faces of 1958 (featuring Eartha Kitt, Alice Ghostley, and Paul Lynde). *Oh, Calcutta*

Revues reflect a variety of subjects, themes, and forms. The popular *One Mo' Time*, for example, is a 1920's black vaudeville musical with a New Orleans jazz flavor.

and One Mo' Time are other examples of revues centered around a theme. Some revues are worked out through improvisations and then scripted. My students at Hunter College, for example, devised revues with a "magazine" format. *Hot Headlines*, for instance, featured various "departments" of a newspaper: Letters to the Editor; Horrorscopes; Faces and Places in the News. *Dragons and Daffodils*, another revue, centered on the fantasy worlds of children.

Subject-to-Change, a New York-based comedy ensemble, performs revues based on eccentric twists in everyday life. One skit, for instance, entitled "The Shrink," concerns a patient in a psychiatrist's office. The patient strolls in feeling great, but leaves in a totally unnerved condition. Why? The shrink's efforts to make her patient talk about his problems has turned him into a sniveling neurotic.

For a group like Subject-to-Change it is important to be writing new material all the time. Having a steady flow of new material gives the group more opportunities to improve a show and to create new ones. But getting the juices flowing is another question altogether. Here's how one of the founders, Irwin Kuperberg, describes the group's creative process:

Since we all started out as amateurs it was very hard, at first, to write anything. It is one thing to have a funny idea, but quite another to translate that idea into a script which is later turned into a scene. Our method for doing this came through trial-and-error. After preparing a few scenes we started to ask ourselves questions like: Which were successful? What was good about them? How can we duplicate the successful elements? In addition the three of us who formed the writing core of the group (Mike Dash, Wendy Schecter, and me) began to look at what our individual talents were: How could each of us fit most effectively into the writing process':

One of the Subject-to-Change's most popular scenes is entitled "Houseplants," a piece in which a group of houseplants on a windowsill come to life and say what is really on their minds. It began as an idea suggested by Mike. "How about a scene about talking plants?" (We have a file of all the ideas that ever pop into our heads.)

We sat down and thought about plants that lend themselves to certain personality types. A prayer plant could be pious. An English ivy could have a Cockney accent. A cactus could be prickly, irritable. Then we wrote character sketches for each one. We tried as completely as possible to define the character's personality. The clearer this was at the beginning, the easier it would be to know what everyone was going to say. As guides we thought not only of what such plants might be like if they were real, but what each member of the group could add.

With the characters established, we created a dialogue between the plants, from which emerged a very interesting variety of contrasts and conflicts.

Finally, the whole group read through the scene with our director, who was able to help all the players discover the essence of their characters and the funniest interpretation of the scene. An important part of this process was experimentation through improvisation. It gave us the opportunity to try out different possibilities and sometimes gave better results than the original material as written.

Audience Participation Revues
"What Do You Do?" [3]

This is a revue that involves a high degree of audience participation. Each week an ensemble of actors present a new topic on a theme, setting (place), prop, or character. Those weekly themes include the World of Work, Public Places, Relationships, School Days, and Fantasies. Each skit is enacted in an appropriate theatre style: musical, comedy, suspense, slapstick, Greek tragedy, horror movie, and so forth. Here is an example of one such format:

Title: "Saturday Night Never?"
Style: Melodrama
Situation: Your boss demands that you come in (Saturday) and get the work done. Your (boy) (girl) friend, who is a news reporter and whom you have not seen in for a bit, calls to say he or she is on his or her way in to spend the day with you. The players enact the skit to a certain open-ended point. The audience is then given four choices:

What Do You Do?
a. Tell him or her you have to work.
b. Call your boss and tell him or her you're sick.
c. Tell him or her to go to the museum and you will see him or her later.
d. Take him or her to work with you.

The audience indicates which ending they would like to see enacted, and the ensemble obliges.

— JUST FOR YOU AND OTHERS TOO —
With some friends/writing colleagues, think of an idea for a topical or satirical revue. Will it be a "collage," a series of vignettes, or what? Jot down some ideas and see if you can come up with a theme.

ONE-PERSON SHOWS

An imaginative two-character play by Amlin Gray entitled *How I Got That Story* got its start as a one-person show in a workshop at the Court Street Theatre of the Milwaukee Repertory Theatre and was later produced at The Second Stage in New York. Gray had a file box of ideas, including a few based on his experiences serving in Vietnam. But none of the ideas seemed to jell. Then he got the idea for a play in which a naive American journalist (The Reporter) is dispatched to mythical Am-bo Land (Vietnam) and encounters twenty-one characters including Madame Ivy, the green-eyed, long-nailed dictator; cynical American officers; Vietnamese call girls; guerrilla soldiers; and a monk who undergoes self-immolation. The surprising thing is that all these characters are played by one person; in effect, The Reporter confronts a whole Historical Event.

The show inventively incorporates elements of realism, adventure, and farce. The stage is fluidly transformed into many scenes, from a dark barroom to a bright hospital to a fetid jungle, using Open Theatre techniques. Some scenes last only 30 seconds, and the longest is ten minutes,

Many one- or two-person shows center around an anthology theme, for example, women characters from Shakespeare's repertory. Other formats have a biographical basis; for example, *Mark Twain Tonight*, *Sojourner Truth*, *Paul Robeson*, or *By George* (George Kaufman). One- or two-person shows generally use very few props or only key ones (in Kaufman's, a phone). The shows are sometimes accompanied by piano, guitar, or other instruments. Sometimes the shows incorporate mixed-media effects, such as slides.

Here is how Jerome Rockwood created his exciting one-person show *Poe*.

One-person shows are a creative and challenging form of playwriting. Here actor-author Jerome Rockwood appears as the title character in *Poe.*

I wanted to do something that would be more than a series of readings of Poe material. I wanted to get inside the man: his life was extraordinary — tortured, wretched. I wanted my show to be a play about his life, his struggles to be recognized, his eventual destruction. I put together pieces of his stories, letters, essays, and interwove them in a way that caused light to be shed on his life . . . bits of his letters reflect on why he wrote certain pieces, and by placing them next to each other,

one illuminates the other. It is a rather impressionistic evening, with the reality of his letters blending into the fantasy of a story or poem. I have beautiful background music composed and performed by a colleague on the bass recorder . . . fellow named Tom Wilt. (See Appendix E, page 179, for more on one-person shows.)

——— JUST FOR YOU ———
Do you have an idea for a one-person show? Would you yourself like to perform it? What will it be about? Something that takes place in the past—present—future??

DOCUDRAMAS

If your source is historical, you may decide to use facts as the springboard and not necessarily the substance of your drama. Henry James thought writers had an obligation to follow the truth strictly when recreating history. Others object to writers who take liberties with history and fiction and evade the responsibility of both genres.

Most workers in the theatre generally agree that arranging the facts of history for theatrical purposes does not cause problems for the viewer, who does not have the facts in hand and therefore cannot judge their accuracy. Thus, theatregoers will not be affected by the exact way Shakespeare has Richard III ascend his throne or by the fact that there were 56 signers of the Declaration of Independence and not the dozen or so represented in the musical *1776*. (The essence of the musical is historically accurate, yet it removes the signers of the Declaration from their pedestals and characterizes them and the events surrounding the Continental Congress as very human.)

With emotionally controversial subject matter, however, the issue of historical accuracy is more complicated. Plays about topics such as the Rosenbergs, J. Robert Oppenheimer, and Pius XII's moral responsibility for some of the cruelties of the Third Reich have stirred a hornet's nest of controversy.

In these cases, are the facts being used as the springboard for a play or as the play's substance? Martin B. Duberman wrote the docudrama *In White America* for the stage because he "wanted to combine the evocative power of the spoken word with the confirming power of historical fact . . . to some extent professional history, which aims at the comprehensive, and professional theatre, which relies on selection, are at cross-purposes. A docu-mentary play... must somehow be both good history and theatre . . . " [4]

Another playwright who uses factual material in his plays, Rolf Hochhuth, explains his creative process:

> . . . To intuitively combine the already available fact into a truthful whole becomes the noble and rarely realized function of art. Precisely because he is faced with such a plethora of raw material, as well as with such difficulties in collating it, the writer must hold fast to his freedom which alone empowers him to fit form to the matter . . . [5]

In developing the theme of guilt and individual responsibility during World War II, Hochhuth, author of *The Deputy*, explains that ". . . the action does not follow the historical course of events in a step-by-step manner, like a journalist's account. Condensation has been necessary in the interests of drama... for as far as possible I adhere to the facts; I had to transform the existing raw material of history into drama. Reality was represented throughout, but much of the slag had to be removed. [6]

In summary, therefore, it is safe to say that the playwright can take certain liberties with events based on historical and biographical fact. You do not have to be bound by every aspect and fact of a character's life. Weed out extraneous facts or adjust them honestly. In making your theme come alive then, you may highlight certain aspects of the story and characters and mold them into a work of art as long as you hold true to the soul or essence of characters and events. Never sacrifice the truth of life to the illusion of art.

Example of Docudrama Format
The drama club at JHS 50 in New York, under my direction, devised a docudrama called *A Man Called MARC* (Vito Marcantonio's nickname).

In devising the docudrama, three possibilities

[4] Martin B. Duberman, preface, *In White America* (New York: The New American Library, 1964).

[5] Rolf Hochhuth, "Sidelights on History," *The Deputy* (Grove Press, 1964), p. 288.

[6] Ibid., p. 287.

came into focus:

1) real people in fictional situations
2) imaginary people in real events
3) imaginary people in imaginary situations

All three choices were used. The program, which features drama, dance, and music, was divided into four sections: M for Man (an overview of Marc's life); A for American (his early life in Harlem); R for Radical (how he struggled against great odds to help poor people in his district); and C for Congressman (his work for social legislation). There were four large squares, each with one of the letters on it. At the end of the program, these squares were turned around, placed together, and a full, large photo of Marcantonio materialized. The opening of that script is presented below.

STORY THEATRE

Story theatre was created and developed by Paul Sills as a concept and technique in which the char-

---

JHS 50 PERFORMERS present A MAN CALLED MARC

NARRATION	*ACTIONS*
THE TIMELESS RIVER COURSES ITS WAY ALONG THE EAST SIDE OF MANHATTAN	Make mirror images
	Ensemble becomes a river (bodies and blue fabric)
	Two players become Sun (red fabric)
CARRYING WITH IT... MEMORIES OF THE EARLIEST AMERICANS RESPECTING ITS SPLENDID BEAUTY. SLOWLY, ON THE SHORES OF THE RIVER, A CITY ROSE AND THE RIVER WAS NEVER THE SAME . . .	Four players become native Indians sitting at bank of River (rest of players) looking at river.
	River transforms into "sounds and sights of city" machine. Indians transform into buildings.
	Buildings transform into polluted river (blue materials)
ON DECEMBER 10, 1902, A CHILD WAS BORN TO MR. AND MRS. SAM MARCANTONIO ON 112TH STREET AND FIRST AVENUE.	River and Machine transform into baptismal scene. River becomes water and machine becomes:

(blue fabric)	Father Mother Priest Neighbors

Need: Dialogue

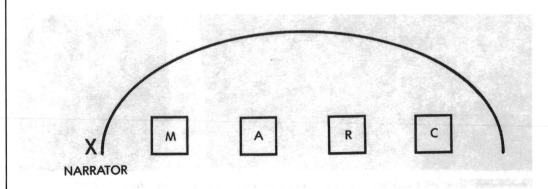

X
NARRATOR

The full scenario may be found in Appendix G

In story theatre, actors tell a story with a variety of nonverbal communication techniques. Here Valerie Harper and Paul Sands use pantomime in *The Golden Goose.*

acters refer to themselves in the third person. Each actor narrates the story in the third person while enacting the part of one of the characters.

For example, at the start of a story theatre version of Hans Christian Andersen's "The Emperor's New Clothes," an actor might enter wearing fancy clothes and announce to the audience, "Many years ago there was an emperor so fond of fine clothes that all his money was spent on them." A small three-piece combo off to one side of the stage might establish a courtly classical mood. The actor playing the emperor continues the story: "He had a different suit for every hour of the day."

Thus, the actor starts the story as an objective narrator but at the same time assumes the traits of the character. For example, the emperor might continue pantomiming putting on clothes or looking into the mimed royal closet. At this point three actors would enter and continue the story:

MINISTER #1: When anybody asked where he was, the answer was not . . .
MINISTER #2: With his wise counselors in the council room . . .
MINISTER #3: But in his dressing room . . .

(Here we might have some pantomine showing the three ministers huddling together officially, while on the other side of the stage the emperor would dismiss court business in favor of trying on more clothes.)

Now two of the actors, instead of continuing the narrative thread, could break into first-person "invented" dialogue:

MINISTER #1: Looks like the emperor needs some new clothes.
MINISTER #2: I know. Two strangers are outside . . . they claim they have some special thread.

Then the two rascal weavers enter, each narrating part of the story and acting roles in it. These actors assume their first-person dialogue only after they have introduced themselves in the third person.

Additionally, some of the less-used actors might become some of the key objects in the story: for example, a throne for the emperor, or the door to the closet, or the actual loom for weaving the cloth.

In story theatre, a great deal of fluidity can be conveyed on stage by cutting through the time-and-space restrictions a traditional play might face. For example, the story "The Devil and Daniel Webster" could be done effectively in story theatre format. *Example of Correct Story Theatre Format.* "The Golden Bird" adapted for the stage by Helen Scourby, one of my former students, from the story in the Grimm Fairy Tales Collection:

(Golden Princess & Golden Prince (Fox) Enter U.R.; cross U.R.C.)

GOLDEN PRINCESS & GOLDEN PRINCE
Once upon a time . . .

GOLDEN PRINCE (Fox)
There was a young prince . . .

GOLDEN PRINCESS
And a young princess . . .

GOLDEN PRINCESS & GOLDEN PRINCE
(Fox) Who lived in a beautiful golden palace, and loved to take long walks together in the forest next to their father's land . . .

GOLDEN PRINCESS
And pick wildflowers . . .

GOLDEN PRINCE (Fox)
To decorate their rooms.

(Golden King enters U.R. crosses U.R.C. to R. of Prince and Princess.)

GOLDEN KING
But their father had warned them, "Never go into the land at the North end of the forest, because it belongs to the wicked witch who does evil deeds to anyone who trespasses on her property."

GOLDEN PRINCE AND GOLDEN PRINCESS
And they said, "Of course, father, we will follow your advice and never go there." (Golden King exits U.R.)

GOLDEN PRINCESS
But one day the Golden Princess was sick. "Oh, my head hurts, and I can't stop sneezing." (She sneezes.) "I think I'll go to bed." (She sneezes herself offstage & exits U.R.)

GOLDEN PRINCE (Fox)
And the Golden Prince thought, "I shall take a walk and find the most unusual wildflower to bring to my sister as a present." He walked and he walked through the forest. (He walks around and around the stage in a huge circle.)

─────────── JUST FOR YOU ───────────

Do you have a favorite story that you think would lend itself especially well to story theatre? Who will be the central and opposing characters? Can you articulate the conflict and theme? What visual ideas do you have for your approach?

──────────────────────────────────

MIXED-MEDIA ELEMENTS

The creative mixture of dance, shadow theatre, large and/or small puppets, music, and other elements can produce truly creative dividends. It is important, however, that the multimedia elements not be used haphazardly just for the sake of making a great effect. Any and all effects must be organically worked into the entire concept of the show with thought and design. For example, Peter Schumann and his Bread and Puppet Theatre Company are masters of integrating stunning visual wizardry with meaningful content. I recall seeing a beautiful Christmas show in which Joseph and Mary were portrayed as little puppets, being refused entry into a cozy inn. At other times, you will see Peter and his troupe on stilts as giants or as a vivid mounted horse-and-rider, accompanied by a spirited band. André Gregory's *Alice in Wonderland* [Manhattan Theatre Project] involved all kinds of visual treats including inventive uses of actors' bodies (e.g., croquet wickets and balls).

The summer I was writing this book a creative group of youngsters (living in Croton Park Colony in Peekskill, N.Y.) under my direction devised a show improvisationally called "Pinocchio Goes to Peekskill." Pinocchio, played by a seven-year-old, can't make up his mind whether or not to go to a summer camp in America. A rep from the camp visits Geppetto's toy shop and shows Pinocchio a slide show (featuring the actors in the show as themselves) of camp activities. Pinocchio is still not impressed, but is willing to go if he can take along some of the toys in the toyshop. One of the toys (live actors), a pet frog, breaks, and while it is being fixed, Geppetto puts on a puppet play showing how Pinocchio came to be. Thus the live Pinocchio and puppets were integrated into the theme involving community participation.

You may enjoy experimenting with ways in which you can incorporate mixed-media elements even for a select portion of your play. For example, when director Tom O'Horgan directed *Lenny* [Bruce], he began the production with the mythic presentation of primitive censorship (huge fantastic creatures) performed in dance and stunning mime ritual.

IN SUM AND LOOKING AHEAD

Coming back to the primitive origins of drama reminds us that the history of playwriting has always been an experimental adventure in search of new directions.

In this chapter we have talked about such forms as revues, musical productions, docudramas, experimental drama, one-person shows, story theatre, and mixed-media possibilities. We have also discussed workshop and market possibilities for your first play.

Now that you have completed your play, you can look forward to new plays and varied writing experiences. Keep stretching your imagination, exploring your feelings, searching for new forms as you focus on dramatic stories. My colleagues and good friends Howard Berland and Mark Berman, who have attempted virtually every form—mysteries, comedies, historical pieces, dramas, musicals — recommend that playwrights use the same strategy to develop skills. You may also wish to investigate the possibility of writing for radio and the television and film media.

I recall being greatly moved by Edward Albee's stunning play *The Zoo Story*, a realistic, compassionate two-character play. Several decades later I enjoyed another work by Albee, *Seascape*, with a completely different form — a play about a couple of humans transforming into lizards through a fantastic process of evolution. Albee's playwriting process has been equally fascinating to observe through the years, as he continues to explore a rich variety of themes and styles. When I first began playwriting, 1 recall seeing a rather pleasant, "well-made" play called *Five Finger Exercise* by Peter Shaffer. Through the years I have been touched by Shaffer's expanding virtuosity revealed in such beautiful plays as *The Royal Hunt of the Sun, Black Comedy, Equus, and Amadeus.*

But rewarding as most well-known plays are, what I most look forward to is the work of unknown, arising playwrights — including yours!

In the years I have been teaching playwriting I have marveled at the progress of writers (some of whose work is reported in this chapter), searching for new themes and exciting ways to express them.

I hope that you and I will have an opportunity to carry on the dialogue we started at the beginning of this book:

MEP: (Brightly.) Well, hello-goodbye.
YOU: (Guarded excitement.) I want to show you something . . .
MEP: I have an idea . . .
YOU: (Proudly taking out ms.) See, it's all about . . .
MEP: (Looking at your manuscript—a little "dog-eared," teared with spots of sweat and hard work.) I see . . . I see . . .
YOU: It's all there . . . the vision and the revisions . . . the dreaming . . . and the construction work—like they say in *Barnum*—one brick at a time . . . and more dreaming and . . .
MEP: Beautiful . . . you got the last word . . . go ahead.

Experimental theatre, as seen in this production of the highly acclaimed Manhattan Project's *Alice in Wonderland*, reminds us that playwrighting has been an experimental adventure from the earliest times.

JUST FOR YOU
————AS THE CURTAIN FALLS————

PLAYWRIGHT'S PAGE

1) What did you enjoy most about writing your play?

2) What did you enjoy least about writing your play. Why?

3) What technique in this book did you find most helpful?

4) Are there any forms discussed in this chapter you would especially like to try?

5) What will your new play be about?

MORE **RAW** MATERIALS

Read . . . some scenes from your play. Also see and read revues, docudramas, story theatre scripts. They're right in your library.

Act . . . With some friends, actors, colleagues, act out some of the scenes in your play.

Write! . . . (and rewrite) That's what it's all about.

—— SUGGESTIONS FOR CLASSROOM ACTIVITIES ——

Many playwrights believe a play is not really finished until it has some form of a stage production. Remember, there are varied phases and levels of performance possible, which include workshop readings, staged readings, and informal classroom productions. You will be surprised to find that real opportunities in the theatre may be available nearby.

Discuss
• the possibilities of producing your play in class or in a community workshop. A number of professional/working playwrights take their plays on tour to regional theatres where they can work with an eye to improving them. Then, when they feel the play is ready, they will bring it to New York or some other commercial venue as did, for example, two Pulitzer Prize-winning dramatists, Margaret Edson, with *Wit*, and August Wilson, with *Fences*. You can create your own version of touring regional theatres with Creative Caravans. In this concept, a director, actors, and you tour classes in your school or at your community center site. This way, when you feel the play is ready for it, you can get the satisfaction of sharing it with others and also get some feedback for improving it. What specific auditions, liaison arrangements, and scheduling details will have to be arranged?
• whether or not nontraditional casting is an issue in producing plays. Do you think some roles have to be race/culture, gender or age specific, or should they be nontraditional in casting? Explain.

Read
• Look over your Playwright's Page again (page 158). Are there any questions or thoughts you would like to add?
• Conduct staged readings of your play and/or group play. Where will the actors sit? What kind of movement of the actors do you anticipate — standing sometimes, planned movement, or sitting for the most part? Should some sections of the play be memorized? If so, why? Regardless of the stage conventions you follow, remember that staged readings are not usually a finished product for an audience to see but are for the benefit of the playwright to improve his or her script.

Act out some scenes from your play in class or in a community setting. Get feedback (See Appendix D Giving and Receiving Feedback) on what works and

NOTEBOOK (OR JOURNAL) FEATURE

Jot down your thoughts about how you got the idea for your play, the process of writing it, and where you intend to go with it. Remember the words of author Walter Mosley, "Keep your mind and heart open to the work." What did you like most about the writing process? What did you like least? What things might you still want to improve? Why? What have you learned about yourself and others in the process of writing and communicating about writing? Poet Nikki Giovanni expressed her feelings about poetry, as you can feel from this excerpt from "Poetry":*

Poetry is motion graceful
as a fawn
gentle as a teardrop
strong like the eye
finding peace in a crowded room . . .

Now write what drama or a play feels like to you. You may wish to share this with the class. Look again at the poem (Suggestions for Classroom Activities, Chapter II, page 40) you wrote as a group and possibly do another one.

* Nikki Giovanni, *The Selected Poems of Nikki Giovanni* (New York: HarperCollins, 1996), p. 175. Reprinted by permission of HarperCollins Publishers, Inc.

what doesn't. Make notes that you can assess later for improving the play. Remember to listen with an open mind.

Write or e-mail queries regarding information about playwriting contests, workshops, and conferences. Drama bookstores often have books or ads for such events. (See page 149 for more information.)

Not exactly Broadway's *The Lion King*, but this production of humans and puppets provided great satisfaction for playwright, performers, and audience.

MORE PLAYWRITING OPPORTUNITIES

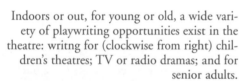

Indoors or out, for young or old, a wide variety of playwriting opportunities exist in the theatre: writng for (clockwise from right) children's theatres; TV or radio dramas; and for senior adults.

CAST YOUR VOTE ABOUT CASTING

In readings, workshops, and production of your plays, questions relating to casting may come up. Throughout the playwriting process you have been encouraged to build characters with specific traits in mind. Many believe that with classic plays (such as *Julius Caesar*, shown above), the ethnic roots of the actors should not make a difference. Others feel strongly that in race-specific plays (as in Shirley Lauro's *Open Admissions*, above) the race of an actor should be taken into consideration. Gender is often a consideration too. In some classic and contemporary works (as in Neil Simon's *The Odd Couple*, seen here), the same characters are portrayed by men and by women, following the basic plot with variations in characterization. Often such racial and gender (as well as age) casting considerations are worked out with the playwright and director with possible input from actors. In workshops and staged readings, nontraditional casting is often followed.

When it comes to productions before audiences, however, the issue of nontradtional casting can become a heated one. Some producing companies believe in totally realistic casting. Others do not have a problem with nontraditional casting. For example, David Herskovits, artistic director of the Target Margin Theatre, observes that the presence of an actor's race will always be apparent and rightfully so. An audience can experience "both the racial mix of performers, and, at the same time, the action of the play." He remarks that both aspects of the experience are celebrated.* Do you believe that any qualified actor, regardless of color, gender, or age, can or should be able to play any of your play's characters? Why or why not?

* David Herskovits, "Tilting Artfully: An Off-Broadway Manifesto," *The New York Times*, Arts and Leisure, November 1999.

Arata, Esther Spring and Rotalis, Nicholas John, eds. *Black American Playwrights, 1800-Present.* Lanham, Maryland: Scarecrow Press, 1976.

Archer, William. *Play-Making: A Manual of Craftsmanship.* New York: Dover Publications, 1960. Written in 1912.

Baker, George P. *Dramatic Technique.* Westport, CT: Greenwood, 1970.

Bentley, Eric. *The Life of the Drama.* New York: Applause Theatre & Cinema Books, 1991.

Benét, Stephen Vincent. *The Devil and Daniel Webster and Other Writings.* New York: Viking Penguin, 1999.

————. *The Devil and Daniel Webster.* New York: Dramatists Play Service, 1943.

Brooks, Cleanth, and Heilmann, Robert B. *Understanding Drama.* New York: Holt, Rinehart and Winston, 1961.

Butcher, S. H., ed. *Aristotle's Theory of Poetry and Fine Art.* New York: Dover, 1997.

Cerf, Bennett, and Cartmell, Van H., eds. *24 Favorite One-Act Plays.* Garden City: Dolphin, 1963.

Clay, James H., and Krempel, Daniel. *The Theatrical Image.* Lanham, Maryland: University Press of America, 1985.

Cole, Toby, ed. *Playwrights on Playwriting.* New York: Hill and Wang, 1995.

Dickson, Michael Begelow and Volansky, Michele, eds., *25 Ten-Minute Plays From Actors Theatre of Louisville.* New York: Samuel French, 1989, 1992, 1995.

Duberman, Martin B. *In White America.* New York: New American Library, 1964.

Egri, Lajos. *The Art of Dramatic Writing.* New York: Simon and Schuster, 1972.

Engel, Lehman. *Words With Music.* New York: Macmillan Co., 1980.

Ewen, David. *The Complete Book of the American Musical.* New York: Holt, Rinehart, and Winston, 1970.

France, Rachel, ed. *A Century of Plays by American Women.* New York: Richards Rosen Press, 1979.

Friederich, Willard J., and Fraser, John H. *Scenery Design for the Amateur Stage.* New York: Macmillan Co., 1950.

Gassner, John, ed. *Producing the Play.* New York: Dryden Press, 1953.

Grebanier, Bernard. Playwriting. *How to Write for the Theatre.* New York: Thomas Y. Crowell Co., 1961.

Halpern, Daniel. *Plays in One Act.* New York: HarperCollins, 1997.

Hatch, James V. and Shine, Ted. *Black Theatre USA: Forty-Five Plays by Black Americans, 1847-1974.* New York: Free Press, 1974.

Hatlen, Theodore W. *Orientation to the Theater.* New York: Appleton-Century-Crofts, 1962.

Hochhuth, Rolf. *The Deputy.* New York: Grove Press, 1964.

Hogan, Robert, and Molin, Sven Eric. *Drama: The Major Genres.* An Introductory Critical Anthology. New York: Dodd, Mead & Co., 1962.

Jones, Robert Edmond. *The Dramatic Imagination.* New York: Routledge, 1987.

Kerr, Walter. *How Not to Write a Play.* New York: Simon and Schuster, 1955.

Klaus, Carla, H., Gilbert, Miriam and Field, Branford, Jr. *Stages of Drama: Classical to Contemporary Theatre.* New York: St. Martin's Press, 1995.

Lawson, John Howard. *Theory and Technique of Playwriting.* New York: Hill and Wang, 1936; revised 1960.

Longfellow, Henry Wadsworth. *The Courtship of Miles Standish.* New York: The New American Library, 1964.

MacGowan, Kenneth. *A Primer of Playwriting.* Westport, Connecticut: Greenwood Press, 1981.

McCalmon, George, and Moe, Christian. *Creating Historical Drama.* Carbondale: Southern Illinois University Press, 1965.

Miles, Julia, ed. *Playwriting Women: Seven Plays From the Women's Project*. Portsmouth, New Hampshire: Heinemann, 1993.

————. *Here to Stay: Five Plays From the Women's Project*. New York: Applause Theatre & Cinema Books, 1997.

Milgram, Sally-Anne. *Dealing With Life's Dilemmas: Exploring Values Through English and Drama*. San Jose, CA: Resource Publications, Inc. 2001.

Miller, Arthur. *Collected Plays*. New York: Viking Press, 1957.

Poggi, Jack. *The Monologue Workshop: From Search to Discovery in Audition and Performance*. New York: Applause Theatre & Cinema Books, 1997.

Polsky, Milton E. *Let's Improvise: Becoming Creative, Spontaneous and Expressive Through Drama*. New York: Applause Theatre & Cinema Books, 1998.

Priestly, J. B. *The Art of the Dramatist*. London: Heinemann, 1973.

Rattigan, Terence. *The Browning Version*. New York: Samuel French, 1975. (Also in Cerf and Cartmell, *24 Favorite One-Act Plays*.)

Rowe, Kenneth Thorpe. *A Theater in Your Head*. New York: Funk and Wagnals, 1960.

Simonson, Lee. *The Stage Is Set*. New York,1946.

Spolin, Viola. *Improvisation for the Theater*. Evanston, Illinois: Northwestern Press, 1999.

Styan, J. L. *The Elements of Drama*. New York: Cambridge University Press, 1960.

————. *The Dramatic Experience*. New York: Cambridge University Press, 1965.

Wager, Walter, ed. *The Playwrights Speak*. New York: Delta, 1967.

Wilkerson, Margaret B. *New Plays by Black Women*. New York: Penguin Books, 1986.

Wilson, August. *Three Plays*. Pittsburgh: University of Pittsburgh Press, 1991.

Young, Glenn, ed. *The Best Short Plays of 1998-1999*, New York: Applause Theatre & Cinema Books, 2001.

APPENDICES

appendix A:
EXAMPLE OF PLAYSCRIPT FORMAT

appendix B:
ADDITIONAL EXAMPLES OF PLOT ELEMENTS

appendix C:
SELF-EVALUATION CHECKLIST

appendix D:
GIVING AND RECEIVING FEEDBACK

appendix E:
MORE ON MONOLOGUES, ONE-PERSON SHOWS, AND
WRITING BRIEF PLAYS

appendix F:
SCENES FOR PRACTICE

appendix G:
SCENARIO FOR DOCUDRAMA: MARC

appendix H:
PLAYWRITING TERMS

EXAMPLE OF PLAYSCRIPT FORMAT

THE BALLAD OF "BOX" BROWN *

by

Milton Polsky

SYNOPSIS OF SCENES

Scene 1:   Headquarters of Anti-Slavery Society, Philadelphia, 1853.
Scene 2:   Richmond, Virginia, Brown's home, early morning 1849.
Scene 3:   On road to tobacco factory, immediately following.
Scene 4:   Inside the factory, immediately following.
Scene 5:   Dream Interlude.
Scene 6:   Inside the factory, late afternoon.
Scene 7:   On the road home, immediately following.
Scene 8:   In the tobacco factory, later that evening.
Scene 9:   Inside Smith's Shoe Shoppe, the next morning.
Scene 10:   Porto-Montage, Brown's journey.
Scene 11:   Headquarters of Anti-Slavery Society, Philadelphia,. 1853.

The use of scenery which suggests the locales and atmospheres of the different settings is encouraged rather than attempts to recreate them realistically.

A suggested visual metaphor is the use of live actors (from the chorus) to become through movement and mime—the various modes of transportation Henry Brown rides on while in the box.

THE BALLAD OF "BOX" BROWN
A Musical Play for the Whole Family
Cast of Characters (In Order of Appearance):

WILLIAM STILL . . . . A leader of the Underground Railroad (URR)
LAURA ROBERTS . . . . About 10, member of the URR
MRS. ROBERTS . . . . About 30, Laura's mother, an ex-slave
HENRY BROWN . . . . In early 30's, slave—later abolitionist
JONAH . . . . About 10, Henry's nephew

* Adapted from The Narrative of Henry "Box" Brown

NANCY . . . . Late 20's, Brown's wife
CALEPH . . . . Late 20 's, Jonah's father and Nancy's brother
WILLIAM . . . . 30's, Brown's "master," owner of the factory
SAMUEL SMITH . . . . In 40's, shoe dealer and agent for the URR

Members of the chorus can play the agents of the URR, the sailor, young man, young woman, Allen's friend, Man-in-Cape, and Peter Roberts.
Doubling of actors is encouraged for minor roles.

MUSICAL NUMBERS

Scene 1:	"The Ballad of Box Brown"
Scene 2:	"Wake Up Jonah" (and dance)
	"Cow"
	"Like Leaves"
Scene III:	"Where-O-Where-O"
Scene IV:	"Working Tobacco"
Scene V:	"The URR" (and dance)
Scene VII:	"Like Leaves" (reprise)
Scene IX:	"Make a Break"
Scene X:	"The Ballad of Box Brown"
Scene XI:	"Oh, Freedom" (traditional spiritual)
	"The URR" (reprise)

THE BALLAD OF BOX BROWN   (starts new page)
A Musical Adventure on the URR
Scene One: Philadelphia, 1853

Headquarters of the Anti-Slavery Society in Philadelphia, 1853. A pulpit, a few crates and a sign:

URR STOCKHOLDERS
MEETING TONIGHT! ALL ATTEND!

WILLIAM STILL, a proud man dressed in minister's robes, enters, goes to pulpit and addresses the audience.

STILL
Stockholders of the Underground Railroad, gather 'round. Esteemed friends of the URR, praise the Lord. The "Express" train rolled in this morning at 3 a.m. The goods have been delivered!
(The CHORUS of about 6-8 antislavery agents, including LAURA, about 10, enter and sit on crates placed around STILL.)

LAURA
Another meeting of the stockholders of the URR, Reverend Still?

STILL

Yes, as sure as you're standing there, Laura Roberts.

LAURA

Do I have to pass out the handbills later?

STILL

(indicating the audience)
To the new stockholders? Yes, that's your job, Laura.

LAURA

Can I guard the new "parcel" instead?

STILL

Oh, he's doing fine. Resting from his trip on the URR.

LAURA

I never get to do anything exciting around here. Just pass out handbills. I'm not a child, you know.

MRS. ROBERTS

(as she enters)
Laura Roberts, you got enough nerve to paper this whole room. You know it's way past your bedtime.

LAURA

But Momma — this here's something special. Mr. Brown's in town! And I never even met him.

MRS. ROBERTS

Hush, I don't want no stuff out of *you*, Laura Roberts.

(pause)
I know Mr. Brown's in town. And I know it's way past your bedtime, too.

STILL

Mrs. Roberts . . .

(delicately interceding)
A word, please.

(takes her over to the side)
The Sisters have been doing a wonderful job raising funds for our important mission. Mr. Brown appreciates it, we all do.

MRS. ROBERTS

Well, we're doing our best . . . and so are you. All right, young lady, you can stay.

(to STILL)
Give the signal, Mr. Chief Conductor . . .

STILL

(He sings.)
Come on everybody,
Gather 'round
I'm gonna tell about Henry Brown.

He rode from Richmond
In a box
To Philadelphy town!

ADDITIONAL EXAMPLES OF PLOT ELEMENTS

Examples of Major Goals:
- In Ibsen's *A Doll's House*, Nora Helmer wants to leave her husband and establish a life of her own.
- In Guare's *The House of Blue Leaves*, Artie wants to go to Hollywood and become a famous songwriter.
- In Chekhov's *The Cherry Orchard*, Madame Ranevskaya wants to hold onto her cherished land and way of life.
- In Williams' *A Streetcar Named Desire*, Blanche DuBois wants to find shelter, sanctuary from harsh, cruel reality.
- In Lanford Wilson's *Hot L Baltimore*, Paul Granger III wants to find his grandfather.
- In Shepard's *Buried Child*, Vince wants to be recognized by his family.
- In O'Neill's *Long Day's Journey Into Night*, Mary Tyrone wants to escape from reality by retreating into memories of the past through taking drugs.
- In Mamet's *American Buffalo*, Donny Dubrow's goal is to make a good profit by breaking into a house and stealing a rare American Buffalo coin.

More Visible Stakes
- In *American Buffalo*, the American Buffalo coin Bob brings Donny dramatizes the business goal—the empty values that threaten their friendship.
- The fence Troy builds in August Wilson's *Fences* symbolizes and shows the personal and family barriers he has to overcome.
- In *Buried Child*, the baby skeleton, wrapped in blankets, carried onstage by Tilden dramatizes the sins of the family's past.
- The men's phalli show how frustrated they are in Aristophanes' *Lysistrata*.
- Sheridan Whiteside's wheelchair—his throne,

his seat of power in *The Man Who Came to Dinner*.
- The disease-ridden capital ("Pestilence sweeps the country") which Oedipus governs in *Oedipus Rex*.
- In *The Little Foxes*, Horace's medicine bottle—as long as he lives, Regina's dreams will be obstructed.
- The wagon that the title figure in Bertolt Brecht's *Mother Courage* must pull through war and pestilence even as she tries to pull herself and children through the war.
- In Arthur Miller's *The Price*, the attic holds piles of furniture that is being sold by two alienated brothers after their father has died. In addition to dividing the proceeds from the sale, the brothers meet to confront each other over the price paid for the life choices they have made.
- In *The Glass Menagerie*, Laura's glass animal collection represents her unique sensibility, her fragility, and the family's need for fantasy: Amanda's fantasy, the Gentleman Caller; Tom's, the memories and picture of his father.
- The model of St. Phillip's Church that John Merrick builds throughout *The Elephant Man*. Its completion signals his poignant death.

More Examples of Point of Attack
- In Mamet's *American Buffalo*, Donny tells Bob he doesn't want him to do the job. This action commits Donny to the central thematic conflict—business vs. friendship.
- In Williams' *A Streetcar Named Desire*, Blanche implores Stella to leave Stanley. She refuses but Stanley overhears—now he's determined to get Blanche out of the house.
- In Odets' *Golden Boy*, Joe tells his father he is quitting music and pursuing boxing. This begins the play's central action.

• In *Lysistrata*, Lysistrata urges the women to go on a sex strike, convincing them this is the only way the men will stop fighting.

• In *Long Day's Journey Into Night*, Mary comes downstairs—apparently she has returned to her drug addiction. The Tyrone family must now confront reality and deal with their own escape from reality.

• In Shepard's *Buried Child*, Vince tries to get Dodge, his grandfather, to recognize him as his grandson. Dodge treats him like a stranger.

• In Lanford Wilson's *Hot L Baltimore*, the residents of the hotel receive eviction notices that the hotel is going to be torn down.

Examples of "Dramatic Clocks"

• When Sheridan Whiteside in Hart and Kaufman's *The Man Who Came to Dinner* is given fifteen minutes to leave the house, he must act fast to help his secretary recover her love life.

• The czar's decree for the Jewish townspeople to leave Anatevka within a month in Joseph Stein's musical *Fiddler on the Roof*.

• In *The Little Foxes*, Ben tells Regina the contract will be signed in a week; if Horace doesn't come home now and join the deal, Regina will be cut out. This ultimatum incites Regina to action.

• The dramatic action of *The Glass Menagerie* is a flashback framed by Tom's narration. A memory play, *Menagerie* is a personal look at the past. The weekend visit of the Gentleman Caller gives the play dramatic immediacy.

• In *The Emperor Jones*, the natives' drumbeats sounding louder and louder as Jones runs out of time intensify the suspense.

Dramatic Questions

• *Fences*: Will Troy resolve his inner conflict with his father and come to terms with his wife and son?

• *Lysistrata*: Will the women's sex strike end that war?

• *Trifles*: Will Mrs. Hale and Mrs. Peters discover who the murderer is?

• *A Raisin in the Sun*: Will Mama Younger be able to move into the neighborhood of her choice while keeping her family together'?

• *Tartuffe*: Will Orgon's family rid themselves of Tartuffe?

• *American Buffalo*: Will Donny sacrifice friendship to business?

• *The House of Blue Leaves*: Will Artie go to Hollywood and become a famous songwriter?

• *A Streetcar Named Desire*: Will Blanche find shelter?

• *The Hot L Baltimore*: Will Paul Granger III find his grandfather?

Crises or Turning Points

• In *Waiting for Godot*, the boy tells Vladimir and Estragon that Godot will not be coming today.

• In *Long Day's Journey Into Night*, Mary Tyrone comes downstairs holding her wedding gown. The family is again confronted by reality—Mary's relapse.

• In *Trifles*, Mrs. Hale and Mrs. Peters discover the dead bird in Mrs. Wright's sewing box, confirming she has murdered her husband.

• In *Lysistrata*, the Athenian magistrate and the Lacedaemoian Herald meet and agree that the men's frustrations can no longer be endured; they must make preparations for a peace conference.

• In *Fences*, Cory challenges his father Troy's supremacy in the family.

• In *The Glass Menagerie*, The Gentleman Caller tells Laura he is engaged. This shatters Amanda's dream of marrying off Laura.

• In *The House of Blue Leaves*, Billy asks Bunny to be his companion and rejects Artie's songwriting.

• In *American Buffalo*, Teach bets Bob. The action leads to Donny's decision to call off the job.

• In *Buried Child*, Vince returns drunk, violent and savage, threatening to take over the house. Now, the family acknowledges him as a member.

Examples of Climaxes

• In *Fences*, Troy wrestles for his life with Death.

• In *Long Day's Journey Into Night*, Edmund tries to penetrate his mother's somnolence with the harsh fact that he doesn't have a cold — he has consumption. But Mary is lost to the past.

• In *A Raisin in the Sun*, Walter Younger asserts his dignity and tells off Mr. Lindner.

• In *Lysistrata*, at the Athenian-Spartan peace conference, Lysistrata settles the peace terms. Athens and Sparta become allies.

• In *Trifles,* Mrs. Hale snatches the sewing box from Mrs. Wright and quickly hides it.

• In *The House of Blue Leaves*, Artie strangles his wife, Bananas. Trapped with a crazy woman, "too old to be a young talent," Artie does not achieve his goal.

• In *American Buffalo*, Donny calls off the job.

• In *Buried Child*, Dodge wills the house to his grandson Vince. Shelly leaves and Dodge dies.

Resolutions

• In *Long Day's Journey Into Night*, Mary Tyrone is lost in the past, the family is faced with the reality of her addiction. The family's illusions have been exposed. Their hopes are revealed as futile; but they have gained compassion and insight.

• In *Lysistrata*, the sex strike is terminated. The men are invited to a peace banquet by the women. They sing, dance, and solidify the peace.

• In *A Streetcar Named Desire*, Blanche ironically does find shelter but not the kind she would choose. She is taken away to a mental institution.

• In *Buried Child*, Tilden carries the buried child into the house while Halie, his mother, describes that a once barren garden is fertile again. The family will go on now—the past sins are uncovered.

• In *The House of Blue Leaves*, Artie plays the piano and sings his song. He is happy, content, in his element. His dream goes on.

• In *American Buffalo*, Teach assures himself that Donny is not angry at him. Bob apologizes to Donny, and Donny forgives him.

SELF-EVALUATION CHECKLIST

I. THEME

• Is the play worthwhile in the sense that it says something dramatically? Truthfully?

• Holds interest?

• Moves one to think, laugh or cry — engages the emotions?

• Does the theme gradually emerge from the interactions of the characters, never directly stated or announced by you?

II. PLOT

• Is the plot clearly developed with either a forward-moving progression or other kind of shape?

• Is the plot (or structure) dramatic, with conflict, complications, crises, and climax?

• Is the structure esthetically whole, adding up to a theatrical experience?

• Is each scene essential to the play as a whole and organic to the other scenes?

• Is the exposition as brief as possible?

• Does a dramatic question (or problem) sufficiently hold the interest of the audience?

• Does the plot move along—too slowly; too quickly? Is there a natural rhythm and pacing'?

III. CHARACTER

• Do character and plot interact, one developing from the other'?

• Do the central and opposing characters have sufficient delineation of character traits?

• Are the objectives of each character clearly developed?

• Are relationships between characters clear when they're supposed to be?

• Are the reasons (motivations) for all character actions clear when they're supposed to be?

• Are there any wasted or extraneous characters?

IV. DIALOGUE

• Does dialogue delineate character, move the plot along, and/or illuminate the dramatic problem or question?

• Is dialogue vital and true to character?

• Is dialogue natural, economical; does it grow out of character and have its own character?

• Does dialogue convey the spirit of the times or period?

• Does dialogue reflect your "voice" and style of expression?

V. MUSIC

• For a musical, is song not only related to the action, but a part of it as well?

• Do the song and its lyrics contribute to the dramatic action, delineate character, and/or help establish a mood?

• Do the lyrics grow out of character and have a basic structure?

• Do the lyrics sound as if they belong to the character?

VI. VISUAL ELEMENTS

• Have you discovered a dramatic metaphor for your play?

• Is the visual style clear?

• Are vocal/visual elements of your script in harmony?

• Are your stage directions brief and clear and used only when important to delineate character, advance the plot, or help establish a mood?

VII. GENERAL

• Do you like your script so far?

• Are there any *specific* parts you do not like?

• Are there *specific* ways you can improve your play? How?

● ●

SAMPLE PLAYWRITING RUBRIC

Use this rubric to help you revise your play or evaluate it. Feel free to adapt this rubric or create one of your own.

Take a Bow!
• The characters are now believable, with individualized distinguishing traits.
• The plot has a plausible conflict that is clearly developed.
• All of the dialogue is true to character.
• This is a script written for the stage.

Lights Up
• Characters are more believable and defined.
• The plot has motion and conflict, but needs more clarity.
• Some of the dialogue is true to character.
• There is now more of a sense that this is a stage play, not a TV or movie script.

Curtain Down
• The characters are not believable.
• The plot is static, lacking conflict — or else overstuffed with incidents.
• The dialogue is stiff or stilted and not true to character.
• This is more of a TV or movie script than a play written for the stage.

● ●

Thanks to John A. Shorter for his help in developing this rubric.

GIVING AND RECEIVING FEEDBACK

FEEDBACK — WHEN, WHY, AND BY WHOM

It's up to you, as the playwright, to ask for feedback on your play — when you feel you are ready for it. This feedback might be about your main idea. It could be about a particular problem you're having while writing your play or hearing it read aloud during the final stages of its creation. Make sure that you are ready to receive the feedback — perhaps by working with just one person or with a small group of people whose opinions you value. Remember, it is *your* play. Be careful that people giving feedback don't change your ideas so much that it becomes their version instead of yours.

On the other hand, you may not want feedback at certain times. You may prefer wrestling with the emerging problems yourself, not because you don't value constructive advice from others, but because you know that as you keep on rewriting, the problems will be cleared up. It was not until J.K. Rowling had almost finished a draft of a Harry Potter book that she realized that she would have to go back to the middle and rewrite from that point on to reach the novel's revised ending. This is part of the painful pleasure (or pleasurable pain) of being a writer — seeing how messy parts become less messy and clearer as you draft and revise. Learning to trust the process of rewriting is something all writers go through.

"Final draft, William? Surely ye jest!"

Giving Feedback

Be sensitive to what the other playwrights are trying to do. As a playwright yourself, you are aware of the process of writing. You know that some of the problems will be figured out later. Avoid personal or vague destructive comments, such as "I didn't like it," or "too corny." Be specific about your objections and word them in a constructive way. Sometimes, just a simple suggestion or even a few words can trigger encouraging results. I know this is true in athletics: tennis star Venus Williams was advised merely to bend her knees a little more, and by doing so her forehand stroke improved greatly. A lifeguard suggesting that I simply cup my fingers "miraculously" improved

Student in New York University's "Looking for Shakespeare" Project receives feedback on her monologue from another student and project head, Alistair Martin-Smith. (See page 180.)

my swimming stroke. Also, be sensitive to how extreme your suggestions might be. Carol Dixon, a writer and teacher at The Writers' Voice in New York, advises that if there is too little pushing, the artist never improves but "too much, and off the cliff he goes, spirit crushed." Above all, in the feedback process, respect each other and the evolving work. Questions can be open-ended, but I prefer the questions to be structured. For example:

1. What do you like about the scene/play/character? Be specific. ("I can relate to that because . . .")
2. What parts are unclear? Repetitious? Not developed enough? Be specific.
3. Is the major conflict in the scene/play clear? Strong? Real? Explain why with some specific examples.
4. What do you remember about the characters? Be specific.
5. Do you think anything should be omitted, added, or clarified more? Why? Be as specific as you can.

CONSTRUCTIVE WAYS TO PHRASE COMMENTS

Sample Comments

If you're thinking:
    "This part here doesn't make sense . . ."
You might ask:
    "How can you make this section clearer?"

If you're thinking:
    "There just isn't enough information about this character."
You might ask:
    "Why does _____ do that? How could you add some dialogue or action to show what you mean?"

If you're thinking:
    "The ending doesn't resolve the main conflict. It seems forced."

You might ask:

> "What might be a clearer resolution? What is happening? Why?"

Above all, remember that questions and comments are only suggestions. It is the playwright who must finally decide — after taking time to think it over — which changes, if any, should be made.

Receiving Feedback

Listen carefully, even if you disagree with the comment being made — you may change your mind later. Take notes. You do not have to make decisions now. Perhaps at some point you will say, "That's what I thought too — now I hear my point of view confirmed. I'm glad they brought up the questions." One of my playwriting students remarked, "If one person says you're a horse, well okay. But if twelve say you are, head for the stable." I recall how the student had stuck to a point in one instance and she was right. But at all times, she welcomed the suggestions. If they are given in the right spirit, you, too, can benefit greatly.

Readings

Another good way to get feedback about your play-in-progress is to have the play read aloud. These readings can be informal — "cold," or on-the-spot, or "staged readings." The staged readings might also be rehearsed several times. In a staged reading the actors may all sit in chairs and read their parts aloud or they may get up from time to time and do some limited movement, such as entrances and exits. In any case, as with other partner and group feedback sessions, these guidelines can be helpful:

Readers:
- Stay in character.
- Speak up.
- Listen to each other.

Listeners:
- Focus on the readers and listen actively, attentively, and silently.
- Avoid interrupting or calling out. Let the readers do the acting.
- Take notes for compliments or suggestions you may wish to share with the playwright.

When the reading is over, listeners should always first ask the playwright what he or she would like to know from the listeners. Remember, this session is an opportunity for the playwright and the play to grow, not simply to entertain an audience. Sometimes a reading can have other purposes, such as serving as a springboard for discussing various issues the play addresses. But for now, the reading is for you, the playwright, for feedback.

Playwright:
- Take notes, so you can later assess comments. Repeat: you do not have to decide anything now. At times, something deep inside you will tell you what choices are the right ones.
- Check what might be significant, which things to accept or reject.
- Ask questions about anything else you would like to know and need more feedback on. Then, listeners can ask more questions for further discussion and constructive comments, or fill out a questionnaire in which the playwright asks for comments.

Remember, feedback and suggestions for revisions should be constructively worded. Playwriting teacher, Elana Gartner, has this advice: "Charitable flattery does not help the playwright but neither does outright criticism. If you do not find the piece to your liking, for whatever reason, you may wish to assist the playwright in seeing new approaches with your feedback."

MORE ON MONOLOGUES, ONE-PERSON SHOWS, AND WRITING BRIEF PLAYS

MONOLOGUES

Length and Functions
When you think about it, three kinds of writing make up a playscript: dialogue, stage/speech directions, and possibly monologues. Simply defined, monologues in plays are the lines spoken by a character to one or more other characters who remain silent during the speech. (A soliloquy occurs when a character reveals his or her inner thoughts only to the audience; no other characters are present at the time. See, for instance, the "To be or not to be" soliloquy in *Hamlet,* Act III, scene 1.)

Monologues in plays can be relatively short, comprise a whole scene (as in the "Where Are We Going?" speech Dr. Heidi Holland gives in Act II, Scene 4 of *The Heidi Chronicles*), or can even make up the entire play, as in August Strindberg's *The Stronger.* Perhaps the most famous full play-length soliloquy is Samuel Beckett's *Krapp's Last Tape,* in which the title character, surrounded by boxes, papers, an old-fashioned tape recorder, and boxes of reel-to-reel audio tapes, spends his days listening to the tapes he made long years ago when he was a younger person. As he lingers on some memories, fast-forwards to other parts of his life, and makes new recordings, we get an intimate sense of a man whose grief, frustration, and abandoned hopes are now but poignant shadows of a vanished, utterly contrasted younger self.

The functions of monologues vary too: framing a play, such as Tom's opening and closing monologues in *The Glass Menagerie;* setting up the background as Salieri does in *Amadeus;* revealing character, as in *Jitney;* serving as the plot's turning point as

in Mark Anthony's famous speech to the Romans; or as the focal point of a play, such as in Rebecca Gilman's *Spinning the Butter,* when the central character, a well-meaning college dean, reveals her inner feelings of racial prejudice during an emotional twenty-minute speech.

Developing a Monologue in Your Play
Regardless of a monologue's length and function, writing it comes back to the same question you would ask about your dialogue: would the character say this at this *particular* time and place to these particular people? Write freely as you would write dialogue. Say the words aloud to yourself, to a partner, or into a tape recorder. Refer back to the character chart on pages 108 and 109 for additional ideas and insights about the character. Does the nature of the monologue call for vivid word pictures or a heightened sensory makeup? As you do with dialogue in the revision process, make cuts, additions, or other changes.

Example of a Monologue As a Key Point
If the monologue is a focal point of a scene or play, you should ask if it builds to an emotional peak. For example, the play I wrote with Howard Berland, *The Spirit of Bleecker Street,* underwent a number of rewrites for a key monologue. The time is 1806, the scene a grog shop (tavern) in Greenwich Village. Major Anthony Bleecker and his wife Margaret have gone there to see the County Clerk (who owns the grog shop and certifies legal matters in the Village) to lay their claim to a piece of land in the area. In walks Tom Paine, the radical hero who was so instrumental in inspiring the troops during the

A well-written monologue can be very effective in a courtroom drama, as is Lt. Col. Nathan Jessup's passionate speech (beginning "We live in a world that has walls") at the end of *A Few Good Men* by Aaron Sorkin in which Jessup is forced to admit that he illegally ordered a punishment that resulted in the death of a marine.

American Revolution thirty-five years earlier. Paine is despised now by the motley crowd of drinkers because of his unconventional religious beliefs. The County Clerk immediately wants Paine out of his grog shop. When Bleecker objects, the County Clerk challenges him to decide between defending Paine or getting his piece of land. Tension builds as Major Bleecker tries to make up his mind, and the County Clerk grows impatient:

COUNTY CLERK

My dear friend, I mean to cause no family strife, but surely you must see that this wretched, old man —

MAJOR BLEECKER

Wretched man???
(*Coming between COUNTY CLERK and PAINE.*)
I see that you're not fit to walk the same ground as this man!

COUNTY CLERK

Sir! I shan't be treated this way — certainly not in my own shop! I don't care how much land you want to buy!

Originally, we had Major Bleecker answer the County Clerk as follows:

MAJOR BLEECKER
(*Deep in memory.*)
Those were the times . . . our soldiers running away every day — all those ragged, starving men — 'til (*To PAINE.*) — your words gave me the strength to go on.

We revised this dialogue into the following monologue:

MAJOR BLEECKER
(*Ignoring the CLERK, lost in reverie as instrumental, "These Are the Times" fades in, B.G.*)
. . . How can I forget those freezing trenches of Pennsylvania — our soldiers were running away every day, rags wrapped around their blistered, bleeding feet — hungry, starving boys . . . Then, like a storm coming from the sky, he came — this man — putting fire in our shattered souls . . . 'Twas this man, sir, who kept our Revolution alive . . .

The monologue now seemed to work — almost. There was something still missing. Several rewrites

Major Bleecker (right) has a hard choice to make — recover his lost ideals and defend Paine (center) or lose the land that is due him.

of the whole play later, we added this one sentence to the end of Bleecker's speech: " . . . without him, none of your mother's sons would be sitting here free, drinking your damn coffee!" We realized that these additional words made a big difference because they are the subtext of why Bleecker says the monologue in the first place. With the added line, both Major Bleecker and the monologue reach a high point, leading Bleecker and the ensemble to sing the song, "These Are the Times," which emotionally culminates the scene.

Checking the Circumstances of Your Character's Monologue

At some point in the writing process, check out the circumstances surrounding a particular monologue for your play by asking yourself these kinds of questions:

- Should this, indeed, be a monologue or be broken up into dialogue? Is this supposed to be funny, sad, both, or what? Is the character saying or revealing too much--or too little?
- Where and when is the monologue being said? (under any special environmental conditions?) What has just happened before the monologue — and after it is said?
- To whom is it spoken and why?

In musicals, the most important or conflicted or comical moments in the dramatic highlights of each scene are typically built up into songs, often soliloquies, which heighten the dramatic impact with the enriched effect of the combined mediums of music and theatre.

On the next page we see Carmen James (see page 175 as she receives feedback on her monologue) play 42-year-old emigre Anna Berman, whose monologue begins: "I can feel the little spiders of excitement crawling up my skin/And the colorful butterflies of anticipation in my stomach/Oh, I feel like I'm the budding age of twenty-two again . . ."

ONE-PERSON SHOWS

Values and Examples

One-person shows afford wonderful creative opportunities for both writing and performing. You may decide to write the show and have another person perform it, or perform it yourself.

One option is to put together a show about some aspect of your life consisting of monologues and dialogue between a variety of characters. Or you can create a cast of wholly fictional characters as Whoopi Goldberg does in her one-person shows on television and a number of others do on stage. For example, in his *Wake Up and Smell the Coffee*, Eric

Original monologues can become a vital part of a revue or play. For example, students, ages 12-17, created a show called "A Midsummer Night's Rave (or What You Will)" presented as part of the "Looking for Shakespeare" theatre workshop sponsored by the New York University Program in Educational Theatre. The concept synthesized scenes from *A Midsummer Night's Dream* and *Twelfth Night* with parallel original scenes and monologues written and performed by the students.

whose husband was killed during the riot, and dozens more.

In contrast, in a number of one-person shows the central character is the writer, who also plays him or herself. Most noteworthy among these writer-performers are Spalding Gray and Claudia Shear. Gray writes thoughtfully and entertainingly about various aspects of his life, while in *Blown Sideways Through Life*, Shear relates her own story of how she supported herself through the years by taking sixty-four menial jobs, ranging from short order cook to a receptionist in a brothel.

Developing a One-Person Show

Here is some valuable advice by Jack Poggi, author of *The Monologue Workshop*. He recommends developing the one-person show over a period of time and trying out the stories in performance. For example, Bogosian develops one piece or sketch at a time, sometimes improvising into his tape recorder and testing it in public. This is the time to ask such questions as: Does the show move along? Is it clear? Does it get laughs when it's supposed to? Does it capture and hold the audience's attention?

Once the raw materials you plan to develop are collected, the arrangement of the pieces is the next step. If you are presenting a story about yourself or perhaps about someone else (e.g., Edgar Allan Poe), telling it chronologically might be one way to go. However, you might want to jump back and forth in time, as Tim Gregory, playing Orson Welles, the famous writer-actor-director, does in a one-person

Bogosian portrays, in a steady stream-of-consciousness manner, diverse characters, ranging from Texas millionaires to big-city drug addicts.

Anna Deveare Smith, in her one-woman performance pieces, portrays an array of real people she has interviewed. Probably her most well-known performance pieces are *Fires in the Mirror*, an examination of racial violence in Crown Heights, Brooklyn, New York; and *Twilight: Los Angeles 1992*, dealing with the aftermath of the Rodney King verdict. Smith plays, with voice and mannerisms, people who were affected by the events leading to and after the incident, including former Chief of Police, Daryl F. Gates (who explains why he left police headquarters to attend a fund-raising party). Her other characters include a Beverly Hills real estate agent, an inner-city teenager, a Korean woman

Here Anna Deveare Smith is seen portraying Reverend Al Sharpton in *Fires in the Mirror*.

show written by Daniel Mark Feldman. The action starts in Welles' dressing room as he prepares to deliver a speech after accepting an award. Then the incidents flash back and forth into his life, always returning to the base in his dressing room. At the end of the show, by the time Welles is ready to accept his award, we know the unpredictable artistic maverick quite well.   Poggi advises that continuity in a one-person show can be provided by " . . . one of the characters you're playing, or simply as yourself, the narrator."* Poggi suggests that you experiment with whichever format works best for the show and with connecting links you need in order to make the format work smoothly. Some one-person shows become more or less set quickly, while others continue to grow with successive performances.

Visual Elements

An advantage of producing a one-person show is that it is relatively easy to assemble. The performer takes charge of the scenic background, which may be nothing all, or relatively simple (writing table and books for *Edgar Allan Poe*) or a very complex visual backdrop (such as the detailed visual multi-media setting in *Twilight: Los Angeles, 1992*). Props, especially, must be selected for an artistic economy of means. By quickly taking off glasses and donning a

hat, Smith in *Twilight* goes from Beverly Hills real estate agent to inner city teenager.

Sarah Jones, in her one-person show, *Women Can't Wait*, uses only one prop, a delicately fine sari, to help instantly establish the idenities of the eight women she portrays. Wearing the sari on her head, she is a shy Indian woman trying to talk with her husband after being beaten by him; wearing it as a scarf around her neck, she is a vivacious French woman trying to establish her independence. She also wears it as a shawl over her shoulder and then around her waist, as still other women.

Some writer-performers, such as Pamela C. Gien and Claudia Shear, like to work closely with a director when deciding costume and prop details.

In her powerful one-woman play, *The Syringa Tree*, writer-performer Pamela C. Gien wears the same simple dress for nearly two hours on stage. And on stage, there is only one prop, a swing. Yet with a heartfelt personal story to tell, and with evocative acting, she alternately transforms her body, voice, and soul into twenty-four very different characters, including young and old, black, white, Zulu, Jewish, English, Afrikaans, Xhosa — from the early Sixties South African apartheid to present day free South Africa.

*Jack Poggi, *The Monologue Workshop* (New York: Applause Theatre Books, 1995)

WRITING BRIEF PLAYS

The writing of one, three, five or ten-minute plays has become very popular in recent years. And no wonder. Short works in other media are popular, so why not in drama too? The haiku, consisting of only three lines and seventeen sylllables, is a strikingly brief form of poetry. The Japanese author and Nobel Prize in Literature recipient Yasunari Kawabata has written lovely one-page short stories he calls "palm of the hand stories."

You have (I trust) already written some one-minute and three-minute plays as exercises in this book. In schools and writing workshops, more and more people are writing ten-minute plays, individually and as a group activity. You and some other playwrights may wish to put together an original play festival of short works.

To get the "feel" for the length of a ten-minute play, think of a half-hour television comedy or drama which consists approximately of two ten-minute acts. To be practical, limit yourself to only a few characters in your ten-minuters, in the hopes of making them easier to get produced. Next, choose a single simple setting for their tightly focused interaction. For example, my *Delaney vs. Dewey* has two characters — a disturbed school librarian and a teacher whom she naggingly tries to manipulate after she has been harassed by some students in the library. The play is set in her small office (with only a chair, table and small bookcase). *Exit the Maven From Mott Haven*, about a nephew's painful job of picking up his elderly uncle to take him to a nursing home, also uses only two characters and is set in an almost bare room of the uncle's Bronx apartment.

But don't feel you must always have such a small cast or limited set. In my ten-minute play, *Fame Is Fleeting*, which is about promise and betrayal, a high school girl's prize-winning essay is totally revised, without her knowing, by the publisher. Three fluid shifts of tables and chairs transform the stage into her house, school, camp setting, publishing house and writer's apartment as four actors play six markedly different characters.

My process is simple. Usually, the idea gets me — it just flashes in my mind and when it does, I quickly write a first draft in one sitting. After awhile, I add, cut, get some feedback from writing friends, revise and polish, and then aim for some sort of production or workshop.

When you get your idea for a ten-minuter of your own, I suggest you freely write a first draft and/or jot down an outline — and then write it quickly. Come back to it later for revisions and polish and then have some classmates or friends read and/or stage it. I would advise keeping the scenery and props simple and minimal. In *Delaney vs. Dewey* all that is needed is a table and some library books; for *Exit the Maven from Mott Haven*, just one small table and a telephone. I heartily recommend that you see ten-minuters and read them, while dashing off a few yourself. They can be fun!

Try your hand at writing these kinds of scenes that appear frequently in drama:

1) One character has a definite objective (tangible or intangible) and the other character either opposes it or has a counter-objective. For example, in Act III of Lillian Hellman's *The Little Foxes*, Regina forces her husband Horace's heart attack. He desperately asks her to get his medicine, which she cruelly denies, causing his death and ensuring her inheritance (or so she thinks). The two rock-poet musicians, Hoss and Crow, in Sam Shepard's *Tooth of a Crime* compete face-to-face in a life-and-death contest for supremacy.

2) Two characters have a specific relationship at the beginning and another one at the end, displaying some alteration in the relationship. Donald Margulies' Pulitzer Prize play, *Dinner With Friends*: At the beginning: the host couple display a brightly vibrant marriage; at the end: A mutual marital weariness where they dutifully repeat time-worn intimate gestures, without conviction. In Henrik Ibsen's *A Doll's House*, Nora is dutifully devoted to her husband, Helmer, but, at last, having come to the realization that she must be her own independent person, she leaves him forever.

3) One or more characters has a definite attitude, feeling, or opinion which is clear to the audience but is never expressed in words by either character. Biff undergoes sullen disillusionment in the hotel scene with Willy in *Death of a Salesman*. In Susan Glaspell's *Trifles*, Mrs. Hale and Mrs. Peters discover Mrs. Wright's dead bird in her sewing box and realize that she has, indeed, killed her husband. But they never directly express to each other this new-found knowledge, instead communicating it only through furtive eye contact.

4) One character knows something which the other does not. In *Othello*, Iago conceals from Othello the true cause of Desdemona's loss of her handkerchief. In Ben Jonson's *Volpone*, Volpone's fooled creditors are unaware that his "illness" is feigned.

5) The scene has a time limit — a "clock" on it — where something is expected or must be completed before the end. In *Plaza Suite*, parents Karen and Roy must convince their daughter Mimsy to get out of the bathroom she's locked herself in, keeping them all impatiently waiting for her wedding to begin. In *The Tempest*, pressed by Ariel to be freed, Prospero promises early on, setting a time limit: "Thou shalt be as free/as mountain winds/After two days/I will discharge thee." Intermittently repeating his promise, he does not free Ariel until the end — the very final line of the final speech (Act V, Scene 1). Prospero: "My Ariel, Chick,/ . . . then to the Elements/Be free and fare thee well."

6) The scene ends with an air of urgency or expectancy; we want to know what happens next. In *A Streetcar Named Desire*, the penultimate scene ends with Kowalski's rape-seduction of Blanche. How will she react? In August Wilson's Pulitzer Prize-winning play, *Fences*, at the end of Act II, Troy has a bitter, realistic fight with his son, Corey, who then leaves home. Troy symbolically taunts Death to a fight for life. What is going to happen to Troy?

7) The scene has reversals of position regarding the character, information, or forces in the play. In the musical adaptation of *Les Miserables*, Jean Valjean, a

Sheridan Whiteside, the title character of *The Man Who Came to Dinner* by Hart and Kaufman, needs time to undo the mischief he's done to his loyal secretary's love life. But Mr. Sheridan, the man whose house Whiteside has aggressively taken over, finally rebels and demands that Whiteside leave his house in fifteen minutes.

mistreated prisoner, escapes and becomes a respected mayor of a town. In August Strindberg's *Miss Julie*, the title character starts as a haughty aristocrat, to whom servant Jean is submissive. Finally, Miss Julie becomes utterly submissive instead to Jean and goes off to kill herself in total despair.

8) It's a love scene! In Edmond Rostand's *Cyrano de Bergerac*, The title character, hidden in Roxanne's garden, poetically pours out his heart to her, nobly allowing handsome nitwit Christian to take credit for his heartfelt feelings; In *A Raisin in the Sun*, Walter Younger, at bitter odds with his mother, shows his love for her in the scene in which he gives her garden tools for her birthday.

9) A scene brings out a strong character trait. In *Richard III*, Richard exposes his villainous ambitions in the opening soliloquy. Shortly before the murder of Duncan in *Macbeth* (Act I, Scene 7), in a vehement outburst of cold-bloodedness, Lady Macbeth provokes her hesitant husband to do the deed. In *My Fair Lady*, Eliza reveals her defiant resentment toward Henry Higgins in the song, "Just You Wait." (Beneath Eliza's anger is her hurt at being mistreated by him as if she were just an object, not a person.)

10) The more important character in a scene speaks less than the other. In Strindberg's *The Stronger*, the more important character, Miss Y, is silent throughout Mrs. X's hostilely searching monologue. Though Mrs. X decides she is the stronger, our attention stays focused on the enigmatic personality of Miss Y. In Act II of *A Raisin in the Sun*, Walter Younger endures Mr. Linder's insulting racist ploy of paying the Younger family off not to move into the white neighborhood until the last scene, when Walter refuses the offer and restores his sense of family and racial pride. In Harold Pinter's *The Dumbwaiter*, "hired guns" Ben and Gus are waiting for an important call. Ben is smarter, talks little, but knows something is going on, while naive Gus keeps nervously talking and talking.

11) A scene acts as exposition — to give background or historical information. In Ionesco's *The Bald Soprano*, Mr. and Mrs. Bobby Watson, in their coyly absurd British modesty, recap, as if strangers, details of their train trip, their house, their room, their bed,

before finally concluding they are man and wife. The actor-interviewers in Moises Kaufmann's (and company) *The Laramie Project* reveal vital things about themselves as well as the town that they are visiting, Laramie, Wyoming, site of the murder of Matthew Shepard.

12) The scene may have a strong subtext — something below the surface, an undercurrent, which permeates it but is not (and should not be) explicit. In *The House of Bernada Alba*, there is a sustained undercurrent of hostile tension due to sexual repression of four unmarried daughters. In *Waiting for Godot*, the polarities of staying and longing and the hovering shadow of an anticipated controlling presence give the play a sustained edge of tension.

SCENARIO FOR DOCUDRAMA: MARC

JHS 50 MANHATTAN PERFORMERS present A MAN CALLED MARC

NARRATION	ACTIONS
THE TIMELESS RIVER COURSES ITS WAY ALONG THE EAST SIDE OF MANHATTAN	Mirrors Ensemble becomes a river (bodies and blue fabric)
CARRYING WITH IT . . . MEMORIES OF THE EARLIEST AMERICANS RESPECTING ITS SPLENDID BEAUTY. SLOWLY, ON THE SHORES OF THE RIVER, A CITY ROSE.	Two players become Sun (red fabric) Four players become native Indians sitting at bank of River (rest of players) looking at river. River transforms into "sounds and sights of city" machine. Indians transform into buildings.
AND THE RIVER WAS NEVER THE SAME . . . ON DECEMBER 10, 1902, A CHILD WAS BORN TO MR. AND MRS. SAM MARCANTONIO ON 112TH STREET AND FIRST AVENUE.	Buildings transform into polluted river (blue fabric) River and machine transform into baptismal scene. River becomes water and machine becomes—

Father
Mother
(blue fabric) Priest
Neighbors

Need: Dialogue

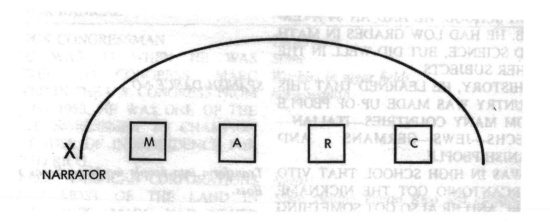

"A MAN CALLED MARC"

NARRATION	ACTION
(1) THE BOY WHO USED TO PLAY BY THE RIVER WOULD GROW UP TO BE	*Scene: MARC looking at river* *Different levels*
(2) A FIGHTER	
(3) A FIGHTER FOR BETTER JOBS	
(4) FOR BETTER HOUSING	
(5) A FIGHTER FOR PEACE	*and positions on stage*
(6) A FIGHTER FOR PEOPLE	
(7) HIS NAME: VITO MARCANTONIO	
(8) M IS FOR MAN	TURN PANEL TO M
(9) A IS FOR AMERICAN	TURN PANEL TO A

VITO MARCANTONIO 'S PARENTS WERE ONLY TWO OF PERHAPS 200,000 ITALIAN AMERICANS LIVING IN EAST HARLEM AT THE TIME.	(Green & white scarves)
THE COMMUNITY WAS RICH IN CUSTOM AND CULTURE.	*All: Tarantella*

THE PEOPLE LOVED LIFE AND WORKED HARD IN THE COAL YARDS ON THE BANK OF THE RIVER, 1N STORES AND FACTORIES FOR VERY LOW WAGES. VITO'S DAD WAS A CARPENTER.	*Mime of various occupations—* *and carpentry* (Father: Remember, son, the shortest distance between two points is a straight line.)

VITO WENT TO ELEMENTARY & JUNIOR HIGH SCHOOL IN EAST HARLEM. HE WAS ONE OF TWO BOYS WHO GRADUATED JR. HIGH TO GO ON TO HIGH SCHOOL. HE HAD AN 84 AVERAGE. HE HAD LOW GRADES IN MATH AND SCIENCE, BUT DID WELL IN THE OTHER SUBJECTS.	*Transform into classroom.* *An actual lesson in math or science (Vito not doing that well.) (Shortest distance between two points is a straight line.)*
IN HISTORY, HE LEARNED THAT THIS COUNTRY WAS MADE UP OF PEOPLE FROM MANY COUNTRIES—ITALIAN—CZECHS—JEWS—GERMANS AND SPANISH PEOPLE.	*SPANISH DANCE NO.*
IT WAS IN HIGH SCHOOL THAT VITO MARCANTONIO GOT THE NICKNAME MARC AND HE ALSO GOT SOMETHING ELSE: HE GOT ANGRY AS HE SAW MANY PEOPLE NOT GETTING FAIR TREATMENT .	*Transform into people working—Scene with Boss.*

NARRATION	ACTION
. . . WHEN IT COMES TO JOBS AND BETTER HOUSING	*LIFT UP PANEL*
	" " "
M IS FOR MAN	*TURN PANEL*
A FOR AMERICAN	
R FOR RADICAL	

MANY PEOPLE WERE NOT SATISFIED WITH WORKING AND HOUSING CONDITIONS. MANY PEOPLE WANTED REFORM *NOW*. WHEN HE WAS ONLY 18, MARC ORGANIZED A RENT STRIKE FOR THE EAST HARLEM TENANTS LEAGUE.	*Scene* *MARC and tenants confronting landlord-withhold rent until improvements were made.*

MARC SPENT SOME TIME AT HARLEM HOUSE TEACHING. IT WAS THERE HE MET HIS WIFE, MIRIAM. SHE WAS 5" TALLER AND 11 YEARS OLDER AND HIS STAUNCHEST SUPPORTER. MARC WENT ON TO LAW SCHOOL AND WORKED FOR FIORELLA LaGUARDIA, WHO WOULD LATER BECOME MAYOR OF NEW YORK.	*MARC is boxing at Harlem House,* showing off for MIRIAM. He gets knocked out. "I sure went a short distance that round."
MARC ALSO LED AN UNEMPLOYMENT STRIKE FOR MORE JOBS. MARC WAS ARRESTED FOR THIS ACTION. BUT THOUSANDS AND THOUSANDS OF PEOPLE IN THE COMMUNITY LOVED AND RESPECTED HIM.	*Scene* *Song: "United We Stand"* *MARC on street corner, speech, and then being arrested. Wife there at his side.*

M IS FOR MAN	*Lift Panel*
A IS FOR AMERICAN	*Lift Panel*
R IS FOR RADICAL	*Lift Panel*

C IS FOR CONGRESSMAN	*Turn Panel*
MARC WAS 33 WHEN HE WAS ELECTED	*Scene*
TO CONGRESS. MARC SERVED IN THE U.S.	*Workers in sugar fields*
CONGRESS FROM 1936 TO 1950. HE WAS	*hot —*
ONE OF THE FEW CONGRESSMEN TO CHAMPION THE CAUSE OF INDEPENDENCE FOR PUERTO RICO.	
4 LARGE AMERICAN CORPORATIONS	*Need:*
OWNED MOST OF THE LAND IN PUERTO	MARC visiting Puerto Rico and challenging
RICO—MARC HAD NEVER BEEN TO ITALY	Governor.
BUT VISITED PUERTO RICO. HE WAS INSTRUMENTAL IN REMOVING THE	
UNFAIR	*Scene: In Congress, with actual excerpts from speech.*

NARRATION	ACTION

AMERICAN GOVERNOR, AND HE INTRO-
DUCED THE FIRST BILL IN CONGRESS
FOR PUERTO RICAN INDEPENDENCE.

IN ADDITION TO LIVING IN WASHING-
TON WHERE HIS OFFICE WAS OPEN 7
DAYS A WEEK, MARC MAINTAINED A
SMALL APARTMENT IN EAST HARLEM. HE
WOULD OFTEN WORK UP TO 20 HOURS A
DAY.
MARC SUFFERED A FATAL HEART ATTACK
ON AUGUST 9, 1954.

Scene: Man being evicted from apartment coming to MARC's small place.

HIS FUNERAL WAS HELD NOT FAR FROM
WHERE HE WAS BORN. LINES FORMED
FOR BLOCKS AND BLOCKS. YOU COULD
SEE THE RIVER, THE RIVER MARCANTO-
NIO LOVED SO WELL, CARRYING WITH IT
MEMORIES OF A MAN CALLED MARC.
PAUL O'DWYER SAID: MAY HE REST IN
PEACE. IT WOULD BE A GREAT DAY FOR
NEW YORK IF TEN MORE MARC 'S WERE
TO RISE TO TAKE HIS PLACE. SO FAR, THE
LIKES OF HIM HAVE NOT APPEARED ON
THE POLITICAL SCENE.

Song:
    Words from funeral
Reverse panels one at a time.
Large photo of "MARC"

ANTAGONIST — In this text called the opposing character, the main opponent of the protagonist or central character.

AUDIENCE — All those experiencing the play being performed, read aloud, or worked on during a rehearsal. Audience can also include the performers themselves as they reflect on the action, events, and characters during a performance or rehearsal.

CHARACTERS — These can be a person — real or fantastic, animal, or symbolic entity in a story, play, or scene. They possess specific physical, mental, and behavioral traits.

CHARACTER TRAITS — These include externals (age, sex, and physical attributes), socioeconomic background (ethnic, family, occupational considerations); and psychological attributes (feelings, values, shortcomings and strivings).

CHARACTERIZATION — The process of making a play's characters in performance real and believable through the fleshing out of the above traits by playwright, actors, and director.

CLIMAX — The peak of dramatic action and tension which leads to a resolution of the play's major dramatic conflict or problem.

COMPLICATIONS — The engaging twists and turns in which new developments are added to the evolving conflict between the central and opposing characters.

CONFLICT — The major struggle between central and opposing characters over clashing values and objectives that lead to the eventual climax and resolution of the dramatic action.

CRISIS — A major turning point in the dramatic action, most often when the central character has to make a vital decision concerning a momentous course of action.

DIALOGUE — What is spoken by the characters in their interaction, revealing their thoughts, motivations, plans, and plot developments.

DRAMATIC IRONY — When the audience knows something that is in stark contrast to what the character believes.

DYNAMIC CHARACTER — This is a character who significantly grows or undergoes some kind of change during the course of the play. A STATIC CHARACTER does not grow, staying more or less the same throughout the course of the play.

ELEMENTS OF DRAMA — According to Aristotle, plot, character, theme, dialogue, music, spectacle (visual elements)

EMPATHY — The experience of sharing the emotional state of a character on stage, so that the audience identifies closely with that character.

EXPOSITION — Things that need to be known, and established early in a play through dialogue, in order for the audience to have a better understanding of characters, their circumstances, or the setting and time of the play.

GIVEN CIRCUMSTANCES — Also called the 5 W's, basic things an actor must know:
WHO — a character's physical, mental, behavioral attributes;
WHERE — the play's setting or locale;
WHAT — the character's wants in the play or in a scene;
WHEN — the specific time of day, season, year;
WHY — a character's motivations for an action or lack of action; if known by actor.

INCITING INCIDENT — An incident in the play that changes the current status of the central character's life, putting into motion the main conflict or problem he or she must deal with.

MOTIVATION — A character's reason for doing or not doing something or for saying or not saying something.

OBJECTIVE — A character's main goal through-

POLSKY'S PERSONAL PLOTTING POINTS

Pissed — central character has a problem

Fist — central character has a conflct with at least one other character

Twist — complications that deepen the conflict or problem

Gist — crisis, or turning point of how a central character deals with the conflict/problem

Hissed/kissed/missed — conflict/problem is resolved or stalemated

out the entire play (called super objective) or in a scene (called scene objective) that motivates the character to take or not take an action.

OBSTACLE — A character or thing that blocks another character from achieving his or her objective, so that, in the process, conflict and tension are generated.

PLOT — In this text referred to as dramatic structure — *Beginning*: A problem is introduced, usually between characters; *Middle*: The problem is deepened by complications which lead to a major conflict. *End*: The conflict, reaching the peak of crucial tension, is finally resolved. (However, some dramatic structures do not rely on plotting, as much as on developing character and mood.)

PRESENTATIONAL STYLE — A theatrical style in which the actors acknowledge the presence of the audience, and, in fact, may talk directly to the audience at times.

REPRESENTATIONAL STYLE — A theatrical style in which the actors convey the illusion of " real life" on stage and do not acknowlege the presence of the audience looking into a "fourth wall."

RESOLUTION — After a play's climax, the final solving of the problem or conflict between the central and opposing characters.

SCENE — Not to be confused with setting, it is part of an act (sometimes the whole act) in which the dramatic action unfolds; a FRENCH SCENE consists of two characters interacting on stage;

when one of them leaves and another comes on stage, it is the beginning of another French scene. (See page 85.)

SCENARIO — An outline, flow chart, or chart of the scene-by-scene action of the play.

SPECTACLE — All the visual elements of a play, such as stage sets, costumes, lighting, props and physical movement, including dance. Also might include the spectacle of video or film projections.

SPINE — The overall, dominating objective or thrust of a central character that creates or contributes to the major conflict and resolution of a play.

STAGE AND SPEECH DIRECTIONS — These provide cues and clues regarding a character's gestures, movement, vocal intensity and tone in dialogue and monologues.

SUBTEXT — What is implied rather than spoken directly by a character; underlying feelings beneath the actual words in the script; subtext can include nonverbal gestures and tones of voice which ironically contradict or reveal what is spoken on the surface by a character.

THEME — The main or central idea of a play that is not stated directly by a playwright, but is instead revealed dramatically through the interaction of the characters. Playwrights rarely start with a theme they wish to express, but rather with a character who has a problem to face and overcome.

RECOMMENDED READINGS

A. PLAYS

For your reading pleasure, here's a list of half a dozen or so of some of the world's most famous plays from each of half a dozen different periods, places, and styles. Discuss with your friends what other important classics you would like to be added to this list.

I. MODERN AMERICAN CLASSICS

Edward Albee — *The Zoo Story, Who's Afraid of Virginia Woolf.*

Eugene O'Neill — *The Iceman Cometh,* one-acts

Lillian Hellman — *The Little Foxes*

Arthur Miller — *Death of a Salesman, The Crucible*

Lorraine Hansberry — *A Raisin in the Sun*

Tennesee Williams — *A Streetcar Named Desire, The Glass Menagerie*

David Mamet — *American Buffalo*

Sam Shepard — *The Buried Child, True West*

Wendy Wasserstein — *The Heidi Chronicles*

August Wilson — *Fences, The Piano Lesson*

II. NEW FORMS, BEYOND REALISM

August Strindberg — *The Dream Play*

Luigi Pirandello — *Six Characters in Search of an Author*

Frederico Garcia Lorca — *Blood Wedding*

Jean Giraudoux — *The Madwoman of Chaillot*

Samuel Beckett — *Waiting for Godot*

Eugene Ionesco — *The Bald Soprano*

III. FROM THE RECENT PAST

Henrik Ibsen — *A Doll's House, Hedda Gabler*

Lady Gregory — *Spreading the News*

Oscar Wilde — *The Importance of Being Earnest*

John Millington Synge — *The Playboy of the Western World*

Anton Chekhov — *The Cherry Orchard, The Three Sisters*

Maxim Gorki — *The Lower Depths*

George Bernard Shaw — *Major Barbara, Pygmalion*

IV. POST-RENAISSANCE CLASSICS

Pedro Calderon de la Barca — *Life Is a Dream*

Moliere — *Tartuffe*

Jean Racine — *Phedre*

William Congreve — *The Way of the World*

Oliver Goldsmith — *She Stoops to Conquer*

Johann Wolfgang von Goethe — *Faust*

V. THE ELIZABETHAN GOLDEN AGE

Christopher Marlowe — *Dr. Faustus*

Ben Jonson — *Volpone*

William Shakespeare — *A Midsummer Night's Dream, Hamlet, King Lear*

John Webster — *The Duchess of Malfi*

VI. ANCIENT CLASSICS

Aeschylus — *Prometheus Bound*

Sophocles — *Oedipus*

Euripides — *Medea*

Aristophanes — *Lysistrata*

Kalidasa — *Shakuntala*

Plautus — *The Menachmi*

P.S. These classics offer more than pleasure — they are part of your basic preparation as a playwright. In addition to your favorite classics, it is recommended that you read plays of your peers. Here are some suggestions:

Meeting the Winter Bike Rider and Other Prize-Winning Plays from the 1985 and 1986 Young Playwrights Festival.

The Grand Zero Club and Other Prize-Winning Plays from the 1985 and 1986 Young Playwrights Festival.

Sparks in the Park and Other Prize-Winning Plays from the 1987 and 1988 Young Playwrights Festival.

Information regarding the purchase of single plays since 1988 is available by writing to Young Playwrights, Inc., 306 West 38th Street, Suite 300, New York, NY 10018.

B. BOOKS BY OR ABOUT PLAYWRIGHTS

Gibson, William. *Two for the Seesaw: A Chronicle of the Stage Production.* New York: Limelight Productions, 1984.

Gussow, Mel. *Conversations With Pinter.* London: Nick Hern Books, 1994.

Gussow, Mel. *Conversations With Stoppard.* New York: Limelight Editions, 1995.

Gussow, Mel. *Conversations With and About Beckett.* New York: Grove Press, 1996

Gussow, Mel. *Edward Albee: A Singular Journey, A Biography.* New York: Applause, 2001.

Hart, Moss. *Act One: An Autobiography.* New York: Random House, 1959

Laurents, Arthur. *Original Story By: A Memoir of Broadway and Hollywood.* New York: Applause, 2001

Lerner, Alan Jay. *The Street Where I Live.* New York: Limelight Press, 1994

Miller, Arthur. *Timebends: A Life.* New York: Grove Press, 1987

Simon, Neil. *Rewrites: A Memoir.* New York, Simon and Schuster, 1996.

Simon, Neil. *The Play Goes On: A Memoir.* New York: Simon and Schuster, 1999

Williams, Tennesee. *Memoirs.* Garden City, New York: Doubleday and Company, 1975.

PHOTO CREDITS

Telecommunication Arts and Technology. Louis H. Nemec, director.

p. 78   Courtesy Melissa Gilbert.

p. 83   Courtesy Carl Junction High School. Brian Hauck, director. Photo: Kyle Cleveland.

p. 84   Courtesy Roundabout Theatre Company, Geare Feist and Michael Fried, producing directors. Stephen Porter, director. Photo: Martha Swope. Thanks to Susan Bloch and Company.

p. 90   Courtesy, Linda Howard Westhampton High School. Linda Howard, director. Photo: Linda Howard.

p. 90   Courtesy David Rothenberg Associates and Melting Pot Theatre, Larry Hirschhorn, Artistic Director; Joe Brancato, director Photo: Kevin Fox.

p. 90   Courtesy The Movie Channel.

p. 91   Courtesy Orion Pictures Corporation.

p. 92   Courtesy Zenon Kruszelnick and Actors Studio Drama School, New School University. Zenon Kruszelnick, director. Photo: Scott Wynn.

p. 97   Courtesy University of North Carolina-Greensboro, Department of Communication and Theatre. Richard Mennen, director.

p. 99   Courtesy David Powers and original Annie company. Photo: Martha Swope.

p. 103   Courtesy Jacqueline Greene, American Broadcasting Companies.

p. 105   Courtesy Hunt, Pucci Assoc. Melvin Bemhardt, director. Photo: Martha Swope.

p. 107   Courtesy Cinemobilia.

p. 110-111   Courtesy Jerry Ohlinger's Movie Materials Store, Inc.

p. 112   Courtesy Milton Polsky and LaGuardia High School for the Performing Arts. Gregory Schneider, director. Photo: Baruch Katz.

p. 115   Courtesy Seymour Krawitz & Co. Patrick Garland, director. Produced by Don Gregory and Mike Herrick.

p. 117   Courtesy Hunter College and Milton Polsky.

p. 123   Courtesy Department of Theatre, California State Polytechnic University. San Luis Obispo. Michael Malkin, director.

p. 124   Courtesy John Springer Associates, Inc. John Dexter, director. Photo: Van Williams.

p. 126   Courtesy Richard Kornberg Associates and Second Stage Theatre Marion McClinton, director Photo: Craig Schwartz.

p. 126   Courtesy John Bielenberg, Binghamton University. Judy Friel, director. Scenic Designer, John Bielenberg.

p. 127   Courtesy Milton Polsky, Hunter College. Milton Polsky and Carole Rosen, co-directors. Photo: Peter Munch.

p. 128   Courtesy Milton Polsky, Hunter College. Photo: Terry Buchalter.

p. 127   Courtesy Milton Polsky, Washington Irving High School. Photo: Roberta Polsky.

p. 129   Courtesy Milton Polsky, Hunter College. Photo: Alex Gersznowicz

p. 130   Courtesy Coleman Jennings, Department of Theatre & Dance, University of Texas at Austin.

p. 133   Courtesy Max Eisen and original *Raisin* company. Set by Robert U. Taylor.

p. 135   Courtesy Playward Bus Theatre Company. Jim Mapp, director. Photo: Fran Lightmah.

p. 139   Courtesy John Shorter, Manhasset High School Theatre Department. John Shorter, director. Photo: Michael Sansone.

p. 143   Courtesy John Shorter, Manhasset High School Theatre Department. John Shorter, director. Photo: Emmy Kane.

p. 147   Courtesy John Shorter, Manhasset High School Theatre Department. John Shorter, director. Photo: John Cline.

p. 150   Courtesy Art D'Lugoff and Original *One Mo' Time* company. Photo: Ben Andrews.

p. 152   Courtesy Jerome Rockwood.

p. 155   Courtesy Zev Bufman. Paul Sills, director. Photo: Steve Keull.

p. 158   Courtesy The Manhattan Project's *Alice in Wonderland*. Andre Gregory, director. Photo: Avedon.

p. 160   Courtesy, Milton Polsky and Croton Park Colony Children's Theatre Company, Milton Polsky, director. Photo: Roberta Polsky.

p. 160   (playground) Courtesy Milton Polsky and

Hunter College. Milton Polsky, director. Photo: Bob Cannistraci.

p. 160 (radio) Courtesy Milton Polsky and Hunter College Photo, courtesy Milton Polsky.

p. 160 (senior adults) Courtesy Milton Polsky and Hunter College Brookdale Drama Project, Milton Polsky, director. Photo courtesy, Milton Polsky.

p. 161 Courtesy Bert Andrews. Photo: Bert Andrews.

p. 161 Courtesy Bert Andrews. Photo: Bert Andrews.

p. 161 Courtesy John Shorter, Manhasset High School Theatre Department. John Shorter, director. Photo: Myrna Schein.

p. 161 Courtesy John Shorter, Manhasset High School Theatre Department John Shorter, director. Photo credit: Myrna Schein.

p. 175 Courtesy Alistair Martin-Smith and New York University Program in Educational Theatre and "Looking for Shakespeare," Project Alistair Martin-Smith, director. Photo: Sebastian Piras.

p. 178 Courtesy Showtime, Inc.

p. 179 Courtesy Milton Polsky and The UFT Players. Louis H. Nemec and Suzanne Lamberg, co-directors. Photo: Jack Miller.

p. 180 Courtesy Alistair Martin-Smith and New York University Program in Educational Theatre and "Looking for Shakespeare" Project. Alistair Martin-Smith, director. Photo: Sebastian Piras.

p. 181 Courtesy American Playhouse.

p. 184 Courtesy John Fredericksen, Mamaroneck High School John Fredricksen, director. Photo: George Goldstein.

INDEX